Beethoven and the Construction of Genius

Beethoven and the Construction of Genius

Musical Politics in Vienna, 1792–1803

Tia DeNora

UNIVERSITY OF CALIFORNIA PRESS
Berkeley · Los Angeles · London

University of California Press
Berkeley and Los Angeles, California

University of California Press, Ltd.
London, England

Library of Congress Cataloging-in-Publication Data

DeNora, Tia
   Beethoven and the construction of genius :
musical politics in Vienna, 1792–1803 /
Tia DeNora.
        p.   cm.
   Includes bibliographical references (p.   ) and
index.
   ISBN 0-520-08892-1 (alk. paper)
   ISBN 0-520-21158-8 (pbk: alk. paper)
   1. Beethoven, Ludwig van, 1770–1827—
Appreciation—Austria—Vienna.   2. Music and
society.   3. Vienna (Austria)—Intellectual life.
I. Title.
ML410.B4D36   1995
780'.92—dc20   94-32544
                                     CIP
                                     MN

Printed in the United States of America

9   8   7   6   5   4   3   2   1

The paper used in this publication meets the
minimum requirements of American National
Standard for Information Sciences—Permanence
of Paper for Printed Library Materials, ANSI
Z39.48-1984. ∞

Contents

Figures

Tables

Preface

This book is as much about the problem of social identity as it is about Beethoven. I use the history of Beethoven's initial success as a tool for considering the interrelationship between identity (both reputation and self-identity), social structure, culture, and action. My aim is to reexamine, from a critical standpoint, some of our often deeply embedded assumptions about value, talent, and creativity.

The image of Beethoven—haughty, scowling, and disheveled, as he is depicted in numerous portraits and busts—has been a part of the popular iconography of genius since the early nineteenth century. These images, and at least some of Beethoven's works, are familiar to many people who are otherwise unacquainted with the world of "high culture" music. As a part of our cultural common sense, Beethoven's identity as an exceptional musician appears transcendent. Beethoven is the quintessential genius of Western culture, and the history of how his reputation became established should interest sociologists, social psychologists, and cultural historians, because that history cannot be addressed fully by conventional musicological discourse alone.

In this volume I explore how Beethoven's reputation was initially established, what some of its social consequences were, and, to the extent that it can be answered, why Beethoven's renown took the form it did. I focus on how Beethoven's identity as an extraordinary musician was communicated to audiences outside his initially small circle of aristocratic admirers, and how, over the course of his first decade in Vienna, Beethoven became a culturally authoritative figure. I discuss the practical

ways in which Beethoven, his patrons, and other supporters can be understood as involved (though not always intentionally) in projecting an
image of Beethoven as universally admired and as the heir to Mozart,
and I contextualize these activities in terms of the social, organizational,
and cultural structure of Vienna's musical world during the 1790s.

The first aim of this book is to provide an account of Beethoven's
success that remains at the level of social activity and its milieu. This
ethnographic history provides a springboard into the second and major
purpose of this work—to document the structuration of the Viennese
musical field as this structuration occurred in and through the development of Beethoven's prestige. In other words, we can observe Beethoven's
cultural authority interacting with and influencing the criteria against
which it was judged. I examine this reflexive process by considering some
of the ways Beethoven's increasing reputation contributed to the initial
emergence of an ideology of "serious" (as opposed to light) music. During the final years of the eighteenth century, amateur-oriented, dilettante
musical values were increasingly challenged and obscured from within
by a connoisseur culture of musical production and consumption. By
following the history of Beethoven's success as it unfolded, I try to identify some of the links between Beethoven's eminence and the articulation
of the notion of master composers in Vienna during the early part of the
nineteenth century.

Even now, artistic standards and canons of taste are being debated in
and outside of musical and academic fields, and programs for cultural
reform abound. These programs range from suggestions for "reshuf-
fling" personnel within the canon, to suggestions for substitutions, to
appropriating official members of the canon for new social concerns, to
abolishing canonic structures altogether in favor of postmodernist aesthetics and local and community arts. While these programs obviously
vary in levels of ambition, they share a concern with the ways exclusive
or "high" cultural forms are both inaccessible and inappropriate to the
lived experience of a large proportion of the people to whom they are
upheld as aspirational.

I too share this concern, but I will not address here the issue of which
works or composers should be "in" or "out" of a musical canon (or
whether there should even be a canon); that is a task for cultural critics.
I prefer to step back from these issues and investigate instead the social
processes through which authoritative aesthetic claims are established in
the first place. By implication, this focus undercuts hierarchical ways of
organizing artistic production and reception. It attempts to treat with

dignity the perspectives of those for whom (and for whatever reasons) Beethoven's extraordinary talent was not self-evident, and it does not do violence to the often-overlooked qualities of the numerous musicians who existed in Beethoven's shadow.

My intention is by no means to debunk Beethoven. Within the cultural framework devoted to its appreciation, Beethoven's music is rich and rewarding of close attention, as I continue to discover. At the same time, a deep appreciation of Beethoven need not be coupled with the idea that his works are "transcendent." Such a view appears vain when considered in a cross-cultural or historical context; more insidiously, it leaves unexamined the ways in which "great" men or women exist inevitably at the expense of other possibilities. Genius and its recognition require social and cultural resources if they are to be cultivated, and these resources are often micropolitically charged. I hope this exploration of Beethoven's artistic career will enlarge the potential for thinking about talent and genius as fundamentally social achievements.

Acknowledgments

The initial research for this book began in 1987 when I was a graduate student at the University of California, San Diego. My interest in developing a sociological understanding of genius arose out of work that my Ph.D. supervisor, Hugh ("Bud") Mehan, had recently completed (in collaboration with others) on the classification of pupils in schools (Mehan, Hertweck, and Meihls 1986). I owe Bud an enormous intellectual debt for introducing me to the sociological power of the constructivist perspective. I am also grateful to Bennett Berger for his characteristic insistence that the sociology of culture provide straightforward answers to straightforward questions and that it ground its answers at the level of social action. I also thank Charles Nathanson, who provided close critical reading and helped me begin to articulate several of the ideas developed in this book, and Jann Pasler, who helped me relate my efforts to her own discipline of musicology and shared her views on the topic of artistic reputation. Discussions with the late César Graña in 1985 and 1986 were also useful to my early investigations into the relationship between culture and social structure. Thanks also to John Wills, Barry Saferstein, Kathryn Henderson, and Evan Adelson at UCSD.

I am also grateful to the staff at the University of California Press for their support and guidance. Thanks in particular to Naomi Schneider, Rose Anne White, Ruth Veleta, William Murphy, and Do Mi Stauber.

A consequent pleasure of this research has been that it brought me into contact with the members and culture (to me, often exotic) of a second discipline, eighteenth-century music scholarship. While the following individuals are by no means responsible for what I say in this book, they have rescued me from some of the wilder surmises that, from their point of view, often characterize sociological studies of music. I have incurred more debts in this area than I can acknowledge here, but I particularly thank William Weber, Margaret Hood, Else Radant Landon, David Wyn Jones, and Evan Baker. I also thank Mary Sue Morrow and Bruce Brown for corresponding with me on certain points, and the participants in the International Conference on Music in Austria, 1750–1800 (Cardiff) and in the symposium Beethoven in Vienna 1792–1803: The First Style Period (at the University of Connecticut, Storrs). I would especially like to thank Dexter Edge, who knows so much about the archival picture of Viennese musical life during the late eighteenth century and who has been exceptionally generous with both his time and his own in-progress research on Viennese musical life during the 1780s. Julia Moore, whose research (Moore 1987, n.d.a., n.d.b.) into the socioeconomic position of Beethoven and his patrons is intimately related to the issues developed here, has been a friend, critic, colleague, and collaborator. My debt to her work over the years has grown to the point where it is no longer measurable; it is evidenced on nearly every page.

The University of Wales, Cardiff, provided time and financial support in the shape of a University Fellowship from 1989 to 1991.

Many sociologists and other scholars have read and commented on portions of this work. In the United States, thanks are due to Judy Balfe, Paul DiMaggio, John Kitsuse, and Theodore Sarbin. In the United Kingdom, I thank Paul Atkinson, Sara Delamont, Anne Murcott, the Cardiff Critical Theory Seminar, the Sociology Seminar at Manchester University, members of the British Sociological Association's Music Study Group, students in the International Organization for Advanced Studies in Interpretive Sociology Summer School and in my Sociology of Culture course, and especially fellow sociologist of music Pete Martin. I extend a very warm thanks to my friend and colleague at the University of Exeter, Robert Witkin, who read the penultimate draft of the manuscript and generously shared his ongoing work in the sociology of art. This collaboration has stimulated and encouraged me greatly throughout the final stages of writing.

Finally, my husband, Douglas Tudhope, took time off from his work to read, reread, and generally live this book with me in its various incarnations. This volume has been his project as much as it has been mine and it is dedicated to him with love and gratitude.

Portions of this book have appeared in the following publications and appear here (in revised and adapted form) with permission of the original publishers:

Portions of chapters 2 and 3 appeared in earlier form as "Musical Patronage and Social Change in Beethoven's Vienna," *American Journal of Sociology* 97 (September 1991): 310–46, and have since been substantially revised.

Portions of chapter 6 appeared in "The Social Basis of Beethoven's Style," in *Paying the Piper: Causes and Consequences of Art Patronage,* edited by J. Balfe (Urbana: University of Illinois Press, 1993).

Part of chapter 1 originally appeared in "Beethoven, the Viennese Canon, and the Sociology of Identity, 1793–1803," *Beethoven Forum* 2 (1993): 29–54.

Beethoven and Social Identity

In the autumn of 1792 Beethoven set out for Vienna, where he had been invited to study with Haydn. The son and grandson of court musicians, Beethoven had, over the previous ten years, achieved a degree of distinction within the relatively homogeneous, court-oriented Bonn music world. After some preliminary (and rather severe) study with his father, he spent the years after 1780 as a pupil of Christian Gottlieb Neefe, who helped secure for Beethoven the position of deputy court organist in 1782. Throughout his time in Bonn, Beethoven continued to work at the court in several capacities. He also gained repute, through the Breuning family's private concerts, as a talented improvisational pianist. By 1792 he had produced about three dozen compositions, among them the two ambitious cantatas on the death of Joseph II (WoO 87) and the elevation of Leopold II (WoO 88), both commissioned by the Bonn Lesegesell-schaft, one of the several groups to which he was informally linked.

These early distinctions, in addition to his age (he was not quite twenty-two), made the idea of travel to Vienna and a final apprenticeship with Haydn seem like a logical next step. In fact, Beethoven had already visited Vienna in 1787, but his stay was curtailed when he was called back to the bedside of his dying mother in Bonn. The object of this second trip was to enrich his artistry through study with Haydn and, perhaps more important, to gain the imprimatur of the celebrated composer; then he would return to Bonn to assume a key position in court music affairs. His Bonn circle had no reason to believe his leave was permanent, and it was the elector himself who paid for Beethoven's travel and living expenses.[1] As Neefe noted in a 1793 issue of the *Berliner Musik-Zeitung,* Beethoven "went to Vienna at the expense of our Elector to Haydn in order to perfect himself under his direction more fully in the art of composition" (Thayer and Forbes 1967, 1:113).

Considering Beethoven's accomplishments up to December 1792, one could easily envision his continued success—a career not unlike that enjoyed by his teacher Neefe, his grandfather Ludwig, or any other of the many successful but now forgotten musicians of the late eighteenth and early nineteenth centuries. One could also imagine that, in the later words of his teacher Haydn, Beethoven might eventually "fill the position of one of Europe's greatest composers" (Landon 1959, 141). What was not so clearly foreseeable was the unique way Beethoven came to be identified during the subsequent decade and a half as the author of unconventional, often "difficult," and sometimes unprecedentedly lengthy works such as the sonatas "quasi una fantasia" of 1801, the "Waldstein" and "Appasionata" sonatas of 1803, the "Eroica" Symphony of 1805, and the "Razumovsky" quartets of 1806. Despite Beethoven's apparent attempts to emulate and extend compositional practices of his predecessors (in particular, Haydn and Mozart), his contemporary supporters and opponents alike perceived his works as unusual and even bizarre. The history of Beethoven's reception is punctuated by resistance to what were viewed as the composer's musical idiosyncrasies.

BEETHOVEN AND THE PREHISTORY
OF THE MUSICAL CANON

Beethoven is often regarded as a "revolutionary" composer, a pivotal force in the development of music. The term *revolutionary* is strong but imprecise as an indicator of Beethoven's place in music history; moreover, it explains almost nothing. For a more comprehensive understanding of Beethoven's success among his contemporaries we need to view Beethoven's impact in the context of the changes that characterized high cultural musical life during the late eighteenth and early nineteenth centuries. During the years Beethoven lived and worked in Vienna, between 1792 and 1827, interest in "eternal" standards of excellence in music were articulated and disseminated, and concert repertories increasingly featured the works of Haydn, Mozart, and Beethoven as a musical trinity of master composers. Music historians have often referred to this period as the "prehistory" of the musical canon—the formative years in which new models for the fundamental transformation in the assumptions of taste were initially articulated (Weber 1986).

During the 1980s, other scholars have outlined the contours of this trend toward musical "classics"[2] and, more generally, the emergence of the category "high art" as it occurred in both Europe and the United States (Zolberg 1981; DiMaggio 1982; Levine 1988; Tuchman and Fortin, 1989; Abrams 1985). Most work on the topic has focused on the middle and later nineteenth century, although, as several music scholars have remarked in passing (Weber 1986; Rosen 1972; Kerman 1983), developments in late eighteenth-century Viennese music ideology are best viewed as prototypical of the subsequent and eventually international shift.

A specific look at Beethoven's career can further illuminate this important reorientation in the early period of Viennese canon formation. As William Weber (1986) and Mary Sue Morrow (1989) have observed, Beethoven's special position in the Haydn-Mozart-Beethoven trinity was reflected in contemporary music programming practices. Later in the nineteenth century, it was with Beethoven's symphonies that the traditional eighteenth-century practice of programming a wide and, from the modern viewpoint, frequently incongruous mix of opera arias, sonatas, improvisations, overtures, and symphonies began to give way to the more formalized practice of programming only symphonic music (Weber 1986, 366). Moreover, Beethoven was the only composer whose works were celebrated regardless of their genre.[3] As Weber notes, "It was Beethoven's role that was special; Haydn and Mozart took second place, despite their seeming equality in the pantheon" (1986, 368).

Beethoven was not the first musician to write difficult or "connoisseur's" music. The gap between *Kenner* (expert) and *Liebhaber* (amateur) existed well before Beethoven arrived in Vienna. Rather, the late eighteenth century witnessed a shift toward a more highly articulated, self-conscious ideology of artistic greatness, as applied to secular music. Within this mindset of serious music, the composer-as-genius was reconceived as a figure who could command unprecedented autonomy and deference. Not until later in the nineteenth century, with the professionalization of the music occupation (and with the proselytizing activities of upper middle-class music aficionados), was this ideology disseminated internationally. Yet some of its earliest manifestations appear in the development of Beethoven's career in Vienna.

The particularities of Viennese musical culture were crucial to the shape of Beethoven's success. Vienna was the first European city where a contemporary and youthful composer could be viewed as the heir to a canonic tradition that included not only Haydn and Mozart, but also J. S. Bach and Handel. The manner in which Beethoven was celebrated by his contemporaries thus helped to formulate an understanding of the musical canon that was, during the early years of the nineteenth century, unique to Vienna. By contrast, the English canon consisted of a growing historical consciousness of music within which the works of seventeenth- and early eighteenth-century composers (especially Handel) were revered, predominantly by aristocratic patrons. Whereas in Vienna previous "great" composers (Bach and Handel) were viewed as leading up to Mozart, Haydn, and Beethoven, in London contemporary musicians stood outside the canon. True, the English musical canon was predominantly aristocratic and during the eighteenth century it was increasingly articulated as a self-conscious ideology. However, the English canon was defined in opposition to contemporary music, which was conceived by its advocates as vulgar and decadent (Milligan 1983, chap. 1). In Paris, meanwhile, the musical canon emerged out of practical musical activity long before it was articulated as an ideological stance within the arts. It developed from the need to program standby works that companies knew and could perform with little rehearsal (Weber 1984a; 1992).

To understand Beethoven's success, we need to view it in the context of a wider reorientation of musical taste, as this reorientation occurred in a specific social and geographical setting. Furthermore, we need to consider how Beethoven's success affected the setting within which he operated. Exploration of the initial appearance of serious music ideology thus needs to include the impact of Beethoven's success on the shape and texture of musical life. In this study I illustrate how Beethoven's emergence as a genius composer depended on and simultaneously helped to construct a more general and specifically modern notion of creative musical genius. We need to understand the emergence of these two phenomena—music ideology and Beethoven's success among his contemporaries—as reflexively linked. Doing so illustrates some of the ways music history does not simply evolve or develop, but is rather articulated "from the inside" by real individuals with reference to institutional, cultural, and practical contexts and in light of local contingencies. By following the ways that particular individuals "made" music history, we can extend our understanding of the relationship between musical forms and social life.[4]

TOWARD A SOCIOLOGY OF BEETHOVEN'S REPUTATION

Beethoven's music was anchored to a new—or, for the time, alternative—set of aesthetic criteria and stylistic conventions. The newness of Beethoven's works was contested. Appreciation of his compositions was neither spontaneous nor universal. Beethoven's eventual success was the product of social mediation, and it would be unfair, for example, to accuse Beethoven's contemporary opponents of philistinism or musical ignorance or to argue that opposition to Beethoven consisted simply of conservative reactions. Equally unfair is attributing the failure of some of Beethoven's contemporaries to appreciate his work to "psychological inhibitions" (Graf 1946, 144; Slonimsky 1965, 3). Similarly, it is fallacious to argue that the artistic steps Beethoven took were those of a giant, and that if his contemporaries were unable to perceive their inherent value it was because they were too small or lacked vision. To account for Beethoven's talent in any of these ways is to hold a view that flatters the present-day viewer's so-called more advanced perspective; it also imposes our own aesthetic evaluative terms on a group for which they are not necessarily appropriate.

The crux of the problem with most Beethoven literature as it addresses the composer's reputation is that, to varying degrees, that literature consists of retrospective accounts that isolate the quality of Beethoven's works as the cause of his recognition. In these accounts, greatness emerges out of a kind of temporal conjuring trick. As the sociologist of science Michael Mulkay writes regarding scientific discovery (here understood as the product of individuals—of scientific "geniuses"), "The apparent temporal priority of discovery is something of an illusion. It is an illusion in the sense that discovery is socially accumulated over time, sometimes over . . . long periods . . . and *it is interpretively projected backwards upon earlier events*" (Mulkay 1986, 173; emphasis added). Discovery is, in other words, a trope or figure of discourse, a rhetorical mode of accounting for what gets done in science. So too within the arts, the tropes of genius require critical examination.

There is a precedent for this type of deconstructive work within musicology. In an essay entitled "Innovation, Choice and the History of Music," Leonard Meyer describes the "covert causalism" of many studies of musical influence (Meyer 1983, 3; see also Becker 1982). These studies, he suggests, often fail to make the issue of composer choice problematic in its own right, and thereby tend to depict the issue of influence as purely musicological; in retrospect, influence is conceived as independent of the local, often mundane conditions under which composition occurs. This misconception of influence leads to overidealized and musically imperialistic conceptions of the compositional process, which sidestep the issue of social circumstance.

Just as compositional choice does not occur in a vacuum, neither does reception. Beethoven's recognition, for example, is often explained in ways that overemphasize his "own" talent at the expense of the social bases of his acceptance and celebration.[5] Yet it is through these bases that the layers of pro-Beethoven mythology and culture have "accumulated" (in Mulkay's sense) and enhanced Beethoven's image over time.

Posterity has been good to Beethoven. He has been beautified in both the plastic arts[6] and music scholarship, where so much of the field of Beethoven studies is occupied by hagiography. Mainstream musical history has therefore ensured a bias in favor of Beethoven's genius, an unacknowledged but nevertheless elaborate set of instructions for his appreciation. Because pro-Beethoven culture is so extensive, the experience of his music can be a very rich one. Yet to the extent that our attention to genius and its products (whether these are scientific discoveries or works of art) occurs from the perspective these cultures of appreciation provide, we are blinded to visions of how music history could have been otherwise. We close off from inquiry the issue of how and why some individuals, findings, and enterprises are celebrated over others, why some are perceived as exemplary and others not.

The social resources that make the identity of genius possible (beyond practical and material conditions) include such factors as what an audience will accept as legitimate, and when and from whom it will accept certain types of work. To ignore these issues is to mystify genius, to take it out of its historical and interactional contexts. Moreover, to decontextualize genius is to elide the moral and political character of many or most quarrels over what counts as "valuable" work—to preclude, in this case, a sociological consideration of aesthetics and of art forms, their social uses and social consequences.

We may, in other words, perceive Beethoven as the composer of truly great works, but this does not mean that the contemporaries who objected to his style were "wrong." We cannot assume that our responses will resemble those of the individuals we happen to study.[7] Rather, we need to build on the notion that classificatory schemes are socially constructed, and we need to make the reception and construction of mean-

ing problematic. As Pierre Bourdieu suggests, "Whatever may be the nature of the message—religious prophecy, political speech, publicity
image, technical object, etc.—reception depends upon the categories of
perception, thought and action of those who receive it" (1968, 594n.).
Categories of perception are located in particular times and places; what
is set aside as valuable and, indeed, the structure of value and how it is
allocated will also vary (for example, the degree of contrast perceived
between *best* and *worst*). To make this structuralist observation is not
to imply culture as deterministic, however—it is not to deny the ways
that cultures are created and transformed by actors. Culture (or categories of perception) is constitutive of the reality we perceive and take for
granted, but these categories are themselves created and recreated by socially located individuals and groups.[8] Sociological inquiry can therefore
focus on the issue of how actors attempt to mobilize and manipulate the
structures through which phenomena are apprehended.

In the case of Beethoven's reputation, this process requires a consideration of the ways musical criteria—the categories of perception
through which reception occurs—were themselves subject to change and
manipulation. This point is crucial to our understanding of Beethoven's
reception since, as I discuss throughout this volume, Beethoven's evaluation entailed a two-way process of alignment between his works and the
categories of musical value. I also explore the resources and activities
that helped to authorize accounts of Beethoven's talent and to deflect and
suppress hostile reactions to Beethoven's work. This approach entails a
focus on practical activities, on how alignments between Beethoven and
categories of musical worth were articulated, authorized, and disseminated. At the most general level, I consider the question, How is aesthetic authority produced and sustained?

To answer this question, it is necessary to gain distance from commonsense images of reception. That imagery depicts talent as residing solely
in individual composers and works and as recognized by independent
and separate individual "receivers" as a transcendent and immutable
form of artistic truth. By contrast, I explore the ways reception is actively
structured. From this perspective, talent is conceived of neither as independent of the interpretive acts of those who recognize it nor as reducible
to those acts. Rather, talent is understood as emerging from and con-
stantly renewed through the reflexive interplay, bit by bit, between perception and its object. In other words, Beethoven's artistic development
and the reception of that development should be conceived as feeding

each other in a virtuously circular relationship, one which was capable of producing both greater appreciation of Beethoven's compositions and further scope for his future productions.

An analogy to love (whether civic, familial, or erotic) is relevant here: two or more individuals may collaboratively produce for each other a context in which they can act or be viewed felicitously, each being constructively occupied with making, mobilizing, and allocating resources for the acts (and the appreciation of acts) of another in virtuously recursive ways. Such virtuous circularity generates increasing devotion to its object, which in turn creates the space and confidence for future creative activity. Resources mobilized to nurture the artistic or love relationship are deflected from other potential relationships (and other love objects). This conception of how talent emerges and is nurtured enhances the traditional musicological understandings of a composer's work. It enables more explicit theorizing of the interrelation between the social production of taste and the social production of artworks themselves. This framework is crucial for the study of Beethoven's reputation, because only within it can the study of Beethoven's career avoid simply reinforcing the "Great Man" approach to music history.

THE IMPORTANCE OF BEETHOVEN'S PATRONS

Popular and contradictory imageries of Beethoven's status in Vienna during his lifetime abound and continue to accumulate. On the one hand, Beethoven is sometimes portrayed as having been ignored and unappreciated, which, as we will see, could not have been further from the case during Beethoven's first decade and a half in Vienna. Alternatively, he is portrayed as a composer "of the people," which is also inaccurate. When Baron Peter von Braun, the manager of the Theater an der Wien, appealed to Beethoven in 1806 (in reference to the audiences for *Fidelio*) to try to fill the entire house and thereby increase ticket sales, Beethoven's reply was, "I don't write for the galleries!" (Thayer and Forbes 1967, 1: 397–98). Chapter 2 describes the first fifteen years of the composer's career in Vienna, when Beethoven's musical public was primarily aristocratic. His lighter and more popular compositions aside, Beethoven was not, during these years, particularly concerned with appealing to middle-class audiences. His more esoteric and explicitly oriented seriousness was marked both by the ways his contemporaries compared his work to that of his fellow musicians and by his own attempts to define the quality

of his relationship with his patrons and his public. Public and more genuinely popular reception of Beethoven consisted of fleeting support during
the years around 1814 and the Congress of Vienna—support, it should
be noted, based on works (such as "Wellington's Victory") that modern
music scholars often classify as potboilers.

Thus Beethoven's career was mainly private. It consisted of first, an
approximately twenty-year period, punctuated by participation in public concerts for his own and others' benefit, during which he was well
insulated within the world of aristocratic soirées, and during which he
was extremely productive; second, a brief phase as a popular composer;
third, by 1819, a retreat from public life and an increasing alienation
from the public taste for the lighter styles of composers such as Johann
Nepomuk Hummel and Louis Spohr; and fourth, a period during his last
years in which there was a resurgence of interest in his work.

Neither Beethoven's middle-period popularity nor his ultimate recognition as the greatest of musical masters could have occurred without his
initial lionization by aristocratic society during the 1790s and early
1800s. It is therefore important to view Beethoven's "first decade of un-
broken triumphs," as Maynard Solomon calls it (1977a, 57), more
closely—specifically, to understand the basis for elite receptivity to
Beethoven. In addition, we need to inquire into how these aristocratic
patrons, Prince Karl Lichnowsky in particular, assisted Beethoven in
progressing from pianist, to pianist-composer, to, starting around 1800,
a major Viennese and eventually international figure and a composer of
large-scale symphonic works.

I explore the social circumstances of Beethoven's success by first presenting (in chapters 2 and 3) an outline of the cultural, economic, and
organizational contexts of music making in Vienna when Beethoven arrived in 1792. Chapter 2 sketches some of the changes in musical culture
to which Beethoven's success was reflexively linked. I describe the transition in musical taste, from dilettante values to values of musical seriousness, and consider the vicissitudes of Mozart's reception as well as
the activities of one of Vienna's most active patrons in light of changes in
musical aesthetics and practice between 1787 and 1805. In chapter 3 I
examine the changing economic basis of musical patronage and the implications this change had for music's aristocratic patrons, in order to
consider the extent to which the aristocratic predilection for "serious"
music may have been linked to a concern with maintaining prestige in a
changing patronage climate. I then outline how the organizational basis

and cultural outlook of late eighteenth-century aristocratic musical life created a predisposition toward musical stars and toward the notion of musical genius.

Beginning with chapter 4, I turn my attention to Beethoven himself and describe his connection to prominent Viennese patrons. By comparing Beethoven's early career to that of Jan Ladislav Dussek, I examine resources that were available to Beethoven but beyond the reach of most of his fellow musicians, and I suggest that it was because of a variety of social and cultural forms of capital that Beethoven was well positioned to become "the next Mozart." In chapters 5 through 8 the focus shifts to the level of social action, specifically to some of the more mundane tasks that contributed to the construction of Beethoven as both a successful composer and a creative genius. Chapter 5 describes how early claims of Beethoven's special promise were substantiated and mobilized to present Beethoven as an extraordinary talent. A particular mythic account of Beethoven's relation to Haydn was elaborated over time, and I consider some of the reasons why Beethoven and Haydn were willing to collaborate to produce a fiction that became a resource for the construction of Beethoven's greatness. Chapter 6 addresses Beethoven's place in the life of Vienna's aristocratic salons. I discuss how his music was experienced by its contemporary hearers and some of his patrons' activities that ensured his music was heard sympathetically. It was in this world of aristocratic salons that a claim to Beethoven's greatness was initially constructed and where he was first produced as an authoritative figure. Chapters 7 and 8 are devoted to particular aspects of Beethoven's career and success. Chapter 7 examines an important but overlooked moment in the history of Beethoven's reputation and the success of the discourse of musical genius. That event is Beethoven's piano duel with the Austrian pianist-composer Joseph Wölffl in 1799, which I discuss in order to explore the terms in which high culture music was debated, and also to locate the social ideology for which Beethoven stood. Chapter 8 considers how a pro-Beethoven aesthetic was initially routinized through two forms of music technology, the piano and musical critical discourse in the then leading German-language music periodical, the *Allgemeine Musikalische Zeitung*. Finally, in chapter 9, I summarize the contributions that a study of the social bases of Beethoven's success and abilities can make to the more general topic of the construction of identity. I discuss the implications of this study both for the shape and texture of high cultural musical life today and for the ways we conceive of the identities of individuals, in social research and in everyday life.

CHAPTER 2

The Emergence of Serious Music Culture, 1784-1805

In 1784 Georg Friedrich Richter, Ludwig Fischer, and Mozart collaborated in offering a series of subscription concerts to feature their works. Mozart was pleased with the success of this venture, noting that he had managed to attract 174 subscribers, 30 more than the two of his partners together (Jahn 1882, 2:287; Morrow 1989, 56). He wrote exuberantly to his father: "The first concert on March 17th went off very well. The hall was full to overflowing; and the new concerto [possibly K. 449] I played won extraordinary applause. Everywhere I go I hear praises of that concert" (Anderson 1938, 1:872). During the middle 1780s Viennese concert life was booming and Mozart was at the height of his fame, giving more confirmed concerts than any other musician in Vienna (Moore 1991, 95).

Mozart's popularity was also clearly reflected in the music press.[1] In 1783, for example, the Viennese correspondent for Cramer's *Magazin der Musik* (one of the earliest German-language music periodicals) described a performance of *Die Entführung aus dem Serail* (*The Abduction from the Seraglio*) as follows: "It surpassed the public's expectations and the author's taste and new ideas which were entrancing received the loudest and most general applause" (Deutsch 1965, 214). A month later in the same periodical, a writer reported that the sonatas K. 376, 296, and 377–80 for piano and violin were "rich in new ideas and traces of their author's great musical genius. . . . Amateurs and connoisseurs should first play them through for themselves and they will then perceive that we have in no way exaggerated" (ibid.).

By 1789, however, Mozart's fortunes had changed. Attempting to mount another subscription series, Mozart was able to find only one subscriber, Baron Gottfried van Swieten, who is discussed later in this chapter. After circulating a subscription list for two weeks, Mozart was forced to abandon the plan. On the basis of this evidence, numerous scholars (myself included) have suggested that Mozart's reputation and his popularity declined in the later years of his career.[2] While there does appear to have been a shift in Mozart's fortunes, new light shed by current and ongoing research into Mozart's reception during the years after 1787 has contributed to a more complex picture than that portrayed in previous accounts.

On the basis of his recent discovery of the box office receipts for *Così fan tutte* and the revival of *Le nozze di Figaro* in 1789, the music historian Dexter Edge (1991) has suggested that Mozart's operas remained well attended during the later period of the composer's career. Edge has documented how performances of Mozart's operas compared favorably, in financial terms, with performances of operas by other composers. If Mozart experienced any "failure" in later life, this lapse needs to be seen in the more general context of public concert life during the late 1780s, which was apparently experiencing a temporary decline. (The ebbing in interest began around 1788 and lasted until about 1797.)

In two recent studies (Braunbehrens 1989; Moore 1992), scholars have observed that concert activities dropped off during the later 1780s. Julia Moore suggests that

> the apparently small number of public concerts in Vienna during the later 1780s was related to the extraordinary public concert activity there during the mid-1780s—namely public concerts were wildly fashionable for a few years until they became tiresome, when the upper aristocracy then turned to other sorts of musical activities. What these new activities may have been is a subject for further research and discussion. In other words, Mozart was very, very lucky to be *the* fashionable performer in Vienna at precisely the right moment. (1992, 96)

Thus the failure of Mozart's proposed concert series in 1789 cannot be read as a clear indication of his unpopularity, but should rather be viewed as indicating a more general decline of aristocratic interest in the public concert forum.

These recent reconsiderations of Mozart's reputation in Vienna belie the idea that the composer's popularity waned during the final years of his career. At the same time, the documentary evidence collected in Deutsch 1965[3] does indicate that the reception of some of Mozart's music shifted during the years after 1787, at least with regard to his more connoisseur-oriented and self-consciously serious works. In 1787, for example, a writer for *Magazin der Musik* (which had lavishly praised Mozart four years earlier) describes Mozart as "the most skillful and best keyboard scholar I have ever heard; the pity is only that he aims too high in his artful and truly beautiful compositions, in order to become a new creator, whereby it must be said that feeling and heart profit little." The critic then suggests that the harmonically adventurous *Haydn Quartets* were "too highly seasoned—and whose palate can endure this for long? Forgive this simile from the cookery book" (Deutsch 1965, 290). In 1789, the same magazine compared Mozart with the more senior composer Leopold Kozeluch:

> The works of . . . [Kozeluch] maintain themselves and [in Vienna] find access everywhere, whereas Mozart's works do not in general please quite so much. It is true, too, and his six quartets for violins, viola, and bass dedicated to Haydn confirm it once again, that he has a decided leaning towards the difficult and the unusual. But then, what great and elevated ideas he has too, testifying to a bold spirit! (ibid., 349)

The culinary metaphor (from which our concept of taste is descended) was common in eighteenth-century musical discourse. The *Haydn Quartets* apparently "disagreed" with Prince Anton Grassalkowitz as well; according to a story reported in the *Allgemeine Musikalische Zeitung*, the prince refused to believe that such discords could have been intended by the composer, and he demanded of his musicians to see the score. When he found that the music he had heard did indeed correspond to the notations, he tore up the score in a rage. An Italian purchaser reputedly sent back the score to its publisher, Artaria, believing it full of printer's errors (King 1955, 5).

The Viennese reception of *Don Giovanni* also may have been mixed, judging from references to it in the diary of Count Karl Zinzendorf, who has been suggested by music historians as a typical representative of aristocratic musical taste (Morrow 1989; Edge 1991). Zinzendorf initially notes that he found the music "agreeable and very varied" on 7 May 1788. Then on 12 May he writes, "Mme de la Lieppe finds the music learned, little suited to the voice." On 16 June Zinzendorf notes simply that he had attended the opera and that one of the singers was "informally dressed," and on 23 June, after his fifth or more attendance at *Don Giovanni* (repeated attendance was conventional), he observes that he "was very much bored at the opera Don Giovanni" (Deutsch 1965, 313,

314, 319).[4] In a similar vein, the *Journal des Luxus und der Moden* observes in February 1791 that the opera was "here and there very artificial and overloaded" (ibid., 386). In general, Mozart may have remained popular until his death, but available documentary evidence indicates that some of his work after the middle 1780s was controversial and met with mixed responses. We do know that clear objections to Mozart's music were made in response to Mozart's compositional complexities. These complexities may be understood as reflecting an aesthetic reorientation of Mozart's closest aristocratic patrons during these years—a shift away from an emphasis on music as entertainment and toward the pleasures and values of the musical connoisseur.

Between 1782 and 1789, Mozart began to collaborate more closely with one of the few aristocratic patrons in Vienna actively engaged in promoting the concept of "serious" music, Baron Gottfried van Swieten. During the mid-to-late 1780s, van Swieten was an important court official; as head of the Austrian education department, he played a leading role in the period of enlightened Josephian reform. Mozart took part in van Swieten's Sunday noontime concerts (where participants sang Bach choral music, accompanied by Mozart on piano), and he orchestrated the four Handel oratorios, under instructions from van Swieten to "clothe Handel so solemnly and so tastefully that he pleases the modish fop on the one hand and on the other still shows himself in his sublimity" (Deutsch 1965, 337). Mozart also copied out Bach fugues for performance at van Swieten's. On 10 April 1782 he writes to his father:

> I have been intending to ask you . . . to enclose . . . Handel's six fugues and Eberlin's toccatas and fugues. I go every Sunday at twelve o'clock to the Baron van Swieten, where nothing is played but Handel and Bach. I am collecting at the moment the fugues of Bach—not only of Sebastian, but also of Emanuel and Friedmann. I am also collecting Handel's and should like to have the six I mentioned. I should like the Baron to hear Eberlin's too. (Anderson 1938, 2:800)

On 4 January 1783 Mozart writes:

> Then there are a few counterpoint works by Eberlin copied out on small paper and bound in blue, and some things of Haydn, which I should like to have for the Baron van Swieten to whose house I go every Sunday from twelve to two. Tell me, are there any really good fugues in Haydn's last mass or vesper music, or possibly in both? If so, I should be very much obliged to you if you would have them both scored for me bit by bit. (ibid., 835)

Mozart's contact with van Swieten probably enhanced the composer's interest in contrapuntal forms, an interest we see developed in pieces like the Fantasia and Fugue (K. 394), the Mass in C Minor (K. 427), the Fantasia in F Minor for Mechanical Organ (K. 608), and even the chorale of the two men in armor from *The Magic Flute* (Olleson 1967, 66–67). Edward Olleson has suggested that Mozart's study of counterpoint during these years occasionally "brought about a loss of Mozart's idiomatic personality and perhaps a dryness which is absent from most of his music," pointing in particular to the fugue of the unfinished Suite in C Major (K. 399) (ibid.). While other scholars will no doubt later specify the nature and extent of van Swieten's influence, it is reasonable to suggest that the musicians van Swieten patronized would have been receptive to his concern for "serious" music.

Van Swieten's influence on Mozart may be overrated, but at least two Mozart biographers have observed the notable increase of counterpoint in the works of his last years (Jahn 1882, 2:386–400; Olleson 1963, 1967). Olleson, for example, links the van Swieten influence to the emergence of what he views as Mozart's "masterpieces": "Inspired by Handel via van Swieten, by Bach via Lichnowsky or simply by his own inclination, Mozart produced in the last year of his life some incomparable masterpieces in a contrapuntal, not to say archaic idiom" (1967, 148). It is thus possible that the more learned, difficult aspects of Mozart's later works (as these were perceived by his contemporaries) were oriented to the concerns of van Swieten and his circle (which included Prince Lichnowsky, later Beethoven's closest patron). These connoisseur values would have constituted a minority view in Viennese musical life during the late 1780s, when categories of taste were still generally dominated by the concerns of the dilettante and general listener. Secular music was intended to please—to respond to general tastes and preferences—and "pleasingness," as a writer to the *Chronik von Berlin* notes in May 1791, was "a concept which has gained citizenship throughout the realm of thinking beings" (Deutsch 1965, 390). Mozart may have begun to orient himself to a consciously articulated notion of masterpieces at a time when the prevailing winds of musical fashion were still directed away from (in the words of the contemporary chronicler of music Dr. Charles Burney) the "unmeaning art and contrivance" of J. S. Bach, which, while never entirely out of fashion in Catholic Austria,[5] played a diminished role in secular musical life. The "counter-reform" of musical taste in Vienna had not yet begun.

The ubiquity of pleasingness as a value in late eighteenth-century European music discourse is undeniable. According to Burney, the notion referred to a concern with "nature and facility." In terms of more concrete compositional techniques, these values tended to be translated into music that was relatively easy to comprehend and play and into an aesthetic of amateurism. Johann Ferdinand von Schönfeld, for example, said in his *Jahrbuch der Tonkünst von Wien und Prag* (1796, 390) that he could confidently recommend the works of Leopold Kozeluch, one of the most popular Viennese composers of the 1790s, to "amateurs of the clavier." Similarly, the *Musikalische Real Zeitung* has this to say about the pianist-composer the Abbé Sterkel in 1789: "No excess of modulations to remote keys, no awkward difficulties or neck-breaking passages; but pleasant, flowing melody, well-ordered progress and—what is so rarely achieved by many of today's fashionable composers—tonal unity characterize these sonatas of Herr Sterkel" (Komlós 1987, 229).

As the Haydn scholar Jens Peter Larsen observes, "Scarcely at any other time in European history of music is there such an unmistakable endeavor to write music which is at the same time enjoyable to both [amateurs and connoisseurs]" (1967, 131). Just as musicians had not yet escaped the domestic role that had been shaped for them at the turn of the eighteenth century, neither had music itself moved away from its ancillary role in the settings within which it was made. In secular arenas and in 1780s Vienna, music was meant to entertain; it was not yet commonly conceived as an end in itself. Thus Mozart's cultivation of a learned style may have come at a time when the concept was not generally disseminated and receptivity was scant. During the late 1780s, van Swieten and those who shared his interest in a musical "greatness" constructed from Baroque models were a fringe group within the world of aristocratic music patronage.

Any gap that may have been felt during Mozart's lifetime between his over-learnedness and his more popular works was quickly bridged, however, after his death. During the early 1790s and later, Mozart was hailed (initially in the Prague press[6]) as "immortal Mozart" whose "death came too soon both for [his widow] and for Art"—as Constanze Mozart herself puts it in the announcement of a benefit concert published in the *Wiener Zeitung* on 13 December 1794 [Deutsch 1965, 471). This posthumous rediscovery of Mozart revolved around imagery of the composer culled from his life before his genius had reached its fullest flower. The precise genus and species of that flower became the object of dispute, however, as Mozart's posthumous prestige became a resource for the reputations of potential musical heirs. In other words, association with Mozart became a way of articulating status claims.

During the early 1790s, Prague writers made efforts to highlight their city for its aesthetic foresight in appreciating Mozart. A review of a Mozart concert in the *Prager Neue Zeitung* of 9 February 1794 reads:

> It is easy to imagine how full the hall was, if one knows Prague's artistic sense and its love for Mozart's music. Mozart's widow and son both wept tears of grief at their loss and of gratitude towards a noble nation [i.e., Bohemia]. Thus this evening was fittingly and admirably devoted to an act of homage to merit and genius . . . a small tribute to the unspeakable delight that Mozart's divine tones often drew from us. . . . It is as though Mozart had composed especially for Bohemia; nowhere was his music better understood and executed than in Prague . . . many were the hearts that Mozart's great genius won for itself. (Deutsch 1965, 469–70)

Again, in April of the same year:

> The esteemed Prague public, which well knows how to honour the name of Mozart. . . . The boy Mozart, the son of the immortal man whose divine harmonies will continue to delight us to the end of our days, is to be sent to Prague for the benefit of his education and upbringing; this being at the instigation of his noble patron, His Excellency the Baron van Swieten, who places full confidence in the spirit of the Bohemian nation. (ibid., 471)

Some commentators remained skeptical. In *Teutschlands Annalen des Jahres 1794,* for example, Haydn is favorably compared with Mozart for the former's more explicit attempts to please the public:

> In this year 1794 nothing can or may be sung or played and nothing heard with approbation but that it bears on its brow the all-powerful and magic name of Mozart. . . . That Mozart to a large extent deserves this applause will be disputed by no one. But that he was still in his years of ferment and that his ideas were still frequently in a state of flux, as it were—of this there are only too many instances in his works. If we pause only to consider his symphonies: for all their fire, for all their pomp and brilliance they yet lack that sense of unity, that clarity and directness of presentation which we rightly admire in Jos. Haydn's symphonies. . . . Moreover, one is often tempted, in hearing Mozart's works, to exclaim with the maid-servant in the comedy, "there's nothing natural about me, thank God!" An almost unadulteratedly spicy diet, which spoils the palate if one's taste for it continues; and in the hands of the wretched imitators, who think they need only to Mozartize in order to please, every trace of noble simplicity will finally be banished from music. Such could easily prove to be the final result of this general idolization. (ibid., 472–73)

By the middle 1790s, however, objections such as this were the exception, not the rule; in the German-language music periodicals, at least, the idea of "immortal Mozart" was widespread. Those aspects of his work that were earlier perceived as difficulties or impediments to the wholehearted recommendation of the composer were no longer mentioned: "Posterity does justice to the merits and genius of Mozart; his heavenly harmonies resound everywhere" (*Journal des Luxus und der Moden* [Weimar], July 1795); "During the past few years it has become clearly evident that the taste of our esteemed public has declared itself more and more in favor of Mozart's music" (*Gratzer Zeitung*, 26 August 1795; both sources cited in Deutsch 1965, 475, 476).

By the mid-1790s, Mozart's spirit had become an apparently universal resource and Mozart's death an untimely tragedy. What greater aspiration could there be for a young composer than to receive "Mozart's spirit," to be recognized as heir to the genius of Mozart? Just as Mozart's earlier mixed reception during the late 1780s can be considered as part of a reorientation by some aristocrats (away from the quasi-public concert and toward the more private forums of salons), so too can his posthumous renown. The 1790s' celebration of Mozart as a master composer was part of and contributed to a general reorientation of taste.

VIENNA'S MUSICAL ARISTOCRATS IN THE 1790s

In 1805, a Viennese correspondent to the *Zeitung für die elegante Welt* described the world of Viennese salons and notes of one that "Sunday mornings, and perhaps also Fridays are usually devoted *to true music,* which one never loses sight of here. The string quartets of Haydn, Mozart, Beethoven or Romberg, occasionally of Wranitzsky, are usually played. The easier keyboard music of a Pleyel, Vanhall, Kozeluch is *entirely out of style*" (trans. Morrow 1989, 9). In the sixteen years separating this observation from the 1789 description in *Magazin der Musik* of Kozeluch's accessibility over Mozart's complexity, a partial reorientation of aristocratic musical taste had occurred. This reorientation was articulated in periodicals and is supported by known repertory data. It consisted of a shift away from the prodilettante aesthetic and toward values of musical seriousness and learnedness. The new aesthetic was built primarily around the notions of complexity and of the musical masters, and around symphonic and chamber genre rather than virtuosic showpieces or opera highlights. Within this aesthetic, Mozart, Haydn, and especially Beethoven were highlighted as exemplars of all that was best in Viennese music, while Kozeluch (and numerous other composers like him) were reclassified as lesser contemporaries.

Much of the groundwork for this shift occurred in the private world of aristocratic salons, particularly as activity in these salons centered on Beethoven, who was uniquely celebrated for the expressiveness and complexity of his compositions. Beethoven was known in this arena primarily as a connoisseur's musician and he was increasingly famed for what his contemporaries came to refer to as a "higher style of writing." As one critic writes, "Less educated musicians, and those who expect nothing more from music than a facile entertainment will take up these works in vain."[7]

Who, then, were the members of this world, what were their concerns, and how did they relate to other music patrons who were not Beethoven partisans? As a start toward answering these questions, Table 1 classifies, by social background, the musical dilettantes and patrons listed in Schönfeld's *Jahrbuch*. The small size, not only of this group but of the aristocratic population in comparison to the Viennese population at large, is striking: at this time Vienna was a city of approximately 200,000, growing to 317,768 by 1830 (Moore 1987, 76). According to Johann Pezzl, who wrote a series of guidebooks on Vienna during the

• TABLE I

VIRTUOSI, AMATEUR MUSICIANS, AND MUSIC PATRONS IN THE VIENNESE HIGH CULTURE MUSIC WORLD, AS LISTED IN SCHÖNFELD 1796[a]

First aristocracy by rank		
Princes/princesses	3	
Counts/countesses	19	
Barons	1	(van Swieten)
Total	23	(12%)
Second aristocracy by rank		
Barons/baronesses	8	
Freiherr/freyerrin	6	
"von"	66	
Total	80	(43%)
Middle-class professionals (untitled court officials, doctors, professors, lawyers, painters, architects, intellectuals)	16	(9%)
Businessmen (untitled merchants, factory owners)	3	(2%)
Musicians	64	(34%)
TOTAL	186	(100%)

[a]Based on information contained in Johann Ferdinand von Schönfeld's *Jahrbuch der Tonkünst von Wien und Prag*. I am grateful to Dexter Edge for this information, which he compiled to expand and correct an earlier version of this table that I had published (DeNora 1991, 336, table 4); it will be published along with further analysis in a forthcoming publication by Edge.

late eighteenth century, in 1782 there were twenty-one families of princes, seventy of counts, and fifty of barons (altogether about a thousand individuals); this group, plus members of the then growing newly ennobled "second society," made up approximately 1 percent (2,611 people) of Vienna's population (ibid., 403).

Table 2 lists active concert hosts or organizers during the 1790s for whom there is extant documentary evidence.[8] An in-depth look at Baron van Swieten and his activities provides a clearer picture of the leading aristocratic musical culture during the 1780s and 1790s.

GOTTFRIED VAN SWIETEN: "PATRIARCH OF MUSIC"

Recognized by his contemporaries as the doyen of musical patrons, van Swieten was one of Beethoven's most important supporters during the composer's first decade in Vienna; Beethoven subsequently dedicated his first symphony to him in 1800. Although van Swieten played an important role during the period of Josephian reform, after Joseph II died in 1790 Leopold II annulled many of his brother's economic and political reforms. Van Swieten was, not surprisingly, relieved of his duties (on 5 December 1791, the day of Mozart's death).

Van Swieten's status as a Beethoven supporter was initially unique among Vienna's aristocrats. Until Count Moritz Fries began to patronize Beethoven nearly a decade later, Baron van Swieten was the only member of the initial Beethoven circle of close patrons who, though not born into an old aristocratic family, came to be counted as a member of that world. The son of Empress Maria Theresa's (ennobled) personal physician, van Swieten entered the civil service in 1755, serving as a diplomat in Brussels until 1757. He was then posted to Paris (1760–63), Warsaw (1763–64), and England (1764–69), and thereafter spent seven years in Berlin.

Olleson suggests that "it was perhaps thought that [van Swieten's] musical and literary interests would be a help in dealing with the King [Frederick the Great]. . . . In certain quarters at least, van Swieten's music was seen as his principal quality" (1967, 38). According to Olleson, a story circulated some years later in Vienna that the baron's musical interests were what secured him his position in Berlin. Van Swieten had been sent to Berlin to complete the delicate and complicated negotiations over the partition of Poland between Austria, Russia, and Prussia. When in Berlin he took an active part in a cultural life that differed considerably from Vienna's and was considered by Berliners to be far superior to that

TABLE 2

KEY VIENNESE MUSIC PATRONS IN THE 1790S AND 1800S

Count Anton Georg Appony (1751–1817): Member of GAC; frequent private concert host during the 1790s.

Baron Nathan Arnstein (1758–1818): Ennobled banker and regular private concert host c. 1800. His daughter reportedly played pianoforte music by Steibelt at one of the Arnstein salons.

Prince Auersberg (?–?): Member of GAC.

Count Batthyana (?–?): Member of GAC.

Baron Peter Braun (1758–1819): An industrialist (silk) ennobled in 1795, he was director of court theaters from 1794 to 1807. He stopped leasing them to private artists (making it more difficult for musicians to produce for-profit concerts). He also hosted weekly private concerts and kept a "Harmonie für Tafelmusik" (a table music ensemble).

Mme. Buquoy (?–?): Occasional private concert host during 1790s and 1800s.

Count Franz Josef Czernin (?–?): Member of GAC.

Countess Josephine Deym (?–?): Bimonthly private concert host 1804.

Prince Karl Johann Baptist Walter Dietrichstein (1728–1808): He or his son Franz Joseph (1767–1854) was a member of GAC.

Count Palfy von Erdödy (?–?): Member of GAC.

Count Johann Esterhazy (1774–1829): Member of GAC; occasional private concert host c. 1797.

Prince Paul Anton Esterhazy (1738–94): Though it is not always possible to distinguish among them, one of the several prince Esterhazys was a member of GAC. Other musically active Esterhazy princes during this period were Prince Nikolaus Joseph (1714–90), Haydn's patron and known as "the luxury-loving" prince, and Prince Nikolaus II (1765–1833), who recalled Haydn from London in 1794 and reconstituted the Esterhazy kapelle (ensemble), which Prince Paul Anton had dissolved after the death of Nikolaus I.

Count Moritz Fries (1777–1825): Member of GAC; regular private concert host c. 1799 (Monday evenings). Married Princess Maria Theresa von Hohenlohe Waldenburg in 1800. Haydn's *Creation* was performed at his Vienna palace on 4 April 1800, arranged for septet. He was a noted collector and arts patron, his library contained more than sixteen hundred volumes, and he possessed more than three hundred paintings. Fries's father was an ennobled banker.

Prince Golitzin (1721–93): Russian ambassador to Vienna, he hosted weekly private concerts from 1790 to 1793.

Count Leonard Harrach (?–?): Member of GAC. Schönfeld said he was also a fine dilettante musician (he played the flute).

Count Haugwitz (?–?): Regular private concert host c. 1802–7. In 1807–8 he initiated a series of "Concerts Spirituels."

Prince Ferdinand Johann Nepomuk Joseph Kinsky (1781–1812): Member of GAC; subsequently, along with Archduke Rudolph and Lobkowitz the younger, paid Beethoven an annuity to keep him in Vienna.

(Continued on next page)

TABLE 2 *(continued)*

Prince Karl Lichnowsky (1756–1814): Regular private concert host during the
1790s; after 1795 cohosted Friday morning performances of string quartets
with Count Razumovsky. He was a member of the same Masonic lodge as
Mozart, had been a pupil of Mozart in the 1780s, and had escorted Mozart
on a foreign concert tour. Occasionally he hosted large-scale concerts (*Judas
Maccabaeus* in 1794, according to Zinzendorf's diary). He was married to
Countess von Thun.

Prince Joseph Franz Maximilian von Lobkowitz (1772–1816): Private concert
host as early as 1793; founded a kapelle in 1794 (after 1797 his kapellmeister
was Anton Wranitzky) and hosted premiers of some of Beethoven's
symphonic works. One of the three patrons to provide Beethoven with an
annuity in 1709, he was a keen amateur musician: cellist, singer, violinist, and
composer.

Prince Joseph Maria Carl von Lobkowitz (1725–1802): Member of GAC;
private concert host during 1790s. Married Maria Joseph née Countess
Harrach in 1752. According to Landon (1976–80, 3:294) and Morrow
(1989, 30), he hosted the concert at which Beethoven made his Viennese
debut on 1 March 1795, though it is not clear to what event this claim refers,
unless to a private premier performance of the concerto which Beethoven
performed later that year at a public benefit concert with Haydn. There were
two musically active Prince Lobkowitzes between the years of 1795 and 1802
(there were two lines of the family—see later) and it is not always possible to
distinguish between them in contemporary reports. Zinzendorf refers to the
second as "the younger" (see later).

Prince Paar (?–?): Occasional private concert host during the 1790s.

Herr Paradis (?–?): Weekly concert host 1809. His blind daughter gave
concerts of pianoforte music.

Herr Quarin (?–?): Middle-class occasional private concert host in 1809,
according to Rosenbaum (1968).

Mme. de Rittersberg (?–?): Weekly private concert host 1809, according to
Rosenbaum (1968). Prince Lobkowitz loaned her personnel for her concerts
in 1809, according to Reichardt (1915).

Eleonore and Imanuel Schikaneder (?–?): Directed Theater an der Wien from
1801 to 1806.

Herr Schmierer (?–?): Middle-class regular private concert host c. 1801–3,
according to diarist Joseph Carl Rosenbaum (1968). The concerts tended to
present chamber music rather than larger orchestral pieces, though Haydn's
Creation and *Seasons* were performed here. Rosenbaum's wife performed here.

Hofrat Schubb (?–?): Middle-class regular private concert host (performances
of chamber music) c. 1802–3, according to Rosenbaum (1968).

Prince Josef Johann Nepomuk Schwarzenberg (1769–1833): Member of
GAC (most GAC concerts took place at his home); his wife, Princess Pauline
Karolina Iris von Arenberg-Archot, hosted concerts during the 1790s. The
first performances of Haydn's *Seasons* and *Creation* were held at his winter
palace in Vienna.

Count Sinsendorf (?–?): Member of GAC; not to be confused with Count Karl
von Zinzendorf.

TABLE 2 *(continued)*

Baron Nathan Spielmann (?–?): Weekly private concert host 1802.

Baron Gottfried van Swieten (1733–1803): The son of Empress Maria Theresa's personal physician, he was a civil servant and later diplomat in Brussels (1755–57), Paris (1760–63), Warsaw (1763–64), England (1769), and Berlin (1770–77). In 1777 he returned to Vienna, where he became a commander of the Royal St. Stevens Order and director of the Imperial Library. As head of the Austrian education department, he had a significant impact on cultural matters during Joseph II's reign. He was relieved of this office by Leopold II. Van Swieten was the director and founder of the Gesellschaft der Associierten Cavaliere (GAC) and a private concert host during the early 1780s and the 1790s.

Prince Ferdinand Trauttmannsdorf (1749–1827): Member of GAC; married Princess Carolina née Colloredo.

Baron Raimund Wetzlar (?–?): Son of ennobled banker; hosted the "duels" between Beethoven and Wölffl.

Baron Würth (?–?): Banker and regular private concert host 1804–5, he assembled an orchestra c. 1805.

Sources: Morrow 1989; Biba 1980; Hanslick [1869] 1979; Thayer and Forbes 1967; A. Schindler 1966; Nettl 1956; Schönfeld [1796] 1976; Landon 1970a, 1976–80, vols. 3 and 4; Jahn 1882, vols. 2 and 3; Moore 1987; Griesinger 1968; and Loesser 1954.

GAC, Gesellschaft der Associierten Cavaliere.

---

of their southern neighbors (ibid., 49). Van Swieten's tastes in music, as they shifted over the years between 1770 and 1777, reveal that his encounter with Berlin culture was influential. As Olleson describes the baron's changing interests, in 1770 his preference was for the "lightweight and modern," not the "great and noble" (and old); seven years later, he was an ardent spokesman for the serious in music and the ideology of greatness.

In Berlin literary circles, the Sturm und Drang (literally, storm and stress) movement was well under way by the time van Swieten arrived. Proponents emphasized a rejection of the rules of poetry and glorified feeling as opposed to reason. In the Sturm und Drang perspective, genius became "a slogan for complete rejection of discipline and tradition and was linked with creative spontaneity" (Wellek 1955, 1:176). The modern notion of creative genius appears to have been first articulated in northern Germany during the 1770s and 1780s, often in response to the works of Shakespeare, which were viewed less as theatrical works than as poetry and psychological portraiture (Wellek 1955; Murray 1989). It was also in northern Germany during the eighteenth century that the organicist metaphor was initially applied to creative works. Goethe, in direct opposition to the culinary terms with which Mozart was evaluated, describes what he considers to be the "vile" notion of composition—"as if [an artwork] were a piece of cake made of eggs, flour and sugar. It is a mental creation in every detail, and the whole is of one spirit and act" (Wellek 1955, 1:209).

Although the Sturm und Drang movement and the later interest in the idea of creative genius were primarily literary phenomena, musical life in 1770s Berlin also reflected the concerns with artistic greatness and with the artistic embodiment of emotional life. Music at court had changed little since the 1750s. Two of the principal musicians there, J. Friedrich Agricola and J. Philipp Kirnberger, had been pupils of J. S. Bach, whose works, along with Handel's, were enthusiastically promoted by Frederick the Great's sister Anna Amalia and by Wilhelm Friedemann Bach and Friedrich Marpurg (C. P. E. Bach had left Berlin for Hamburg in 1768). During his residence in Berlin, van Swieten joined the circle around Marpurg and Kirnberger and became acquainted with J. S. Bach's keyboard music and Handel's oratorios. The baron also helped to promote C. P. E. Bach's music internationally by introducing it to the music publisher Artaria in Vienna. Also during the 1770s, the *Phantasie* or expressive, free-form genre was cultivated in northern Germany. The *Phantasie* was a "private" genre and, as a vehicle for personal and emotional expression, foreign to Viennese music culture during these years. This very different flavor of north German musical culture was conveyed by Dr. Burney, who, visiting Berlin in the 1760s, described an encounter with Emanuel Bach:

> After dinner, which was elegantly served and cheerfully eaten, I prevailed upon him to sit down again to a clavichord, and he played with little intermission, till near eleven o'clock at night. During this time, he grew so animated and *possessed,* that he not only played, but looked like one inspired. His eyes were fixed, his under lip fell, and drops of effervescence distilled from his countenance. (1775, 126)

Anecdotal evidence concerning Beethoven's own reception in Berlin in the mid-1790s suggests that this more emotional approach to music had persisted. When Beethoven visited Berlin in 1796, his audience sobbed after his extemporaneous piano performances, a response that, according to Carl Czerny (cited in Thayer and Forbes 1967, 1:185), made him adverse to King Frederick Wilhelm's reputed invitation to stay on as a court musician (possibly as Johann Friedrich Reichardt's replacement). A. W. Thayer reports in another version of this story that Beethoven supposedly observed to an acquaintance in 1810 that his Berlin audience

had not applauded but crowded around him and wept, w
what we artists wish—we want applause!" (ibid., 187).

During his seven years in Berlin, then, van Swieten w
quite different conception of music's role in social life and
to aesthetics that emphasized the notions of creative genius and origina
creation, an approach he later propagated on Viennese soil. Back in Vienna by 1777 and occupied with Josephian reform, the baron cultivated
music perhaps more earnestly than any other Viennese aristocrat. By the
1790s he occupied the position of, as Olleson (1963, 73) has put it, "high
priest of musical taste—a position impregnable after the success of
[Haydn's] Creation and [Haydn's] Seasons" (the mid to late 1790s).
When Johann Ferdinand von Schönfeld (a music publisher and ennobled
businessman) produced a who's who of music in 1796, the *Jahrbuch der
Tonkünst von Wien und Prag*, he described van Swieten in effusive terms.
The baron is,

> as it were, looked upon as a patriarch of music. He has taste only for the great
> and exalted. He himself many years ago composed twelve beautiful sympho-
> nies. When he attends a concert our semi-connoisseurs never take their eyes
> off him, seeking to read in his features, not always intelligible to every one
> what ought to be their opinion of the music. Every year he gives a few large
> and brilliant concerts at which only music by the old masters is performed.
> His preference is for the Handelian manner and he generally has some of
> Handel's great choruses performed. (trans. Thayer and Forbes 1967, 1:157)

The oratorios to which Schönfeld referred were produced by what
was probably Vienna's earliest concert organization, the Gesellschaft der
Associierten Cavaliere (GAC), or associated knights, which van Swieten
founded in 1786 and for which he acted as director. This association was
devoted to the private performances of oratorios, mainly by Handel and
Haydn, which usually were held at Prince Josef Schwarzenberg's palace.
(Each time his works were performed, Haydn received a generous do-
nation from the association.) If a performance was successful, the society
then arranged for a second concert, this time open to the public. The
GAC was active well into the 1800s, growing gradually more powerful
as it took over the direction of three of Vienna's most important public
concert venues.

Van Swieten was apparently a formal man; he wrote several symphonies described by Schönfeld as "beautiful," but which Haydn said were
"stiff as himself" (that is, as van Swieten) (Olleson 1967). Perhaps somewhat pompously, van Swieten offered the following self-portrait in the
first volume of the *Allgemeine Musikalische Zeitung:*

I belong, as far as music is concerned, to a generation that considered it necessary to study an art form thoroughly and systematically before attempting to practice it. I find in such a conviction food for the spirit and for the heart, and I return to it for strength every time I am oppressed by new evidence of decadence in the arts. My principal comforters at such times are Handel and the Bachs and those few great men of our own day who, taking these as their masters, follow resolutely in the same quest for greatness and truth. (A. Schindler 1966, 49)

The fact that Haydn nevertheless collaborated with van Swieten and that he was willing to submit his own compositions, as had Mozart before him, to van Swieten for artistic advice is further testimony to the baron's power in musical affairs.[9] Van Swieten even persuaded Haydn (against his better judgment) to include the imitation of frogs in *The Seasons*—which Haydn subsequently had removed from the later piano transcription. Haydn wrote to August Müller, who was arranging the score: "This entire passage in imitation of a frog did not flow from my pen. I was constrained to write down the French croak. At an orchestral performance this wretched conceit soon disappears, but it cannot be justified in a pianoforte score" (Thayer and Forbes 1967, 1:157–58). As for the process of composing *The Creation,* Franz Grillparzer, the Austrian poet and playwright, said that the baron "had each piece, as soon as it was ready, copied and prerehearsed with a small orchestra. *Much he discarded as too trivial for the grand subject*" (Landon 1976–80, 4: 353; emphasis added).

During the 1780s, van Swieten's preoccupation with musical "greatness and truth" was not always shared by Viennese aristocrats, an indication of some of the obstacles that Beethoven's successful reception faced. To Count Zinzendorf, for example, van Swieten may have seemed too much of a connoisseur—at least there is one diary entry to suggest this may have been the case ("de l'ennui, et Swieten") (Olleson 1967, 225).[10] Olleson observes that contemporary references to van Swieten were often not flattering: he was viewed by some members of Viennese society as "aloof, pedantic and preachy" (ibid., 41). Nonetheless, he had his disciples. The young Prince Karl Lichnowsky, for example, was a regular guest at van Swieten's Sunday morning concerts. It is worth noting that Lichnowsky, like van Swieten, was familiar with Berlin since he was required to visit the Prussian court regularly.

With his earnest enthusiasm for "serious" music, van Swieten was a key figure in promoting a canonic ideology of music in Vienna during the 1780s and 1790s. His contemporaries regarded him as a pioneer of

new conventions of music consumption in the concert hall, and his attempts prefigure patterns of regulating audiences that were later disseminated and institutionalized.[11] Otto Jahn reports that, according to the
composer Sigismund Neukomm, van Swieten

> exerted all his influence in the cause of music, even for so subordinate an end
> as to enforce silence and attention during musical performances. Whenever a
> whispered conversation arose among the audience, his excellence would rise
> from his seat in the first row, draw himself up to his full majestic height, mea-
> sure the offenders with a long, serious look and then very slowly resume his
> seat. The proceeding never failed of its effect. (1882, 2:385)

The taste for "great" music became more central over the course of
the 1790s, and it seems clear that this taste was promoted by Baron van
Swieten. So far, I have documented this cultural development through
anecdotes and reports from contemporary observers and music writers.
While these sources are invaluable for their illustrations of the emerging
culture of musical seriousness, they are less helpful in clarifying the ways
musical predilections were socially distributed during this time. They
show that the taste for serious music was cultivated by Baron van
Swieten, but not how far such taste extended outside the bounds of aristocratic music consumption.

THE VIENNESE PUBLIC CONCERT REPERTORY,
1780–1810

For information on the social boundaries of the taste for serious music
and Beethoven, it is necessary to turn to repertory data and in particular
to the public concert world of subscription and benefit concerts. In comparison with the private realm of salons (and with public music worlds
elsewhere) this arena was relatively small. Nonetheless, examination of
it provides some of the clearest indications of how the serious music ideology was confined initially to Vienna's social elites.

There are at least four reasons for attempting to locate the boundaries
of the new ideology through an examination of public as opposed to
private concert repertories.[12] First, the numbers of both public concerts
and concert locations rose steadily after around 1795 (see Figure 1). Second, because public concerts were, in theory, more accessible to middle-
class patrons, they represent the musical activity of a broader sector of
Vienna's population. The custom of hosting private concerts did begin
to trickle down the social scale during the 1780s and 1790s, but for most

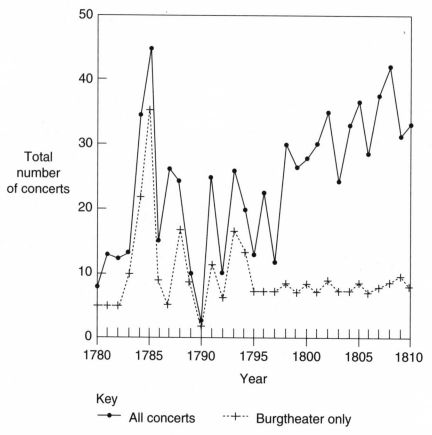

Figure 1. The rise in known public concerts and the decreasing proportion of known concerts at the most important of the court-controlled concert locations (Morrow 1989).

bourgeois in Vienna, the prospect of hosting private salons on a regular basis was—unless one was a musician or could count musicians as acquaintances—financially prohibitive. Even for someone like the civil servant Carl Rosenbaum, who had befriended Haydn and whose wife was a professional singer, a salon was an occasion both costly and (because he and his wife had to do much of the preparation for it themselves) time consuming (Rosenbaum 1968). A ticket or subscription to a concert or series, on the other hand, provided a more realistic alternative. Third, public concerts were at least occasionally used by aristocrats as showcases for composers or performances that had already been premiered privately, a practice to which the circumstances of many Haydn, Mozart, and Beethoven premiers attest. These public concerts, sponsored or organized by aristocrats, communicated the current trends in the world of the private aristocratic salons. Finally (and more practically), there is not enough specific information available on private concert programs (the salons), where composers and works often remain unidentifiable. Indeed, the private concert was a less purposive event—music making in private was entwined with many other social activities, to the extent that the boundaries of what would count as a private concert, in the modern sense, were far from clear. Moreover, because record keeping of public concert programs was often systematic, a greater proportion of extant public concert programs have survived.

The most comprehensive compilation of data on public concert repertories is the one assembled by Morrow (1989) and recently updated and corrected by Edge (1992). Both scholars have helped to reconstruct a public concert calendar, Morrow's for the years 1763 to 1810 (as well as a less detailed private concert calendar for 1761 to 1810) and Edge's for 1780 to 1800. In both calendars data are presented in raw form, by concert and in chronological order, providing a rich source of information for scholars of Viennese musical life. When analyzed, the calendars shed further light on two aspects of the changing ideology of late eighteenth-century musical life. First, they indicate that, with the decline of the hauskapellen or private house orchestras (see chapter 3), attention within the repertory was concentrated on musical stars (Haydn, Mozart, and Beethoven), who were programmed at the expense of most other occupational composers. Second, when the celebration of these composers is explored according to concert location, Morrow's data indicate that the emergence during the 1800s of the taste for explicitly serious music—formal complexity, the so-called higher genre, and a more strict and purposive mode of music reception—emerged primarily among Vienna's elite aristocratic patrons and was clearly not a part of middle-class musical life.

When examined in the context of all public concerts offered in Vienna between 1791 and 1810, Mozart's compositions, along with those of Haydn and Beethoven, occupied a special place in Viennese concert life. Performances of works by these composers were sustained over nearly the whole of this twenty-year period and at a level of intensity higher than for that of any of their contemporaries.[13] These composers can be understood as musical "stars" in the sense that they occupied an exceptional amount of space within the Viennese public concert repertory as a whole; their works occupied a dominant position in the Viennese concert world and signified a growing concentration of attention on musical celebrities (confirming what Morrow [1989] and other scholars have already suggested; see also Moore 1987 and W. Weber 1977, 1984a, 1986).

It would be inappropriate to suggest on the basis of this finding, however, that the works of Haydn, Mozart, and Beethoven were programmed universally across concert locations or that they were all performed with any regular degree of intensity throughout this twenty-year period. On closer inspection, it becomes clear that performances of their works were not randomly distributed, either (in the case of Beethoven) over time, or (in the case of all three) across concert locations. Further qualifying the finding of Haydn, Mozart, and Beethoven as musical stars, therefore, illuminates the social distribution of musical taste in Vienna at this time: explicitly "serious" music was associated primarily with Vienna's old aristocrats but not with the middle class.

The total number of performances of Beethoven's works, for instance, is somewhat misleading, because the distribution of Beethoven's performances was uneven. Thirty-two of the eighty-odd performances of Beethoven's music occurred in 1808 (see Table 3).[14] Moreover, while performances of Haydn and Mozart were more evenly distributed across the twenty-year period, public performances of Beethoven increased after 1800 and were boosted still more in 1808. It is worth inquiring into the circumstances under which the increasing presence of Beethoven in the public concert repertory occurred, and for this it is necessary to examine the distribution of composers' performances according to concert location and, therefore, according to social group.

The 1808 surge in Beethoven performances consisted of five all-Beethoven concerts produced as part of the Liebhaber series (held at the Universitätssaal), the two all-Beethoven concerts that took place at the Theater an der Wien, an all-Beethoven concert held in the Kleine Redoutensaal, and through incidental performances of Beethoven at the Burgtheater.[15] Concerts at all these locations were organized, at this time, by Vienna's old aristocrats. At the Burgtheater, a predominantly aristocratic theater, princes and counts subscribed to boxes, barons and new aristocrats occupied the partier, and intellectuals and lackeys sat up in the gods (O. Schindler 1976; Edge 1991); all subscriptions were dispensed with for special occasion charity performances. Administration of the Burgtheater was taken over by the GAC (the organization van Swieten directed) in 1807, as was that of the Redoutensaal. Tickets for the Liebhaber concerts at the Universitätssaal were distributed by the seventy GAC members to "a carefully chosen audience of subscribers" (Morrow

TABLE 3

PERFORMANCES OF WORKS BY VIENNA'S MOST
FREQUENTLY PERFORMED COMPOSERS, 1791–1810

Year	Haydn	Mozart	Beethoven	Par	Weigl	Cimarosa
1791	5	5	0	0	1	0
1792	3	1	0	0	2	1
1793	10	1	0	0	2	0
1794	3	4	0	0	0	0
1795	4	3	3	0	0	4
1796	12	0	1	0	0	0
1797	1	6	3	0	0	2
1798	11	9	4	0	2	2
1799	9	1	0	0	1	0
1800	13	7	5	4	1	0
1801	14	5	3	0	3	3
1802	9	3	3	12	0	7
1803	5	3	7	4	1	0
1804	4	8	5	5	0	2
1805	16	11	4	3	1	2
1806	3	7	3	9	0	0
1807	7	4	7	2	0	0
1808	5	2	32	2	0	0
1809	8	4	3	2	15	0
1810	4	5	5	4	1	2
Total	146	89	88	47	30	25

Source: Morrow 1989, 238–364.

1989, 62–63)—none were sold to the public. The Theater an der Wien was taken over in 1806 by the GAC. Throughout its irregular existence between 1786 and 1808, the GAC was exclusively aristocratic.[16]

How, meanwhile, did Beethoven fare with middle-class audiences? While none of Vienna's theaters could be classified as entirely middle class, since aristocrats could and sometimes did attend them,[17] the most distinctly middle class of Vienna's concert locations at this time was the Leopoldstadt theater, located in Vienna's suburbs. Ticket prices there were consistently lower than those for similar seats at the court-sponsored Burgtheater or at the Theater an der Wien (Morrow 1989, 131–35). There is no information on Universitätssaal concert ticket prices. Judging from the programs listed in Morrow's public concert calendar, Beethoven was never performed at the Leopoldstadt theater.[18] Although the Leopoldstadt repertory did partially overlap with repertories of other concert locations (see Table 4), the shared music, apart from

TABLE 4
COMPOSERS' FIRST AND LAST APPEARANCES
IN MORROW'S PUBLIC CONCERT CALENDAR,
BY CONCERT LOCATION, 1791 – 1810[a]

		Location		
	Jahn's	Leopoldstadt	Wien	Universitätssaal
Composers held in common by:				
All locations				
Haydn	1798–	1800–	1791–	1807–8
Mozart	1791–	1804–	1791–	1807–8
Cherubini	1806–	1810	1804	1807
J, L, W				
Sarti	1797	1795	1801	
Cimarosa	1795–1802	1795–1804	1792	
Paisiello	1795–1802	1808	1798	
J, W, U				
Beethoven	1797–		1798–	1807–8
L, W, U				
none				
J, L, U				
none				
J, W				
Pleyel	1804–5		1791, 1809	
Hummel	1805		1806	
Kreutzer	1805		1806	
L, W				
Anfossi		1795	1798	
Righini		1801	1798	
Süssmayr		1810	1805–9	
Clement		1810	1805–9	
J, L				
Martini		1802	1801	
L, U				
none				
J, U				
none				
W, U				
none				

Source: Morrow 1989, 238–364.

[a]Listing only those composers who performed at two or more of the following locations: J, Jahn's restaurant; L, Leopoldstadt Theater; U, Universitätssaal; W, Theater an der Wien; concerts at the Universitätssaal took place in 1807 and 1808 only.

Haydn, Mozart, and Cherubini, was generally that of the older-st., Italian composers (Domenico Cimarosa, Vincenzo Righini, Giovanni Paisiello), two of whom continued to be performed at the middle-class theater after they were dropped from the Theater an der Wien. Luigi Cherubini, who was hailed as a "new-style," serious composer, appeared on Leopoldstadt programs later than at the Theater an der Wien. While the middle-class, suburban theater was more conservative with respect to the "aristocratic" composers it performed, it was also known for presenting spectacular programmatic show pieces, such as the battle symphonies of Ferdinand Kauer and the occasionally bizarre antics of the Bohdanowicz family (see Morrow 1989 for details). The Leopoldstadt theater's kapellmeister was Wenzel Müller, a composer of 272 light operettas. The taste for these composer-performers was not shared by the more aristocratic repertories, though the Bohdanowicz family was featured at one of the other more socially mixed concert locations, Jahn's restaurant. Although Beethoven was programmed at Jahn's, he appears on only three separate programs (in 1797, 1798, and 1806) and was not part of the staple repertory, which consisted of Cimarosa, Eberl, and Pleyel. (The last recorded performance of music at Jahn's occurred in 1806 [Morrow 1989].)

Haydn and Mozart were, of course, programmed at the Leopoldstadt theater and Jahn's. Indeed, they appear as "most often programmed" composers at these venues as well as at the Theater an der Wien and the Universitätssaal (see Table 5). It would be wrong to conclude, however, that the taste for "serious" music was distributed evenly across social groups simply because compositions by Haydn and Mozart appeared at all concert locations. A look at the particular works by Mozart and Haydn performed at each location (see Table 6) reveals that the type of composition featured varied from place to place, and this is especially the case with Mozart. Genres which from our twentieth-century preconceptions and stereotypes we characterize as lighter (that is, shorter pieces, or more overtly virtuosic pieces, songs, arias, and overtures) appeared primarily at the Leopoldstadt theater, while the GAC-controlled Theater an der Wien and the Liebhaber-Universitätssaal concerts featured symphonies, cantatas, unstaged versions of opera, and Mozart's *Requiem* instead of (or in addition to) the genres offered at Leopoldstadt.[19]

Thus, while music by the star composers Haydn and Mozart was. common to all of these concert locations, the ways Haydn and Mozart

TABLE 5

COMPOSERS MOST OFTEN LISTED AT FIVE MAJOR LOCATIONS, WITH NUMBER OF PERFORMANCES OF THEIR WORKS AND THE YEARS DURING WHICH THEY ARE LISTED FOR 1791–1810

Jahn's	Leopoldstadt	Wien	Universitätssaal	Burgtheater
Mozart (11), 1791–	Haydn (6), 1800–	Beethoven (22), 1798–	Beethoven (9), 1807–8	Haydn (79), 1791–
Eberl (6), 1804–5	Mozart (5), 1801–	Mozart (13), 1791–	Haydn (3), 1807–8	Par (23), 1800–8
Cimarosa (6), 1795–1802	Cimarosa (5), 1795–1804	Cherubini (12), 1804–		Mozart (22), 1791–
Haydn (5), 1798–	Müller (5), 1796–1808	Haydn (10), 1791–		Beethoven (20), 1795–
	Kauer (5), 1798–1809			Weigl (13), 1791–1807
				Mayer (12), 1802–8
				Paisiello (11), 1791–1804
				Eybler (11), 1794–1804
				Cherubini (11), 1805–
				Salieri (9), 1795–1809
				Auernhammer (8), 1795–1806
				Winter (8), 1796–1810
				Süssmayr (8), 1797–1809
				Handel (8), 1792–1807
				Cimarosa (8), 1793–1810

Source: Morrow 1989, 238–364.
Note: The Liebhaber concerts at the Universitätssaal featured, in addition to performances of Beethoven and Haydn, those of Mozart, Himmel, Cherubini, Rode, and Müller. These composers appeared on Liebhaber programs only once, at the first concert in the series; subsequent concerts were devoted to music of Beethoven and Haydn.

TABLE 6
MOZART PERFORMANCES BY LOCATION AND GENRE

	Wien	Jahn's	Leopold-stadt	Universi-tätssaal
Symphony	2	1		1
Cantata	3			
Opera	3			
Aria	3		2	
Concerto	1	4	1	
Variations	1			
Requiem	1	1		
Vocal trio	2			
Vocal quartet	1	1		
Overture		1	1	
Piano rondo		1		
Four-hand sonata			1	
Total	17	9	6	1

Source: Morrow 1989, 238–364.

were featured varied. The early 1800s version of Mozart, in which he is represented through his lighter works as programmed in the Leopold-stadt theater, more closely resembled a conception of the composer in keeping with that programmed at the Theater an der Wien in the 1780s and early 1790s—the specific works chosen reflected a "successful" and "popular" Mozart, as understood in his lifetime. This representation was also in keeping with the earlier and more universally shared taste for Italianate operatic music and the amateur-oriented aesthetic of "general taste" that aristocrats had begun to abandon during the 1790s. The public concert repertory indicates that Vienna's old aristocrats were closely linked to Vienna's three dominant composers during these years and further, that they were linked to conceptualizations of these composers which emphasized their seriousness.

It seems fair, then, to suggest that a serious music ideology, which took as its exemplars Beethoven and reconstituted, more explicitly "learned" and grandiose versions of Mozart and Haydn, emerged during the 1790s in Vienna, and that this ideology was primarily subscribed to by old aristocrats, not the middle class. This view runs counter to what Arnold Hauser (1962), Henry Raynor (1976), Theodor Adorno (1976), and a host of other scholars have had to say, on the basis of scant evidence, about the origins of serious music ideology, and, as such, it challenges received sociological wisdom and Beethoven mythology concerning the origin of the musical canon.

In recent years, several more detailed social historical studies of Viennese musical life have appeared (Hanson 1985; Morrow 1989; Moore 1987, n.d.b.; Freeman 1987; Edge 1991). The comparative picture they present suggests ever more strongly that, although musical life was certainly thriving elsewhere at this time (in terms of commercial organization and sheer numbers, London musical life was more advanced), it was in Vienna that the new model of musical seriousness based around Haydn, Mozart, and Beethoven was initially formulated.

CHAPTER 3

Musical Patronage
and Social Change

Writing about Austro-Hungarian musical life in the early 1780s, the German musician and traveler Johann Friedrich Reichardt (1915) says, "The court cultivates music passionately and the nobility have an inordinate love and knowledge of music." The motivations Reichardt attributed to these Viennese music patrons (and which subsequently became part of the folklore of music history and a resource for explaining their enthusiastic support of serious music ideology) may have been more flattering than accurate. Eighteenth-century music patronage was born of observance of convention, duty, fashion, and one-upmanship as often as it was of "inordinate love and knowledge." Nonetheless, it was undoubtedly through the efforts of the imperial court and the Viennese aristocrats that, from midcentury and well into the 1820s, Vienna was recognized as a major European music capital, if not for size then certainly for prestige. By 1792 (the year Beethoven arrived in Vienna) the city was at the height of its musical powers, though the social and institutional basis of its music world was undergoing profound change.

In brief, the history of high culture music patronage in eighteenth-century Vienna comprises (1) the rise and fall of the hofkapelle (imperial ensemble) under Karl VI and Maria Theresa, respectively, (2) the rise and fall of aristocratic hauskapellen (house ensembles), (3) the emergence of dilettante forums during the final quarter of the century, and (4) the emergence of freelance musicians and the earliest forms of the Viennese version of the public concert. In his history of Viennese concert life, the nineteenth-century music critic Eduard Hanslick ([1869] 1979) referred to the whole of this phase (1750–1800) as the Patriarchal Era and to the thirty years that followed as the period of dilettante associations. While Hanslick was attempting to call attention to the general decline of private forms of music sponsorship and the subsequent diffusion of patronage to which that decline gave rise, he did not intend to imply that the end of the patriarchal period was characterized by a decline in aristocratic participation in musical affairs. Indeed, he was fully aware that the Viennese aristocrats remained active and, for the most part, dominant in musical affairs well into the nineteenth century (far later than their Parisian or London counterparts), and he described the emergence of these aristocrats as Vienna's "most brilliant" early nineteenth-century dilettantes. In this respect, Hanslick's views tended to reflect the ways these aristocrats were perceived by their contemporary observers (for example, as reported in music periodicals; see Wallace 1986).

Subsequent scholars have tended to reject Hanslick's account and to propose an alternate conception of the relationship between institutional change and aristocratic authority. These reassessments, however, often compartmentalize "eighteenth-century" versus "nineteenth-century" musical life, because they exaggerate the participation and relative influence of the middle classes and underplay the continued importance of aristocratic authority. Nevertheless, these revisionist accounts attained mythical status among late nineteenth-century music scholars, for whom, as the historian William Weber puts it, the "jack-in-the-box" concept of the middle class has functioned as a "historical *deus ex machina*" (1979, 176).

Certainly this myth is nowhere more forceful than in discussions of the acceptance of Beethoven's idiosyncratic and alternative style (Crabbe 1982; Knight 1973). There Beethoven is portrayed as heroically overthrowing "eighteenth-century" aristocratic patronage conventions in order to address his nineteenth-century public more directly and "forcing" hesitant aristocratic patrons to accept this independence; alternately, the aristocrats who supported Beethoven are lauded for their heroic willingness to reject the aesthetic forms, which otherwise buttressed their social position, in favor of what they regarded as the intrinsic and "purely" musical "superiority" of Beethoven's work. As we have seen, Beethoven's fully fledged middle-class public had not yet appeared in the 1790s and early 1800s Vienna and, in fact, it did not emerge until well after his death. Moreover, while Beethoven did attempt to alter many of the conventions that characterized the eighteenth-century composer's relationship with his (aristocratic) patrons, the reasons for his actions are far more complex than such mythic accounts suggest.

Over the past few years, an alternative to the theory of the burgeoning middle-class and declining aristocracy has been proposed (Moore 1987; Morrow 1989). Perhaps because this more recent perspective was developed in response to the "aristocratic demise" theory, however, it has tended to overstate an opposing argument. Insofar as this new theory has focused on demonstrating how aristocrats in early nineteenth-century Vienna were no *less* dominant in music affairs than were their predecessors a quarter century before, it has tended to leave two important issues unexplored. First, this approach has not attempted to look for a potential, perceived, or symbolic (as opposed to statistical or quantitative) middle-class challenge to aristocratic authority. Second, it has tended to base its argument on a before-and-after view of aristocratic authority, following the logic that, because these patrons remained dominant, their position was never subject to challenge.

To what extent can the aristocratic embrace of the new ideology of "serious" music be understood (whether or not aristocrats consciously intended it as such) as helping to conserve aristocratic authority in the face of organizational change? And how serious was the middle-class "challenge" to aristocrats, both in terms of its material consequences (that is, what the new organizational structure facilitated and hindered) and in terms of how it may have been perceived at the time?

VIENNESE MUSIC PATRONAGE IN HISTORICAL CONTEXT

In a sense, Vienna's musical reign began with the accession of Ferdinand in 1619. By choosing Vienna as his primary residence, Ferdinand made it the de facto capital of the empire, which meant that it became one of the centers for hofkapelle performances (Antonicek 1980). As Theophil Antonicek has suggested, Ferdinand was responsible, both on his own and through his Italian wife, Eleonora Gonzaga, for forging the first important links between the Hapsburg court and musicians from Italy, an association that continued for nearly two centuries. In addition, by advocating Baroque rather than Renaissance music ideals (that is, the Italian *stile moderno*—monody plus basso continuo—as opposed to the northern European polyphonic style), Ferdinand helped to dispel the imperial court's sixteenth-century image as the embodiment of musical conservatism (ibid., 716).

It was with Ferdinand that the age of courtly magnificence was ushered in. During the next hundred years, under the emperors Leopold I, Joseph I, and Charles VI, the hofkapelle grew steadily and by 1705 it numbered 107 members; between 1723 and 1740, it swelled to 134 (Moore 1987, 98). In 1746, however, Maria Theresa checked any further growth by dividing the imperial kapelle into two organizations—the hofoper (imperial opera) and the hofkapelle (responsible for all other music production)—and this split led to the decline of the latter organization, which took on a "second-class" status (ibid., 99). By 1822, the hofkapelle was composed of only 20 musicians, most of whom were pensioners (ibid.).

Why so much money was poured into the hofkapelle during the seventeenth century is a fascinating question but beyond the scope of this study. Relevant here is why these funds were curtailed during the eighteenth century and the effect this reduction had on aristocratic musical life. It was not merely coincidental that the rise and fall of the hofkapelle preceded and overlapped with the rise and fall of the aristocratic hauskapellen. These ensembles, especially the smaller and more remote ones,[1] were often composed of musically talented domestic servants who performed double duty (see Mahling 1985; Moore 1987; Morrow 1989). The "heyday," as Hanslick calls it, of these ensembles occurred between 1750 and 1775.[2] By the time Beethoven entered the Viennese music world in 1792, hauskapellen were already a thing of the past. As Schönfeld notes in his 1796 *Jahrbuch*:

> It was formerly a strong custom that our great princely houses maintained their own house orchestras, at which they cultivated the leading spirits (*genie*) of music. Such was the case with Haydn. Only, it is now barren for art lovers, whether for a lessening of a love of music or for want of taste, frugality or for some other cause; in short, to the detriment of music, this worthy custom has been lost—one house orchestra lost after another, so that, apart from Prince Schwarzenberg, perhaps no more exist. (77)

HAUSKAPELLEN AND HOFKAPELLE: RISE AND FALL

So far, two explanations have been offered for the rise of hauskapellen. The most common is the one to which Reichardt alluded—that the Viennese nobility simply had a "love and knowledge" of music. More recently, an additional explanation has been proposed by Moore (1987). Following the social and economic historian Hannes Stekl (1975), Moore argues that the increasing popularity of kapellen was driven as much by aristocratic observance of convention and status-consciousness as by interest in music for its own sake. Aristocrats, in order to conform to their role expectations, maintained ensembles commensurate to their financial means and station. As Stekl notes, "Artists and the public also expected a well-off aristocrat to assume the role of a generous patron, informed collector, appreciative friend of music and painting. Numerous examples of this have been cited by Heinz Gollwitzer" (trans. Moore 1987, 91).

The rise of the hauskapellen, Moore argues, can be best viewed as a kind of fad or fashion in which first the upper nobility and later other aristocrats, major and minor, followed the example set at court. If one was familiar with behavior at court, one could demonstrate one's proximity to the court (and therefore one's status) by imitation. Music, then, was a vehicle (in Vienna, perhaps the most important vehicle, given its conspicuous and social nature) through which one could demonstrate, gain, and even, presumably, lose status; it was a primary medium for the registration of prestige. One could argue that these aristocrats did not need status—ranking at court was based on heredity. Unlike many twentieth-century aristocrats, these hereditary princes already had status. To take such a position, however, is to look at the problem through nonaristocratic lenses. Outside court, ranking was based on cultural consumption and money as well as lineage.

During the middle eighteenth century, the intended audience for aristocratic lavishness was only secondarily the public at large, most of whom, as today, would not be well enough versed in the practices and fashions of the aristocratic subculture to distinguish and appreciate their myriad up-to-the-minute displays. Conspicuous musical consumption, therefore, was not primarily for the benefit of social inferiors; instead, cultural displays were oriented upward and sideways, to those audiences that the patrons wished to imitate or be aligned with, and to audiences they wished to compete with or impress. During the height of the hauskapellen activity, impressing middle-class or minor aristocratic audiences (and thereby distancing themselves from these audiences) was, for high-ranking aristocrats, a relatively minor concern. A letter, for example, from an eighteenth-century nobleman, Count von Sporck, illustrates the importance of these upward and sideways axes in locating one's status position. The count wrote to his friend Count Johann Wilhelm von Thurheim in 1724 and congratulated himself on his ability, as a mere count, to employ an opera company, while his neighbor, a prince, employed only a lutenist:

confess indeed that I have a special fondness for delightful and agree-
music, but this is not the principal reason why I was induced to engage
opera] company. Rather, after I learned that Princess Schwarzenberg was
ke a cure only a mile from here on her husband's estate of Wildschutz . . .
. _ ped that the illustrious princess would remain in the vicinity for the entire
summer. It was decided that the opera singers were to arrive here in the
middle of June at the latest in order to entertain her with operas as well as
comedies. (Freeman, quoted in Moore 1987, 95)

The enterprise of music patronage was socially loaded, and those who
took part in it did so for a variety of intertwined reasons. If we assume
that ideals or goals are frequently articulated with reference to more im-
mediate interests, situations, and available means (Berger 1981; Swidler
1986), it is reasonable to suggest four factors that were, at least in part,
responsible for the rise of the hauskapellen: first, that higher aristocrats
were interested in imitating the imperial court; second, that lower aristocrats were interested in imitating and thereby rubbing shoulders with the
upper aristocrats; third, that the practice became conventional and expected as the century progressed; and fourth, that some aristocrats
would have found musical activity to be of intrinsic interest, but that
interest in and love of music by no means provided the only impetus for
music patronage. This multifactor explanation also serves us better
when we address the issue of the late eighteenth-century demise of the
hauskapellen, especially when we evaluate the various explanations that
have been offered for this decline. If the primary motivating factor for
the proliferation of hauskapellen was love of music, then it is difficult to
explain why by 1796, as Schönfeld observed, nearly all of these ensembles had been disbanded. Was the cause "less of a love for music"—
one of the possible explanations Schönfeld suggested? In that case one
would expect aristocrats to abandon musical life altogether, which
clearly did not occur. What was rejected, in other words, was not musical life itself, but rather its previous social organization. As Morrow observes, "The change did not signify the end of aristocratic patronage of
music or the disappearance of music-making in the home. . . . The custom remained the same; only the arrangement was different" (1989,
1–2).

At this point, it is necessary to consider the other and still dominant
view of why the hauskapellen were disbanded at the end of the century,
for it too is congruent with the "love and knowledge" theory of their
initial rise. This theory suggests that the downfall of the hauskapellen

reflected a corresponding downfall of the aristocracy, an idea espoused (but never sufficiently explicated) in Deutsch 1965, Hellyer 1980, Raynor 1976, Loesser 1954, Solomon 1977a, and Hanson 1985. In brief, these scholars have suggested that aristocratic fortunes were lost or significantly reduced during the later eighteenth century, causing the nobility to turn to more diffuse and socially less exclusive forms of patronage, whereby musicians were engaged on an event-by-event basis as opposed to being kept as full-time members of the domestic staff. Thus economic downfall of the aristocracy is posited as the factor that led to the rise of the public concert and to middle-class dominance in musical affairs.

The hypothesis of an impoverished aristocracy is attractive to scholars attempting to explain not only the decline of the hauskapellen, but also the rise of the larger, more public instrumental musical forms. The idea is that this change led to the "emancipation" of musicians, in that it allowed them to speak directly to a rather anonymous public, and, unencumbered by the constraints imposed by "polite" aristocratic life and their previous role as servants, to produce works of unprecedented complexity and seriousness. Any space cleared for full middle-class participation of concert life, however, was not occupied immediately; the public—that is, the middle classes—did not take control of musical life until much later, if at all, and certainly not before the middle of the nineteenth century. Indeed, Thayer (1967, 1:154) suggests that "out of London, even so late as 1793, there can hardly be said to have existed a 'musical public,' as the term is now understood, and in Vienna at least, with its 200,000 inhabitants, a virtuoso rarely ventured to announce a concert to which he had not already a subscription, sufficient to ensure him against loss, from those at whose residences he had successfully exhibited his skill."[3] But most important, the suggestion that the aristocracy declined economically does not square with the revelations of more recent economic history. Moore (1987, 79–86) has shown that there is no convincing evidence in favor of the hypothesis that the aristocrats lost their fortunes at the end of the eighteenth century, that is, at the time during which kapellen were being disbanded. The economic decline of Vienna's oldest aristocrats that occurs well after 1800[4] can hardly have been the cause of the decline of the hauskapellen. According to Schönfeld, the decline of house ensembles was nearly complete by 1796. Later, it is true, there is more evidence for the hypothesis that landed aristocrats suffered from the effect of Viennese hyperinflation. But in the case of one early nineteenth-century bankruptcy, that of Beethoven's patron Prince Joseph Lobkowitz, it appears that his misfortune was caused mostly by spending on a scale more lavish than his predecessors.[5] It has been argued, however, that even during the early 1800s aristocrats were better off economically than many of their capitalist counterparts, especially after 1809 when the effects of hyperinflation drastically reduced those fortunes not invested in real property (Moore 1987, 82).

Moore has proposed, as an alternative, that the decline of hauskapellen, like their earlier rise, can be understood as a fashion and further, that both rise and decline must be seen in the context of the rise and fall of the imperial hofkapelle. By recognizing the whole kapelle enterprise as a status-conscious endeavor, Moore has suggested, we can understand the rise of the hauskapellen as a response to the court's cultivation of such an ensemble. Correspondingly, the court's subsequent discontinuation of the hofkapelle when it was no longer more lavish than the ensembles of the highest aristocrats followed the principle that "a particular source of prestige, when adopted by a given social class quickly lost its prestige among the next higher social class" (Moore 1987, 100). The court thus became less interested in supporting its kapelle when it could no longer so dramatically outshine those of the aristocrats, and the nobility responded by losing interest in maintaining a practice with which the court was no longer engaged.

As hauskapellen became fashionable, they were imitated by lower aristocrats who, if unable to sponsor orchestral musicians and singers, sponsored *Harmonien* (wind bands) instead. By the 1780s (when the decline of hauskapellen was well under way) these wind ensembles were relatively common, including among the minor aristocracy. There were by then two good reasons for a status-conscious aristocrat to disband his or her hauskapelle: the court had withdrawn from the competition, and the support of a kapelle was no longer an uncommon, and therefore distinctive, practice. Though the higher aristocrats could have distinguished themselves from lower aristocrats through even more ostentatious kapellen—a full kapelle was certainly more magnificent than a wind band—once the court had dropped out of this rivalry, the major reason for having a kapelle in the first place was lost. By discontinuing a custom that was no longer socially useful and by maintaining an active interest in patronage of music through the newer dilettante salon forums, high aristocratic music patrons paved the way (albeit unwittingly) for increasingly broad participation in music affairs.

THE RISE OF SALON FORUMS
AND THEIR SOCIAL IMPLICATIONS

Needless to say, conclusions about the fundamental transformation of the organizational basis of musical life in Vienna remain tentative. When we consider, for instance, the documentary materials available to scholars in some other areas, the evidentiary basis remains comparatively scant. The resources for the study of the years after 1800 (the Vienna of middle-period Beethoven and of Schubert) and before 1790 (before Mozart's death) are more extensive, and these periods have received far more attention from scholars than have the years between 1790 and 1800. Any inferences drawn, therefore, must remain tentative, but on the basis of the evidence that proponents of these theories have marshalled, the conclusion that "nowhere did the aristocracy come tumbling down" (Moore 1987, 47) seems the stronger of the two (other theories could be proposed, such as frugality on the part of aristocrats even if not genuine hardship). It does seem fairly certain that music was a primary medium for acquiring and demonstrating prestige and that the importance of this medium, once participation in music affairs began to broaden socially, was only intensified. Admittedly, the court's withdrawal from instrumental musical support effectively diminished the relevance of attempts on the part of the higher aristocrats to symbolically usurp the court's position as the most lavish of music patrons. Simultaneously, however, the lower aristocratic and upper middle-class entry into musical life necessitated an increasing emphasis on musical forms of exclusion if aristocrats were to remain distinct as musical leaders. The new social organization of musical life posed fresh problems for music's traditional and previously exclusive patrons—Vienna's old aristocrats—by affecting the conditions under which music could be useful in delineating status.

As we have seen, aristocrats continued their involvement in musical affairs after the decline of the hauskapellen. They supported music through events such as salons, after-dinner music, and party music (see Morrow 1989 for an excellent portrait of the private forms of high cultural Viennese musical life of this time), as well as larger performances such as the oratorios produced by van Swieten's GAC. On the surface, this newer, more diffuse form of patronage organization (of which the GAC was an example) appeared to be compatible with the old form of musical life because the events were controlled by old aristocrats and remained, for the most part, private affairs. In comparison with the older organizational structure at its height (the aristocratic sponsorship of permanent domestic ensembles), however, the newer patronage structure did not provide a similar foundation for continued aristocratic distinction and, as the century waned, it gave rise to some changes.

First, the new organizational base was conducive to an increase in independent musicians, most of whom remained dependent on teaching (especially of the piano) as their primary source of income (Morrow 1989; Loesser 1954; M. Weber 1978; Moore 1987). Teaching was important as a way of earning a living (some teachers were paid with room and/or board instead of money) since there were many aspiring dilettantes but not yet much scope for entrepreneurial concert activity. This shift from hauskapellen to dilettante forums facilitated the rise of the "emancipated" musician (Salmen 1985; Mahling 1985), though the change was much more gradual than the "aristocratic demise" theorists have suggested and, in fact, it had more to do with the organizational basis of patronage than with the independent rise of the middle class. In addition, the status of some musicians began to rise as they began the slow transition from servants to autonomous professionals; nineteenth-century kapellen, where they did occur, tended to be composed of professional musicians rather than servants and were as a result more expensive to keep (Moore 1987, 105).

A second change engendered by the new organizational base of patronage was an increase in the number of public concerts (as discussed in chapter 2) and increased participation by the upper middle class and "second society" (ennobled members of the upper middle class) in privately sponsored music affairs. Now, with less of an economic barrier to music participation, those who would not have been able to keep any form of kapelle (not even the *Harmonie,* the poor man's kapelle) could engage in musical life by purchasing a subscription ticket or by hosting or attending a private concert. A cursory examination of Schönfeld's 1796 list of music world participants shows that about 30 percent were middle-class amateur musicians or salon hosts.[6]

Thus the aristocrats who at one time would have been exclusive music patrons now shared or—and this may have been equally important—risked sharing patronage rights over musicians with not only minor aristocrats and new aristocrats, but also members of the middle class. While most middle-class participation occurred in public (for the simple economic reason that private music sponsorship, even on a by-event basis, was expensive), some members of the middle class also sponsored their own salons, as Morrow observes:

> The practice of giving formal private concerts in the home began to trickle down the social scale, with the lower nobility and the wealthy middle class assuming an increasingly active role. By the end of the century, the musical salon had become firmly entrenched in the Viennese cultural world, so that all segments of the population who had the means to participate in the city's cultural life at all could have had access to at least one or two musical coteries. (1989, 2)

THE EXTENT AND QUALITY
OF MIDDLE-CLASS PARTICIPATION

The foregoing discussion leads to the question currently debated by music historians studying this period: To what extent did this additional participation constitute a significant challenge to aristocratic leadership in music affairs? The most recent research has suggested that, in light of the evidence, the actual participation and power of the middle class and second society in musical affairs at the end of the eighteenth century was still relatively insignificant. The private concerts of the old aristocracy, the new aristocracy, and the middle class appear to have been carried on separately but in parallel. The second aristocracy, though they could frequently compete with the old aristocracy in monetary terms, were only rarely admitted to the latter's inner circles (Moore 1987, 61; Matis 1967). Moreover, though some members of the middle class were present at aristocratic salons, it is necessary, as Morrow points out, to

> distinguish between the association of bourgeois and aristocrats as performers and their relationship as members of the audience or as a social group. Musicians had been playing beside their noble employers for centuries without doing any damage to the class system, so that the collaboration in performance does not necessarily signal social change. A mixing of classes on the side of the audience would be a much better indication that a process of democratization was occurring, for though aristocrats necessarily had to associate with middle-class musicians in performance (on whatever basis), they were in no way obliged to fraternize with bourgeois music lovers by inviting them to concerts or by attending concerts in humbler homes. Whether or not they chose to do so is a difficult question to answer, but the diaries of two people who consistently attended concerts—the nobleman and socialite Count Karl von Zinzendorf and the middle-class accountant Joseph Carl Rosenbaum—indicate that the social boundaries were maintained in the various salons. (1989, 24)

Thus, to some extent, it is meaningful to speak of a social distribution of personnel, which suggests that middle-class participants and aristocrats were not on equal footing, even when participating in the same events.

Furthermore, the middle class was at this time relatively disparate and, as William Weber (1978) has observed, it is problematic to consider it a class at all. Those participants from the middle class and especially those who attended salons were members of the upper middle class, such as wholesale merchants, bankers, and higher government bureaucrats. According to Moore's calculations, contradicting Deutsch's statement that "there was a piano in every household" at this time (1965, xv), only members of the old aristocracy, the second aristocracy, and the rich bankers would have been able to purchase a piano with financial ease. Most middle-class aficionados were not rich enough to participate regularly in musical life (see Moore 1987, chap. 1; Morrow 1989, 2).

These recent studies have demonstrated that the democratization of musical life occurred gradually, and that, for the most part, the salons were not instruments of social change but tended to mirror the structure of Viennese society. In this most recent view, aristocrats are depicted as the unchallenged leaders of musical life, in spite of the organizational changes that life had recently undergone, and the limited democratization of musical life is dismissed as relatively insignificant. On the surface, musical life remained essentially unchanged, though perhaps capable of offering to patrons more variety, insofar as they heard less of their personal house ensemble and house composer's works. This view, however, misses one of the most sociologically interesting features of this period. Concluding that the salons were not instruments of social change overlooks the ways the salons (and the music ideology with which they were associated) were not merely neutral mirrors of social structure but also instruments of social stability.

THE CHANGING MEANING OF MUSICAL PATRONAGE

Although aristocratic leadership in music affairs remained constant, the substantive content of that leadership changed. The sources of distinction shifted from simple quantitative expenditure to qualitative demonstrations of discernment and "good taste" and to a heightened emphasis on the appreciation of "greatness," from which derived the notion of master composers. Praising Beethoven was simultaneously, albeit implicitly, praising his aristocratic patrons. Through the pursuit of the greatest composers (whose status depended on recognition by aristocratic, powerful patrons), Vienna's social aristocrats could themselves be identified as aristocrats of taste.

Because scholars have not yet made this music-ideological shift problematic in its own right, interest in the factors that could help to account for the shift has been negligible, and inquiry into the mechanisms for patronage distinction—specifically into the way these mechanisms gradually shifted—has been bypassed in favor of accounts celebrating the change. As Don Randel observes (1992, 11), canonic ideology is "in the musicological toolbox"—it is built in to the analytic strategies that music scholars employ. As a consequence, music scholarship often results in tautological confirmation of the canon's biased principles. Thus there are few tools for showing the extent to which the embrace of the new idea of musical greatness by some of Vienna's old aristocrats may have served as a proactive attempt to maintain status in the face of the loss of exclusive control over the traditional institutional means of authority in music affairs—a way of reconstituting their traditional social identity according to innovative cultural means.

To bring this aspect of aristocratic activity to light, it is necessary to distinguish more clearly between the short-term consequences and the potential long-term implications of the change in the organization of music sponsorship. Accordingly, we should attempt to assess the ways in which the nobility may have experienced these changes—how and to what extent they perceived these effects. So far, discussions of the sources and mechanisms for aristocratic distinction in Viennese musical life have remained theoretically vague. Music scholars have implicitly tended to conceive of aristocratic authority in its active cultural configuration rather than in terms of its structural underpinnings (that is, the institutional means according to which such cultural authority is maintained), and they have ignored the erosion of aristocratic control over the means of the production of musical life. Consequently, the short-term effects of the change have been conflated with the longer-term implications of the change in ways that preclude consideration of how the altered structure may have posed (and did pose) a potential threat to aristocratic authority over the long term.

The short-term social broadening that occurred was indeed limited. The potential long-term threat to aristocratic authority, however—the erosion of the institutional means for distinction—is clear: if, under the new system, distinction via patronage had continued to be constituted solely through quantitative participation, then the ability to achieve this distinction was deregulated to the extent that it was, in principle, opened to anyone who could afford to purchase a concert subscription or to host occasional private concerts. The musical means through which social exclusion could be achieved were being eroded. Incidentally, the dynamics

now permitted, at least in theory, the articulation of a professional ratio-
nale on the part of musicians.

There is no extant explicit testimony from the aristocrats themselves
acknowledging that they perceived their traditional authority to be under threat (the closest example is van Swieten's references to musical
"decadence"). But why should we expect there to be any? Moreover,
even if this aristocratic enterprise were not strategic in its intent, the social consequences—the structuration of status groups—are not to be denied. To expect the nobility to declare or even to hold such an externalist
view of their own situation may be to paint a far too rational portrait of
aristocratic consciousness. At the same time, it is worth speculating on
the cultural context of aristocratic sponsorship and asking how strategic
this form of aristocratic aesthetic entrepreneurship was.

MUSICAL PATRONAGE AND CULTURAL CONTEXT

Late eighteenth-century Viennese society was rigidly hierarchical
(Moore 1987, 58) and often perceived as "haughty" by foreign observers
(Landon 1988, 24). Its members, especially the aristocrats, were keenly
aware of social gradations, and even the most subtle violations of this
hierarchy would have been registered by them. On the whole, the documentary evidence from a number of Viennese and foreign, aristocratic
and middle-class observers supports this view. Reichardt, for example,
emphasized in his observations on Vienna just how difficult it was for
foreign nobility, even of very good houses, to penetrate the inner circle
of this world (Landon 1988, 4). We have already seen the ways in which
the structure of salons reproduced these social barriers. In criticizing
Loesser's exaggerated twentieth-century report that "a piano could be
found in every house in late eighteenth-century Vienna," Moore observes that "reports of drastic changes by contemporary observers
should be evaluated carefully. In these rigidly hierarchical and traditional
societies even quite small increases in size or influence of the middle
classes tended to register disproportionally large shock waves among observers" (1987, 58). In other words, although Viennese social structure
was not significantly altered during the late eighteenth and early nineteenth centuries, this "nonchange" occurred in a cultural climate hyper-
sensitive to change.

Although the number of ennoblements rose during the second half of
the eighteenth century,[7] the Viennese population grew at a higher rate.
Moore has argued that this net decline of ennoblements in relation to the

population at large would have made ennoblements appear less common (1987, 76), but her point is largely irrelevant in this discussion, since the old aristocrats would have been unlikely to have attended to how the growing number of new nobles actually represented a shrinking proportion of aristocrats to the general population. They were most likely to have registered how this growing number appeared in relation to themselves, in which case its significance would have been magnified. Scholars of the history of the Austrian aristocracy have observed that the old aristocrats were actively concerned with distancing themselves from their newly ennobled counterparts (Stekl 1978; Moore 1987). No matter how rich, most ennobled bankers—let alone members of the upper middle class—were still perceived as second-class aristocrats (Moore 1987, 83–84). More important, however, is that the mechanics of the new organizational base of music patronage made it possible for members of the second society and middle class to lead more or less the same sort of musical life as an aristocrat: they could patronize the same musicians and hear music by the same composers (albeit at different times and in different places) as long as they could afford to do so, which, increasingly during the 1790s, they could. They attended public concerts or sponsored private salons, either activity being considerably cheaper than supporting a kapelle. In view of the importance of musical sponsorship for the constitution of aristocratic identity, as evidenced in the discussion of the rise and fall of the hauskapellen, it becomes easier to appreciate that late eighteenth-century aristocrats risked being dispossessed of the primary means for maintaining their identity as leaders of cultural life. Given that it was during this period that aristocratic musical life began to be characterized by the concern for serious music, it is plausible that at least some of Vienna's old aristocrats were conscious of the implications of the change and that their interest and enthusiasm for the new serious music ideology may have developed in part as an attempt to preserve and enhance their status as cultural leaders.

THE WIDENING CONTEXT
OF QUASI-FREELANCE MUSICAL ACTIVITY

Because the decline of the hauskapellen had a destabilizing effect on musical occupations, the new quasi-freelance musicians now had an economic interest in widening their circles of admirers and in furthering their reputations. As the prospect of domestic tenure in an aristocratic kapelle became increasingly remote, career musicians of the 1790s turned of necessity to freelance strategies. During the 1790s and early 1800s, many career musicians wondered how they were to survive in this newer, less regularized economic environment and how a more impersonal clientele could be enlisted. Even Beethoven, who during these years was more securely ensconced in private patronage networks than any other Viennese-based composer apart from Haydn, expressed concern for the need to regularize music economics. As he remarks in an 1801 letter to one of his publishers, Franz Hoffmeister, "There ought to be in the world a *market for art* where the artist would only have to bring his works and take as much money as he needed" (Anderson 1961, 48; emphasis original).

One cause of this new form of economic insecurity for both musical workers and patrons was that late eighteenth-century career musicians, as Moore (n.d.a.) has shown, were operating in a noncash economy. Unlike their predecessors, who would have been tied to particular houses, 1790s musicians benefited far less from *Naturgeld*—the noncash presents of food and other necessary goods and clothing (such as uniforms and livery). As Moore has suggested, the emergence of quasi-freelance forms of income for musicians was not initially accompanied by improved economic status; if anything, the general economic position of musicians declined. During these transition years, musicians had to rely on ad hoc means of producing a living. Not surprisingly, therefore, they remained dependent on the patronage of wealthy aristocrats. Their most common sources of income during these years were teaching (a role musicians had traditionally performed in aristocratic households, churches, and so on), performing in privately sponsored concerts and salons, and small-scale, often subscription, publishing, supplemented with occasional benefit concerts. That the benefit concert remained an anomaly (a musician had to receive permission from the emperor to hold one) testifies to the peculiarly uncommercial character of Viennese musical life. While none of these income-generating practices was new to late eighteenth-century musical life, the importance of each was intensified during the 1790s because they became integral to a musician's economic survival. From a purely financial point of view, late eighteenth-century Viennese musicians would have welcomed opportunities for broadening the public basis of music consumption.

There were, however, obstacles to such a pursuit. First, institutional means for locating audiences were almost nonexistent. Second, the musicians' interest in broadening their public was hardly commensurate with the concerns and projects of music's traditional old aristocratic patrons, whose exclusive and controlling position as cultural leaders could be undermined by such a trend. To restructure patterns of music consumption from private resident ensembles to public and quasi-public concerts, and to do so without correspondingly attempting to relocate musical patronage's exclusionary basis in musical styles and forms of taste, was to erode the organizational mechanism through which distinction was sustained; it had the potential to deprive aristocratic distinction of its organizational and economic basis.

Whether they were aware of it or not, Vienna's aristocrats had a clear interest in impeding any large-scale public and commercial development of musical life by continuing to conduct most of their musical affairs in private. Indeed, the lively salon life of the 1790s did hinder the growth of a public musical life in Vienna (see also Morrow 1989, xv) in the sense that there was no need for public musical life as long as aristocrats were able to continue to conduct their musical lives in private. Although the number of public concerts did increase and facilitated the partial entry of the middle class and second society into musical affairs, this increase was relatively small in comparison with the thriving public concert life of London, which meant that there were limited opportunities in Vienna for occupational musicians. An implicit tension existed at this time between musicians (especially those musicians not singled out for aristocratic patronage) and music patrons. During the late 1790s and early 1800s, this tension was still usually resolved in favor of the patron, which had implications for the types of careers and acclaim available to musicians. This tension can be seen more clearly when we compare Viennese with London musical life.

In the second volume of the *Allgemeine Musikalische Zeitung,* a correspondent observes that "the Englishman . . . has thus gathered together in his country all along such a considerable number of the foremost artists of all types as are able to coexist elsewhere . . . the outward condition of music in England [is] so favorable that it cannot be matched elsewhere, where there is less inclination toward the great and where there are scantier expenditures" (trans. Milligan 1983, 2). The music business was booming in England during the 1790s in part because the English upper middle classes had more money to spend than their Viennese counterparts. England was, in general, more conducive to business enterprise; coupled with the fact that London's wealth tended to draw foreign musicians, this created a climate favorable to entrepreneurship by the musicians. London musical life was, not surprisingly, characterized by diversity: in contrast with Vienna, there was no clearly demarcated aristocracy of taste (though there was a set of tastes—especially for old music—associated primarily with aristocrats). Although aristocrats did play an important part in musical life, musical patronage was a far less centralized, less hierarchical enterprise.

Though the anonymous *Allgemeine Musikalische Zeitung* author pointed to London as the land of "great" music, musical taste there was more flexible, more open to novelty, broader and more diverse, as measured by the sheer size of English repertories during this period. Compared with Vienna of the 1790s, London held far more opportunities for a musician to earn a living without additional private support. Simultaneously, however, London's career musicians were more firmly tied to popular and amateur tastes, a point illustrated in chapter 5, where I compare Beethoven's career with that of Jan Ladislav Dussek, a pianist-composer working in London during the 1790s.

Thus, as Arthur Loesser so aptly puts it, the London music world "cut wide but also shallow" (1954, 251). While there was an emerging ideology of canonic works in London, as the historian William Weber continues to document (1992), this ideology consisted of a growing historical consciousness of music, within which the works of seventeenth- and eighteenth-century composers (especially Handel) were revered, predominantly by aristocratic patrons. Unlike the Viennese, however, Londoners of the 1790s did not so easily extend the canon to contemporary musicians, and its proponents made this clear (Milligan 1983, chap. 1).[8] Although the aristocratic taste for "ancient music" in London was articulated in opposition to contemporary music, considered vulgar and decadent, it was by no means a dominant ideology; opportunities to produce and/or consume diverse musical styles abounded in London during the 1790s through subscription series, benefit concerts, oratorio performances, and garden concerts. In 1793, Doane's directory of musicians in London listed 1,333 "composers and professors" of music, though this list included amateurs, music sellers, copyists, and others. As the economic and social historian Cyril Ehrlich has noted, English musical life of the 1790s is not easily summarized. Three times the size of Vienna, London clearly provided a more extensive range of career opportunities for musicians:

> The gradual commercialization of music allowed [the musician in London] to escape into an open society but imposed new and unfamiliar risks . . . he lost old forms of security and the privilege of making music for a small, intimate and perhaps, cultivated circle. He gained a measure of freedom and access to

diverse and potentially remunerative, if less discriminating, audiences and pupils. (Ehrlich 1985, 4)

In comparison, the structure of the Viennese music world remained conservative. Maynard Solomon (1977a, 65) has observed that the feudal mold was not broken at the time of Beethoven's arrival in Vienna. Rather, it was reshaped and adapted to altered circumstances. Whereas success in London was dependent more on the patronage of fellow musicians (and public concert organizers and impresarios), in Vienna it was virtually impossible for a local musician to build a successful concert career without the patronage of individual aristocratic concert hosts. Viennese musicians, therefore, remained reliant on the quality and quantity of the interpersonal links they were able to forge with private patrons. While aristocratic patronage practices certainly featured in London's richly textured concert life, in Vienna they were the mainstay of the musical scene. Thus aristocratic dominance of musical life in the 1790s, coupled with the decline of the hauskapellen and the subsequent diffusion of aristocratic patronage (and the shift in aristocratic focus to a newly emancipated pool of musicians ready for hire on an occasional basis), created a mismatch between the number of opportunities the Viennese system offered and the number of musicians in need of secure employment (Moore 1987, n.d.b.).

In this interim period, before new public concert institutions emerged and after traditional forums were significantly curtailed, musicians relied more than ever on capturing the attention of the sort of patrons who could offer them concert forums. Without previous private backing from aristocratic patrons, a musician found that the already scarce opportunities to present himself "to the public" became virtually nonexistent.

Just what the notion "public opinion" actually signified in late eighteenth-century Vienna cannot be assumed. While members of the high culture music "public" (the audiences at high culture music events) undoubtedly had opinions, the formulation and public articulation of these opinions were often extremely structured. "Public" success, recognition, and acclaim in late eighteenth-century Vienna should be conceived as inseparable from the selection processes conducted privately through individual channels by a few music-controlling people. We cannot hope to understand the vicissitudes of musical taste, success, and failure in Vienna without attending to the concerns, interrelations, and circumstances of the specific individuals who composed what can be called without exaggeration the city's musical power elite.

Because musical life was dependent on the activities of individuals rather than bureaucratic or commercial organizations, employment opportunities for musicians were far less regular, causing particular hardship for musicians after the hauskapellen were disbanded (Morrow 1989, 63–67; Moore 1987). For a composer like Beethoven, it was advantageous to comply with aristocrats since the institutional mechanisms for commercial musical life that were available during this time in London were not yet present in Vienna, and aristocratic, private support provided the kind of financial stability that most other composers during this transition period were unable to find. At aristocrat-sponsored public concerts, ticket prices were sometimes far higher than at nonaristocratic-sponsored events (Beethoven's 1803 benefit tickets, for example, were twelve times the normal price [see Moore 1987, 319]). In this way an event could remain exclusive while simultaneously providing a substantial benefit for the musician. Thus the absence of a highly articulated organizational basis for commercial musical activity in Vienna maintained the aristocratic monopoly over the consumption of serious music. For Beethoven, there was little economic incentive during the years around 1800 to cultivate Leopoldstadt audiences at the expense of his richer aristocratic patrons and the relative security and performance opportunities they were able to provide.

THE CONVERGENCE OF AESTHETIC
AND SOCIAL PLANES

In chapter 2, I considered the emergence of the serious music ideology in the aristocratic music world between the late 1780s and the early 1800s. To reach a closer understanding of the ways aristocrats may have conceived of that culture, I described the views of its most extreme exponent, Baron van Swieten. Now, in light of the shifting organizational basis of musical patronage and its implications for aristocratic distinction, it is necessary to consider the extent to which van Swieten's vision of musical seriousness may have been linked to a concern for maintaining a special and dominant position in the Viennese music world. Exploring this issue requires speculation about what van Swieten may have meant when he complained about the "new evidence of decadence in the arts." We need, in other words, to find ways of recognizing the possible sincerity of van Swieten's belief in "those select few great men of our own time" while simultaneously recognizing that the cultural practices associated with the baron's musical preferences were socially exclusionary.

From van Swieten's perspective—and from the perspective of his aristocratic GAC associates—the new "decadence" consisted in large part of an aversion to composers' and musicians' limited attempts to broaden their economic basis of support by appealing more overtly to the amateur performer (through easy-to-play pieces) and to new audiences through more flamboyant and virtuosic practices.[9] The new showmanship would no doubt have been perceived as undercutting the relevance of prior musical training and was therefore biased toward those composers with less experience in that they did not demand any special knowledge from their audiences. In musical terms, then, the new flamboyance was not commensurate with familiarity, skill, and study, and, in this respect, one can sympathize with the probable aristocratic concern that the whole enterprise of music making would be characterized by essentially nonmusical—that is, extramusical—features. In this sense, the emergence of the new showmanship could be viewed as "debasing" the participatory, dilettante music-making tradition and as undercutting many of the pleasures of participating in such a tradition. Aristocrats like van Swieten may have been reacting because their musical experience was being narrowed and made subservient to other forms.

At the same time, this view was only one way of understanding the issue. Whether van Swieten recognized it as such, the issue was simultaneously social and political because of the alignment of music patronage with the pursuit and maintenance of status. For the Viennese music aristocrats, the new "decadence" meant not only the deterioration of music but, equally important, the corruption of its audience, via the social broadening of that group. To the traditional heirs of musical taste, this threat, real or perceived, posed a problem of boundary maintenance and therefore of social pollution. It called for the sort of aristocratic response that could consolidate and cordon off the "true" from the "false" music audiences at a time when these distinctions were becoming blurred. Additionally, it meant that music aristocrats had to reconsider the issue of how to define themselves *as* music aristocrats (as opposed to other sorts of music consumers) and by doing so, identify their own level in this social sphere as an aristocracy of taste. One way to dramatize their identity was through the patronage of, as van Swieten put it, "great men"— heirs to "true music" and to the "great" tradition (that is, to the tradition before it became "tainted" with new qualities outside the control and interest of the music aristocrats). In this way, van Swieten's version of an incipient canonic ideology may have coalesced with the practices by which some aristocrats during this period maintained and highlighted their particular position within the Viennese music world.

IDEOLOGICAL AND ECONOMIC PRECONDITIONS FOR MUSICAL GREATNESS

In Vienna during the 1790s, routes to independent commercial success in the musical field remained obstructed and individual aristocrats stayed secure in their role as gatekeepers for public exposure. Existing public forums were usually buttressed or underwritten with private means so that even the benefit concerts and sometimes music publications were not nearly as "public" or self-sustaining as they might appear to the casual observer. Thus the decline of the hauskapellen and the increased competition to which it led concentrated attention on a select few musicians, who were able to enjoy the best of both worlds: increased opportunities for earning a quasi-freelance income from teaching, publications, and public (benefit) concerts, as well as private backing from controlling aristocrats, which could underwrite the credibility of freelance activities. The result was the emergence of an organizational structure conducive to a star system, as Moore observes:

> A peculiar aspect of the new situation was that precisely those few musicians who were still protected by the security of the old patronage system, namely the Kapellmeister, were most likely to reap the financial rewards of the new musical free market, such as frequent access to theaters to give academies, larger publication fees, and so on. Haydn and Salieri are perhaps the clearest examples of artists who had the best of both worlds. The income inequalities outside of permanent positions extended beyond the infrequent opportunities to earn large sums via public concerts and publications, and even the single engagements that appealed to Mozart provided large fees for a few star performers, while the average musician was very badly paid. (1987, 420)

The category of musical celebrity was emerging in the 1790s Vienna independent of Beethoven. It was nurtured by an aristocratic concern with and receptivity to the notion of musical greatness, and given impetus by the shifting economic structure of patronage after the decline of the hauskapellen and before the rise of newer organizational means for musical production and dissemination. As Thayer puts it, "All the conditions precedent for the elevation of the art [of music] were just at this time fulfilled at Vienna and in one department—that of instrumental music—they existed in a degree unknown in any other city" (1967, 1:155).

Independent of Beethoven, then, the stage was set for a qualitatively different kind of musical greatness. I next address how a connection was made between this predisposition and Beethoven, rather than some other musician, and how Beethoven came to be positioned advantageously within the context of aristocratic patronage during the 1790s.

CHAPTER 4

Beethoven's Social Resources

Beethoven was young and relatively unknown to the general public when he arrived in Vienna in November 1792. He was a "foreign" talent in geographical terms (and would have been perceived as such by nonaristocratic Viennese), but he was also already connected to a powerful segment of Vienna's aristocratic patronage network. These connections eased his entry into Viennese concert life.

Austro-Hungarian aristocrats were interrelated through numerous family links which transcended geography and which overlapped with the diplomatic and administrative positions in which family members served. Beethoven's Bonn patron, for example, Count Ferdinand Waldstein, was related through his mother to Prince Liechtenstein, through his grandmother to Prince Ferdinand Trauttmannsdorf, and through his sister to Prince Dietrichstein. Family ties were accompanied by musical alliances; all three princes were members of van Swieten's GAC. Waldstein was also related, through his uncles and aunts, to Prince Kinsky and Count Palfy von Erdödy (also GAC members) and, more distantly, to Prince Lobkowitz the younger (GAC), as well as the aristocratic families of Crugenburg, Wallis, Kaunitz, Kohary, Funfkirchen, Keglevics, and Colloredo-Mansfeld. The Bonn elector, Max Franz, who assumed the post in 1784, was a brother of Emperor Joseph and thus uncle of the next two emperors, Leopold II (emperor from 1790 to 1792) and Franz II (emperor from 1792 to 1806). Beethoven's well-connected position was an important resource for his entry into and acceptance by the

upper echelons of Viennese musical life. As Thayer observes, Be
could

> hardly have gone thither under better auspices. He was Court Organist and
> Pianist to the Emperor's uncle; his talents in that field were well known to the
> many Austrians of rank who had heard him in Bonn when visiting there or
> when paying their respects to the Elector in passing to and from the Austrian
> Netherlands; he was a pupil of Joseph Haydn—a circumstance in itself suffi-
> cient to secure him a hearing; and he was protected by Count Waldstein,
> whose family connections were such that he could introduce his favorite into
> the highest circles, the imperial house only excepted. (1967, 1:156)

At a time when aristocratic connections were still crucial to a musician's economic survival, Beethoven was exceptionally well placed. The
aristocrats with whom he was associated were already receptive to the
notion of musical greatness. In terms of his connections and position
within the musical field, Beethoven was perhaps unique among the composers of his day. The significant differences that social connections like
Beethoven's made to the shape of his career (and to the content of his
work) can be seen more clearly when he is compared with Jan Ladislav
Dussek, a composer whose career and musical style during the 1790s
and early 1800s resembled Beethoven's own. Comparing the two illuminates the ways that similar compositional approaches (as far as surface
stylistic characteristics) were framed differently, and it permits exploration of the impact of different settings and cultures on the ways musical
works come to be identified and valued.

Dussek, who was known during the early and middle part of his career as "le beau Dussek" (Scholes 1955, 308), is often viewed as a musical prophet of Beethoven because his works possess similar dramatic and
expressive characteristics. It has been suggested that Beethoven may have
been influenced by some of Dussek's works during the late 1790s (for
example, Blom 1958; Ringer 1970). Like Beethoven's works, Dussek's
were emotionally expressive and many were composed in the "Grand"
style during the 1790s. Beethoven was almost certainly exposed to Dussek's work by John Cramer, the London-based pianist who visited Vienna in 1798 and who met several times with Beethoven. If so, it is ironic
that Dussek is remembered mainly as one of Beethoven's lesser contemporaries, rather than as a probable source of inspiration to Beethoven. Moreover, commercially Dussek and Beethoven were in the same
league—if anything, Dussek was slightly ahead—even on German soil,
since Breitkopf and Härtel (Beethoven's principal publishers after 1802)

issued Dussek's entire works far earlier than they did Beethoven's.[1] Also like Beethoven, Dussek composed a heroic "rescue opera," which he composed in 1797, eight years before *Fidelio*.

WELL-CONNECTED AND
LESS WELL-CONNECTED MUSICIANS

As Table 7 illustrates, Dussek was a decade older than Beethoven. He spent the 1780s as an itinerant virtuoso, in part because he was unable to secure a post in an aristocratic household. As was the case for many other virtuosi, these foreign concert tours helped to publicize his name. On the strength of this reputation, Dussek was able to secure a position at the French court, where he became a favorite of Marie Antoinette. When political events made his position unstable, he fled in 1789 to London where he had to begin anew. This time though, his French reputation preceded him. Indeed, it served to ingratiate his work with English aristocrats, who looked kindly on musical works with titles such as "The Sufferings of the Queen of France. A Musical Composition Expressing the feelings of the unfortunate Marie Antoinette During her Imprisonment, Trial, &c." (Dussek published this piece with Corri, a well-known London music firm, in 1793).

Like Beethoven, Dussek arrived in a new city at the beginning of the 1790s, and like Beethoven, he arrived there bearing the prestige that ties to foreign aristocrats could bring. Dussek's ties, however, were more diffuse than Beethoven's. Dussek was moving between two fairly distinct patronage worlds, Paris and London, where, despite aristocratic patrons common to both, there was not the same degree of overlap which the family ties of Austro-Hungarian aristocrats created for Beethoven. Moreover, the world of aristocratic patronage in London was only one of several strands in a diverse and more commercially developed musical world. As a virtuoso pianist during the 1790s, Dussek appealed not only to aristocrats (many of whom were preoccupied with the notion of "ancient" music) but also to members of the upper middle class. He was successful in London, appearing often on concert programs as well as with Haydn during the latter's London visits. He was less successful in business, however, and fled to France in 1798 to avoid debtor's prison when the music publishing partnership Corri and Dussek went bankrupt; he never saw his wife or child again.

Unlike Dussek, Beethoven had ties to a court kapelle. First through his father,[2] and later through other members of the court and the kapelle,

TABLE 7
DUSSEK'S AND BEETHOVEN'S CAREERS

	Dussek	Beethoven
Mother	Caslav judge's daughter; harpist	daughter of overseer of food, electoral court, Bonn
Siblings	one of eight	one of three
Father	son of a wagon maker and copper; Caslav organist and elementary school teacher from 1758	son of electoral court kapellmeister; tenor in the court kapelle
Birth	12 February 1760	17 December 1770
Education/ training	elementary school and piano under father; father and son mentioned in Burney 1770, 132–33	elementary school and piano under father, who tries to put him forward as child prodigy; additional study with court organist van den Eeden, 1778; study with Pfeiffer, 1779, at night after wine house; study with Rovantini of Ehrenbreitstein; befriends Franciscan friar and organist and organ builder Koch; also befriends organist of the Minorites, who allows him to play organ for 6:00 A.M. mass
	to Jihlava as boy soprano; further study with relatives; humanities at Jesuit gymnasium, 1772	father stops his education (typical for time and place); concentration on music, 1781; study with Neefe (perhaps arranged for by the elector) begins; appointed deputy court organist, 1782; deputy court harpsichordist, 1783, which gives experience reading scores and of orchestras
	1774–76, further study at gymnasium in Kuttenberg and organist at Jesuit church	assistant court organist, 1784; Bonn musical life cultivated under new elector, Max Franz, 1784
	to Prague; study of liberal arts at New City gymnasium, 1776–77	visits Vienna briefly; possibly meets Mozart
	1778 University of Prague: logic and philosophy; no degree earned; assistance in music from Benedictine monk	attends lectures in philosophy at University of Bonn, 1789
Early patrons and posts	Captain Manner of Austrian artillery takes him to Mechelen (Belgium) where he works as piano teacher, 1778	Max Franz, elector of Bonn (brother of Austro-Hungarian Emperor Joseph II)

(Continued on next page)

TABLE 7 *(continued)*

	Dussek	Beethoven
		von Breuning family, "his first training in social behavior," c. 1784; teaches Eleonore and Lenz von Breuning piano; participates in salons there; through them meets Waldstein
	travels to Amsterdam where invited to The Hague; spends a year with William V, ruler of Holland in 1781	Count Waldstein, brother-in-law to Prince Liechtenstein and favorite companion of elector, after 1788
	travels to Hamburg, c. 1782; from Hamburg in 1782 to Saint Petersburg via Berlin, where he may have studied with Emmanuel Bach	1789 appointed as chamber musician along with others his age; appointment as court pianist
	at Saint Petersburg, a favorite of Catherine II; kapellmeister for Prince Karl Radziwill in Lithuania, at generous salary, for 2 years	unofficial member Lesegesellschaft (aristocrats and burghers; including court musicians and Waldstein), 1789
	1784 returns to Berlin; leaves Berlin on a grand concert tour of German cities; plays piano and glass harmonica; 1786 to Paris; a favorite of Marie Antoinette; a sensation in Milan; back to Paris in 1788; numerous works composed and published; 1789 flees Paris because of links to aristocrats; arrives in London	c. 1790 frequents Widow Koch's tavern, meeting place for artists and intellectuals
1790–99	well established as piano teacher in London, rates are as high as Clementi's and Cramer's, pupils include princess of York and other aristocratic ladies; participates in numerous public concerts from 1790 (benefits; Saloman concerts with Haydn); influences Broadwood piano firm to extend the range of their instruments from 5 octaves (FF to f3) to 5½ (FF to c4); writes compositions "for piano with additional keys"; summer 1791 tours Scotland with Domenico Corri (loans Haydn his piano while away)	

TABLE 7 *(continued)*

Dussek	Beethoven
31 August 1792, marries Edinburgh-born singer Sophie Corri; letter from Haydn to Dussek's father praising Dussek's ability	1792 moves to Vienna (for final study before international concert tour and return to Bonn) under sponsorship of Waldstein and Max Franz
enters into his father-in-law's music publishing business	moves into residence of Prince Lichnowsky, 1792; studies with Haydn, Albrechtsberger, Schenk
1794, frequent association with Haydn in Saloman concerts	
counters Wölffl's "Non Plus Ultra" sonata with his own work, "Ultra"	1796 first letter to Streicher concerning piano reform; pianistic "duel" with Wölffl at Wetzlar's, 1799

Sources: Thayer and Forbes 1967; Craw 1964; Nettl 1956; Frimmel [1926] 1968; Schonberg 1963; *Allgemeine Musikalische Zeitung;* Newman 1963.

he was exposed to a wide variety of teachers and visiting musicians. By contrast, Dussek's only teacher during the early part of his life was his father, who was an organist and elementary school teacher in the Czech town of Caslav. The situation of Dussek's father provides a general sense of the careers of less highly placed provincial musicians during this time. By day he taught young children, then "he spent entire nights with the scores of Caldara, Bach, Fux and Tuma among others which he studied and from which he extracted the most useful exerts [*sic*] for his pupils" (Dlabacz, quoted in Craw 1964, 13). The eighteenth-century pioneer of music history Dr. Charles Burney, who toured the continent during 1772 in preparation for his survey of international musical life, has left a touching portrait of Dussek's father, whom he met when he passed through Caslav:

> The organist and cantor, M. Johann Dulsick [*sic*] and the first violin of the parish church, M. Martin Kruch, who are likewise the two school-masters, gave me all the satisfaction I required. I went into the school, which was full of little children of both sexes, from six to ten or eleven years old, who were reading, writing, playing on violins, hautbois, bassoons, and other instruments. The organist had in a small room of his house four clavichords with little boys practicing on them all: his son of nine [*sic*] years old, was a very good performer.

After this, he attended me to the church, which is but a small one, and played an admirable voluntary on the organ, which is likewise but small, though well-toned. . . . He played an extempore fugue, upon a new and pleasing subject, in a very masterly manner; and I think him one of the best performers on the organ which I heard throughout my journey. He complained of loss of hand, for want of practice, and said, that he had too many learners to instruct, in the first rudiments, to be allowed leisure for study, and that he had his house not only full of other people's children but his own:

"Chill penury repressed his noble rage" which is the case of many a musician, whose mind and talents are superior to such drudgery! yet, thus circumstanced, there is no alternative but a jail.[3] (1775; quoted in Craw 1964, 16)

Thus Dussek's father, a primary school teacher in a small provincial town, was hardly in a position from which he could have arranged for his son the exposure to visitors and teachers or the concentrated attention that Beethoven received. Nor was the younger Dussek, without ties to a court, able to get practical experience with larger instrumental ensembles, as Beethoven could. But perhaps most important, as the grandson of the previous Bonn court kapellmeister, Beethoven was positioned from the start for, at least potentially, a very different type of career. Unlike Dussek, Beethoven did not have to follow the route of boy soprano in a cathedral choir (the typical early path to a music career), or otherwise prolong his formal education in order to gain exposure to potential patrons. Consequently, he could afford to devote less energy to the search for patrons (his existing patrons did that work for him) and instead conserved his time and energy for creative work. When Beethoven's social ties are diagrammed (see Figure 2), it becomes clear that his initial contact with Neefe and Haydn, with Abbé Sterkel, Carl Ludwig Junker, and even Waldstein was facilitated by his position within musical circles at the electoral court. Beethoven was, for example, presented to Haydn by the elector himself, when Haydn stopped in Bonn on his way to London. Haydn's contemporary biographer, A. C. Dies, has reported Haydn's own account of the event. Haydn had attended mass at the electoral court chapel:

Toward the close of the mass a person approached and asked him [Haydn] to repair to the oratory, where he was expected. Haydn obeyed and was not a little surprised when he found that the Elector, Maximillian, had him summoned, took him at once by the hand and presented him to the virtuosi [sic; Beethoven] with the words: "Here I make you acquainted with the Haydn whom you all revere so highly." The Elector gave both parties time to become acquainted with each other, and, to give Haydn a convincing proof of his respect, invited him to dinner. (Thayer and Forbes 1967, 1:101)

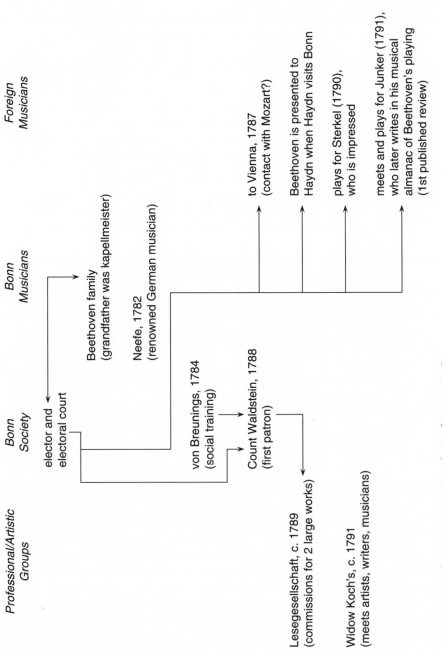

Figure 2. Beethoven's connections during his years in Bonn.

Beethoven's introduction to the Abbé Sterkel (a renowned pianist and musician at the Mainz electoral court at Aschaffenburg-am-Main) also occurred through court connections, the two being brought together by Beethoven's Bonn musical colleagues Ferdinand Ries and Nikolaus Simrock when the Bonn court journeyed to Mergentheim. A third important musician whom Beethoven met through his position at court was Carl Ludwig Junker, chaplain at Kirchberg and a musical servant of Prince Hohenlohe. Junker had been invited to Mergentheim, the capital of the Teutonic Order, where Max Franz and his entourage were spending the autumn of 1791 while the elector chaired a grand meeting of commanders and knights. The author of several musical almanacs and a music "authority" of some influence, Junker subsequently praised Beethoven in the pages of Bössler's *Musikal Correspondenz* in November 1791:

> The members of the chapel [kapelle], almost without exception, are in their best years, glowing with health, men of culture and fine personal appearance. They form truly a fine sight, when one adds the splendid uniform in which the Elector has clothed them—red, and richly trimmed with gold.
>
> I heard also one of the greatest of pianists—the dear, good Bethofen [*sic*], some compositions by whom appeared in the Speier *Blemenlese* in 1783, written in his eleventh year. True, he did not perform in public, probably the instrument here was not to his mind. . . . I heard him extemporize in private; yes, I was even invited to propose a theme for him to vary. The greatness of this amiable, light-hearted man, as a virtuoso, may in my opinion be safely estimated from his almost inexhaustible wealth of ideas, the altogether characteristic style of expression in his playing, and the great execution which he displays. I know, therefore no one thing which he lacks, that conduces to the greatness of an artist. I have heard Vogler upon the pianoforte . . . have often heard him, heard him by the hour together, and never failed to wonder at his astonishing execution; but Bethofen, in addition to the execution, has greater clearness and weight of ideas, and more expression. . . . Even the members of this remarkable orchestra are, without exception, his admirers, and all ears when he plays. Yet he is exceedingly modest and free from all pretension. . . . His style of treating his instrument is so different from that usually adopted, that it impresses one with the idea, that by a path of his own discovery he has attained that height of excellence whereon he now stands (Thayer and Forbes 1967, 1:104–5)

Of this event, Thayer has observed that Junker "showed his gratitude in a long letter . . . in which superlatives somewhat abound, but which is an exquisite piece of gossip and gives the liveliest picture that exists of the 'Kapelle'" (ibid.). Whatever Junker actually may have thought of Beethoven's playing (and it does seem as if he was genuinely impressed), he also had much to gain from being impressed and absolutely nothing to gain from criticizing. For one, he could demonstrate his own close ties to the electoral entourage through this report. He had, as he is quick to report, been invited to hear Beethoven, the elector's favorite, perform in private; moreover, he was "even invited" to propose a theme for Beethoven to vary. Was Junker attempting to depict himself as close to court society? Is that the only reason why, as Thayer notes, "superlatives somewhat abound"? Questions like these can only remain speculative; however, they help to bring into focus the multileveled discourse of contemporary chronicles.

Beethoven's fortuitous position as a court musician advantaged him over his contemporaries. These advantages (such as approval from important people, commissions, and the like) simultaneously functioned as indications of his talent, his promise, and his previous success. It would be overly cynical (and sociologically questionable) to reduce Beethoven's success and the emergence of his talent to mere nepotism: of course Beethoven was musically competent and musically interesting. The point is rather that there were numerous other musicians who, under different circumstances, could also have ended up as celebrities. The importance of Beethoven's initial connections must not be underplayed, especially since by all accounts Beethoven, unlike Mozart, was not recognized as exhibiting many signs of precocious talent early on (see, for example, Wegeler and Ries 1987, 17; Thayer and Forbes 1967, 1:65; Solomon 1977a, 28).

During Beethoven's first four years in Vienna, from November 1792 through 1796 (during which time he became established as a pianist-composer in Vienna), his rise is apparent through his expanding network of patrons and support personnel (see Figure 3). A diagram of Beethoven's acquaintances with various individuals reveals that the majority of his contacts were made either through Haydn[4] or through Prince Karl Lichnowsky. In the following two chapters I consider the ways that contact with these two men helped further Beethoven's reputation. For the moment, however, the important point is that, just as Beethoven's chances of acceptance by these early patrons were increased by his impeccable Bonn credentials and connections (which, it should be noted, would probably have secured him a sympathetic hearing even if the special concerns of patrons had not merged so well with his own background and stylistic predilections), so too his chances of subsequent success in Vienna were significantly increased by the initial backing he received from this growing circle of high-ranking, musically powerful patrons.

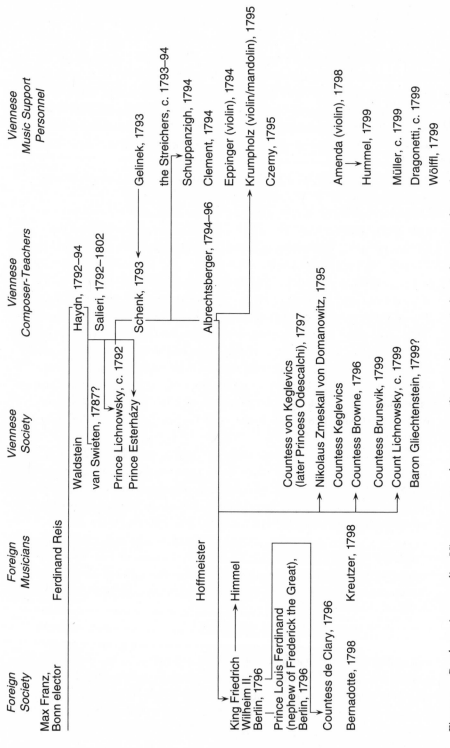

Figure 3. Beethoven's expanding Viennese network, 1792–99 (lines and arrows indicate direction of introductions to Beethoven). (Sources: Anderson 1961, vol. 1; Thayer and Forbes 1967; A. Schindler 1966; Landon 1970a.)

Beethoven arrived in Vienna with a good deal of social and cultural capital in the form of connections and previous honors, which enabled him (to extend the metaphor) to establish "credit" with new and potential patrons in Vienna. Metaphors can be overextended, and the metaphor of capital can be pushed too far. To be sure, Beethoven's success cannot be attributed to his social connections alone; at the same time, his career was underwritten from the start, and this security became a condition for his becoming known as a unique and particularly imposing kind of talent: because he could afford to do so socially, Beethoven took artistic risks. His musical works posed new and increased demands for listener attention. Severed from the forms of security that his connections provided, these works would perhaps have fallen on unsympathetic ears or, more likely, never have been made at all.

"SERIOUS" MUSIC AND ITS RESOURCES

Assuming that Beethoven's compositions were oriented, at least in part, to particular audiences and contexts, we need to explore his patrons' efforts as they were oriented toward comprehending and defending Beethoven's work. We have not understood Beethoven very well if we fail to realize that had he spent the decade of 1792–1802 in London (as did Dussek), his artistic output would have developed quite differently.

It is unlikely that Beethoven in London would have become the prominent figure we know, even with the support of English aristocrats. Dussek, for example, could not undertake certain musical projects because of his different situation. Dussek did not have at his disposal—as Beethoven did—a privately sponsored string quartet and orchestra; therefore his compositional output was mainly for piano (see Table 8). Yet because large-scale instrumental compositions served as the major vehicle for defining oneself as a composer rather than as a *pianist-*composer (less prestigious in both cities), it was more difficult for Dussek than for Beethoven to sustain an international claim as a major composer. Dussek simply did not have easy access to the resources necessary for frequent large-scale productions.

The later nineteenth-century notion of serious and important secular music revolved around large-scale instrumental or operatic works, around particular genres or particular combinations of instruments, and around difficulty of comprehension. To observe, then, that Beethoven was a "more serious" composer than Dussek because of the genres in which he (as compared with Dussek) composed, is to elevate one kind of

TABLE 8
DUSSEK'S AND BEETHOVEN'S
COMPOSITIONAL OUTPUT BY GENRE

	Dussek	Beethoven
Piano solo		
Sonatas	35	32
Sonatinas	12	0
Variations	23 sets	20 sets
Fantasias	3	1
Fugues	1	1
Rondos	23	5
Topicals	6	0
Other		44
Piano duet		
Sonatas	11	1
Fugues	3	0
Other	0	4
Piano and violin	65	10
Piano and cello	0	8
Piano and horn	0	1
Piano and flute	8	0
Piano and mandolin	0	4
Piano trios	24	9
Piano quartets	1	1
Piano quintets	1	1
Other piano chamber	0	6
String quartets	3	17
Songs	12	82
Canons	7	
Operas	1	1
Masses	1	2
Oratorios	0	1
Cantatas	0	4
Other choral and orchestral	0	10
Piano concerti	17	5 (+ 1 early)
Other concerti	4 (harp)	2 (violin and triple) (+ 1 fragment)
Other solo and orchestra	0	3 (1 fragment)
Symphonies	0	9
Wind band	0	10
String ensembles	0	14
Strings and winds	0	9
Total	261	317

Sources: Kerman and Tyson 1980; Craw 1964.

substantive musical material over another, independent of the processes of composition that characterize each internally, and independent of an appreciation of how these composers interacted with the cultures of music reception in which they operated. This view also makes invidious comparisons between two qualitatively different musical approaches. Although valued artists and valued works are not simply appointed, the backing of powerful people can help marshal the resources that make certain artistic claims easier to sustain. When we consider the relation between the organizational structure of Beethoven's and Dussek's respective music worlds and the ways their respective works were produced and packaged for public consumption, this point is clarified. The dedicatees and titles of Dussek's works, their use of preexisting musical material, and their resort to extramusical descriptive devices and to timely subject matter can all be understood in context of the composer's orientation to the particular characteristics of the London—as opposed to Viennese—musical world.

Table 9 lists Beethoven's compositions and their dedicatees during his first seventeen years in Vienna, and Table 10 lists Dussek's dedicatees from 1791 (his first year in London) to 1812, the year of his death. A comparison of the two lists from 1791 to 1812 (Dussek) and 1793 to 1810 (Beethoven) reveals that 9 (18 percent) of Dussek's dedicatees were musicians (only 3—about 6 percent—of Beethoven's works were dedicated to musicians), 26 (52 percent) were to the middle class and/or gentry (it is not always possible to distinguish between these categories for Dussek's dedicatees), 34 (68 percent) were women, and 15 (30 percent) were titled aristocrats. When Dussek's dedications are considered roughly by decade (that is, 1791 to 1800 in London and 1801 to 1812 on the continent), changes in their social composition become apparent: the dedicatees were women 83 percent of the time during the first decade, 54 percent in the second, aristocrats 13 percent in the first decade and 44 percent in the second. By contrast, titled aristocrats formed the bulk of Beethoven's dedications over both decades (67 out of 71); moreover, they were mostly men (68 percent).

In sum, Dussek's dedications went more often to women, were less often repeated (except to Clementi), and went less often to aristocrats but more often to musicians. The data confirm what is already known: that Dussek was an extremely fashionable London piano teacher, that the bulk of London piano students were women (a mixture of aristocrats, gentry, and middle class), and that London concert life was

TABLE 9
BEETHOVEN'S DEDICATIONS DURING HIS FIRST SEVENTEEN YEARS IN VIENNA, 1793–1810

Title and Opus	Date of Composition/Date of Publication (publisher)[a]	Dedicatee
Variations for Piano and Violin WoO 40	1793/1793 (Artaria)	Eleonore von Breuning
Three Piano Trios op. 1	1793–94/1795 (Artaria)	Prince Lichnowsky
Piano Variations WoO 67	?/1794 (Simrock)	theme by Count Waldstein
Three Piano Sonatas op. 2	1793–95/1796 (Artaria)	Haydn
Piano Variations WoO 69	1795/1795 (Traeg)	Prince Lichnowsky
Ab, perfido op. 65	1795–96/1805 (Hoffmeister and Kuhel)	Countess Josephine de Clary
Pieces for Mandolin op. 43a, 43b, 44a, 44b	1796/—	Countess de Clary
Two Sonatas for Piano and Cello op. 5	1796–97/1797 (Artaria)	Friedrich Wilhelm II
Piano Variations WoO 71	1796–97/1797 (Artaria)	Countess Browne
Variations for Cello and Piano WoO 45	1796–97/1797 (Artaria)	Princess Christiane Lichnowsky
Duet for Violin and Cello WoO 32	1796–97/—	poss. Nikolaus Zmeskall von Domanovecz
Quintet op. 16	1796/1801 (Artaria)	Prince Schwarzenberg
Piano Sonata op. 7	1796–97/1797 (Artaria)	Countess Barbara von Keglevics
Songs WoO 121	1796/1796 (Artaria?)	Major von Kovesdy
Three Piano Sonatas op. 10	1796–98/1798 (Eder)	Countess Browne
Three String Trios op. 9	1797–98/1798 (Traeg)	Count Browne
Three Sonatas for Piano and Violin op. 12	1797–98/1799 (Artaria)	Antonio Salieri
Piano Concerto no. 1 in C, op. 15	1795–1800/1801 (Mollo)	Princess Odescalchi, née Keglevics
Trio for Piano, Clarinet, and Cello op. 11	1797–98/1798 (Mollo)	Countess Maria Wilhelmine Thun

Work	Date (Publisher)	Dedicatee
Piano Sonata op. 13	1797–98/1799 (Hoffmeister)	Prince Lichnowsky
Two Piano Sonatas op. 14	1798–99/1799 (Mollo)	Prince Lichnowsky
Piano Variations WoO 73	1799/1799 (Artaria)	Countess von Keglevics
Variations for Piano, Violin, and Cello op. 44	1792–96/1804 (Hoffmeister)	Countess de Clary
Six String Quartets op. 18	1798–1800/1801 (Mollo)	Prince Lobkowitz
Septet op. 20	1799–1800/1802 (Hoffmeister)	Empress Maria Theresa
Piano Sonata op. 22	1800/1802 (Hoffmeister)	Count Browne
Piano Concerto no. 3, op. 37	1800–1803/1804 (Kunst und Industrie Comptoir)	Prince Louis Ferdinand
Horn Sonata op. 17	1800/1801 (Mollo)	Baroness Josephine Braun
Piano Rondo op. 51:2	1798?/1802 (—)	Countess Henriette Lichnowsky
Symphony no. 1, op. 21	1799–1800/1801 (Hoffmeister)	Baron Gottfried van Swieten
Ballet op. 43	1800–1801/1801 (Artaria), 1804 (Hoffmeister)	Princess Christiane Lichnowsky
Violin Sonata op. 23	1800/1801 (Mollo)	Count Fries
Violin Sonata op. 24	1800–1801/1801 (Mollo)	Count Fries
Piano Sonata op. 26	1800–1801/1802 (Cappi)	Prince Lichnowsky
Piano Sonata op. 27:1	1800–1801/1801 (Cappi)	Princess Josephine von Liechtenstein
String Quintet op. 29	1801/1802 (Breitkopf and Härtel)	Count Fries
Piano Sonata op. 27:2	1801/1802 (Cappi)	Countess Giulietta Guicciardi
Piano Sonata op. 28	1801/1801 (Kunst und Industrie Comptoir)	Joseph von Sonnenfels
Variations for Piano and Cello WoO 46	1801/1802 (Mollo)	Count Browne
Piano Concerto no. 2, op. 19	published by Hoffmeister, 1801	Carl Nicklas von Nickelsberg
Symphony no. 2, op. 36	1801–2/1804 (Kunst und Industrie Comptoir)	Prince Lichnowsky
Three Violin Sonatas op. 30	1801–2/1803 (Kunst und Industrie Comptoir)	Alexander I, tsar of Russia
Six Songs op. 48	before 1802/1803 (Artaria)	Count Browne
Piano Variations op. 34	1802/1802 (Breitkopf and Härtel)	Princess Odescalchi
Piano Variations op. 35	1802/1803 (Breitkopf and Härtel)	Count Moritz Lichnowsky
Violin Sonata op. 47	1802–3/1805 (Simrock)	originally for George Bridge, dedicated to Kreutzer
Symphony no. 3, op. 55	1803/1806 (Kunst und Industrie Comptoir)	Prince Lobkowitz
Three Marches for Piano, Four Hands op. 45	1803/1804 (Kunst und Industrie Comptoir)	Princess Maria Esterhazy

(Continued on next page)

TABLE 9 (continued)

Title and Opus	Date of Composition/Date of Publication (publisher)[a]	Dedicatee
Triple Concerto op. 56	1803–4/1807 (Kunst und Industrie Comptoir)	Prince Lobkowitz
Piano Sonata op. 53	1803–4/1805 (Kunst und Industrie Comptoir)	Count Waldstein
Piano Sonata op. 57	1804–5/1807 (Kunst und Industrie Comptoir)	Count Brunsvik
Three String Quartets op. 59	1805–6/1808 (Kunst und Industrie Comptoir)	Count Razumovsky
Piano Concerto no. 4, op. 58	1805–6/1808 (Kunst und Industrie Comptoir)	Archduke Rudolph
Violin Concerto op. 61	1806/1808 (Kunst und Industrie Comptoir)	Stephan von Breuning
Symphony no. 4, op. 60	1806/1808 (Kunst und Industrie Comptoir)	Count Franz von Oppersdorff
Mass in C, op. 86	1807/1812 (Breitkopf and Härtel)	Prince Kinsky
Symphony no. 5, op. 67	1807–8/1809 (Breitkopf and Härtel)	Prince Lobkowitz and Count Razumovsky
Symphony no. 6, op. 68	1808/1809 (Breitkopf and Härtel)	Prince Lobkowitz and Count Razumovsky
Choral Fantasy op. 80	1808/1811 (Breitkopf and Härtel)	Maximilian Joseph, King of Bavaria
Cello Sonata op. 69	1807–8/1809 (Breitkopf and Härtel)	Baron Ignaz Gleichenstein
Two Piano Trios op. 70	1808/1809 (Breitkopf and Härtel)	Countess Marie Erdödy
Piano Concerto no. 5, op. 73	1809/1811 (Breitkopf and Härtel)	Archduke Rudolph
March for Wind Band WoO 18	1809/—	Archduke Anton
String Quartet ("Harp") op. 74	1809/1810 (Breitkopf and Härtel)	Prince Lobkowitz
Piano Sonata op. 78	1809/1810 (Breitkopf and Härtel)	Countess Therese von Brunsvik
Piano Variations op. 76	1809/1810 (Breitkopf and Härtel)	Franz Olivia
Six Songs op. 75	1809/1810 (Breitkopf and Härtel)	Princess Kinsky
March for Wind Band WoO 19	1810	Archduke Anton
String Quartet op. 95	1810/1816 (Steiner)	Nikolaus Zmeskall von Domanovecz
Piano Sonata op. 81a	1809–10/1811 (Breitkopf and Härtel)	Archduke Rudolph
Three Songs op. 83	1810/1811 (Breitkopf and Härtel)	Princess Kinsky

Sources: Thayer and Forbes 1967; Kerman and Tyson 1980.
[a]Beethoven's publishers between 1793 and 1810 were, by city: Vienna: Artaria, Cappi, Eder, Hoffmeister and Kuhel (moved to Leipzig in 1801), Kunst und Industrie Comptoir, Mollo, Steiner, Traeg; Bonn: Simrock; Leipzig: Breitkopf and Härtel, Hoffmeister and Kuhel.

TABLE 10
DUSSEK'S DEDICATEES, 1791 – 1812

1791	Joseph Haydn
1792	Mlle. Bathoe
1793	Mrs. Chinnery; Miss Cornelia Collins
1794	Mrs. Hyde
1795	Miss Shaw; Mrs. F. G. Smyth; Lady Elizabeth Montagu; Miss Anne Thompson; Miss Wheler and Miss Penelope Wheler
1796	Miss de Vismes; Viscount Duncan
1797	Muzio Clementi
1798	Miss Beauchamp; Miss Fairfield; Viscountess Lowther
1799	Mme. Krumpholz; Mrs. Aprecce; Miss Griffith
1800	Mrs. Bartolozzi; Muzio Clementi; Mme. Dussek
1801 Vidal	Mrs. Rose Marshall; the Larrivee Sisters(?); M. and Mme. Louis
1802	Muzio Clementi; Miss Pauling
1804	Prince Louis Ferdinand; Himmel; John Cramer; Mlle. Susette Godefroy
1806	Pio Cianchettini; Himmel
1807	(on the death of Prince Louis Ferdinand); Baroness Klost; M. Wagner, M.D.; Prince Hatzfeld; Princess de Bénévent
1808	Mrs. Barbier
1809	Mlle. Charlotte de Talleyrand
1810	Lady Mildmay; J. B. Viotti
1811	Duchess of Courlande; Lady Mildmay; Countess Perigord; Countess d'Estève; Prince Esterhazy
1812	Mlle. Betsy Ouvard; M. Biancour

Source: Craw 1964.

organized more frequently by entrepreneurs than in Vienna and was conducted mostly in public. We can infer, therefore, that English dedications served a somewhat different function from their Viennese counterparts. Dussek's were made less often to music controllers and more to students. The expected reward of his dedications was less likely to have been a gift or the prospect of a concert location; they may have provided instead a means for enticing further pupils (perhaps because there would always be the possibility that such pupils would receive dedications, a status symbol). Conversely, depending on the pupil, Dussek's dedications may also have provided a way of advertising his own status as a teacher via his pupils (through which Dussek was able to attract fashionable members of London society).

Certainly, Beethoven also taught during these years and his income from pupils was "not inconsequential though difficult to estimate" (Moore 1987, 363). Beethoven's teaching, however, seems to have been important less for its economic remuneration than for its capacity to provide a route to personal forms of patronage by particular families. Teaching was often a means to more intimate relationships with aristocrats, which we see born out in the quality of Beethoven's subsequent friendships with his pupils. When the Countess Susanna Guicciardi presented him with a gift, Beethoven was apparently offended, perceiving it as remuneration for teaching the countess's daughter Giulietta: "I am not exaggerating when I say that your present gave me a shock. . . . It immediately put the little I had done for dear [Giulietta] on a par with your present" (see Solomon 1977a, 64; Tyson 1973, 9). Similarly, Arthur Loesser (though not the most reliable of sources) has suggested that Beethoven may have refused the customary commission from piano manufacturers when he arranged for sales to his pupils, passing the savings on to the pupil instead (1954, 134). Honor, prestige, and more intimate relationships rather than money were the valued currencies in Vienna, where ties to music's aristocrats remained the route for success.

More so than Beethoven, Dussek was an independent, "freelance" musician. What we know about Dussek's career enhances the picture of late eighteenth-century London musical life that I began to sketch in the previous chapter. Set in context of a more diffuse patronage network and a more highly developed "market" for music, relationships between individual musicians and patrons were less personal in London than they were in Vienna.

An examination of the titles of Dussek's London works (see Table 11) extends this theme. Of thirty-nine titles, thirty-two identify the piece in question as making use of one or more of the following: a popular song or tune (thirteen), a well-known opera aria or theme (four), a "favorite" theme or a "favorite" piece (eleven used the word *favorite*), an extramusical or topical event (four), or the so-called Grand style (eight were described in this way).[5] With the exception of this latter description (Beethoven's pieces are sometimes noted on their title pages as "Grand"), Beethoven's composition titles are nearly always plainly stated.[6]

Through their titles, Dussek's pieces are framed to include a fairly wide range of consumers. They advertise themselves as "popular" and

TABLE 11

TITLES OF DUSSEK'S WORKS
COMPOSED IN ENGLAND, 1793–98

1793

A New Year's Gift. God Save The King. with Variations for the Piano Forte

Six Sonatines Pour le Forte ou le Clavecin avec Accompagnement d'une Flutte

Dussek's Sonata Opera 21

The Rosary: A favorite English Ballad in the Midnight Wanderers . . . arranged as a Rondo

A Sonata for the Grand & Small Piano Forte with additional Keys

Dussek's grande concerto as performed at Mr. Salomon's & at the Professional Concerts

The Sufferings of the Queen of France. A Musical Composition Expressing the feelings of the unfortunate Marie Antoinette During her Imprisonment, Trial, &c. The Music, Adapted for the Piano Forte or Harpsichord

O Dear what can the matter be. A favorite Song arranged as a Rondo for the Piano Forte or Harpsichord

Rosline Castle with Variations in which is Introduced the Lass of Peaties Mill

Within a Mile of Edinburgh. A Scotch Song with Variations for the Piano Forte or Harpsichord

1794

A Duetto for the Harp & Piano Forte or Two Piano Fortes (one with additional keys)

Lord Howe's Hornpipe Arranged as a Rondo

Dussek's 2d Grand Concerto in F for the Piano Forte With Additional Keys. Arranged Likewise for those without; as Performed at the Professional, Salomon's Concerts, at the Oratorios, Theatre Royal Covent Garden And the King's Theatre Haymarket

Viotti's favorite pollacca . . . arranged as a rondo for the piano-forte

Six Leçons Progressives Pour Le Clavecin ou Piano Forte Dans Lesquelles se trouvent introduites des airs caractérises de diférentes Nations

1795

Six Sonatas for the Piano Forte with an accompaniment for a Violin

Fal Lal La! The Favorite Welch Air Sung by Mrs. Bland in the Cherokee Arranged and Varied for the Piano Forte

Dussek's Third Grand Concerto in C Composed for the Piano-forte with or without additional keys—as performed at Salomon's & the Opera Concerts

Three Sonatas for the Piano Forte, And also arranged for the Piano Forte with additional Keys in which are introduced The Fife Hunt, A Scotch Reel and the National Air of Rule Britannia as Rondos with an Accompaniment for a Violin or Flute

Dussek's Grand Concerto for the Pedal Harp or Piano Forte with or without Additional Keys . . . as performed at Salomons Concerts Hanover Square

(Continued on next page)

TABLE 11 *(continued)*

Grand March in Alceste, arranged as a Rondo for piano

Madame Del Caro's hornpipe arranged as a rondo for the pianoforte

Three Sonatas, with Scotch & German Airs and Three Preludes for the Piano Forte (with or without additional keys)

Here's a health to them that's awa. A Scotch Air Arranged as a Rondo

1796

The Royal Quick Step. A Favorite Country Dance Arranged as a Rondo for the Piano Forte

The favorite Scythian Dance in the Opera of Iphigenie en Tauride Composed by Gluck as Performed at the King's Theatre in Haymarket Arranged as a Rondo for the Piano Forte

Three Original Sonatas in Which are Introdus'd the Favourite Airs of Whither my Love 'ah whither are Thou gone & I though our Quarrels endeded (*sic*) and set my heart at ease & When to Nina Hapless Maid Her & Oh send Lewie Gordon home and the Lad & Hope told a flattering Tale that & With an Accompaniment For a Violin and Bass

Dussek's Grand Overture For Two Performers on One Piano Forte With the Additional Keys As Performed At Mr Salomon's And other Concerts

A Favorite air *Alla Tedesca* arranged as a rondo

La Chasse, for piano forte

1797

Two Harp Sonatas

Tre Sonate per il Piano Forte composte e dedicate al Suo stimatissimo Amico Muzio Clementi da Giovanni Luigi Dussek

The Naval Battle and Total Defeat of the Grand Dutch Fleet by Admiral Duncan on the 11th of October 1797. A Characteristic Sonata for the Piano Forte

1798

The Grand Military Concerto for the Piano-Forte

A Grand Sonata for the Piano Forte with an Accompaniment for a Violin

The favorite Romance of the Captive of Spilberg as now performing with the greatest Applause at the Theatre Royal Drury Lane the words by Prince (his first name) Hoare, Espq. the music entirely new

A Complete & exact delineation of the Ceremony from St. Jame's to St. Paul's on Tuesday the 19th of Dec.r. 1797 on which day their Majesties, together with both Houses of Parliament went in solemn Procession to return thanks for the several Naval Victories obtained by the British Fleet, over those of France, Spain & Holland. The whole forming an elegant frontispiece to new Music for the Piano Forte composed expressly on the occasion by J. L. Dussek

The Favorite Duett of Tink A Tink as Sung by Mrs Bland & Mr. Bannister Jun. In the Opera of Blue Beard. Arranged as a Rondo for the Piano Forte

The Favorite Concerto for the Piano Forte

Source: Craw 1964.

"familiar" through the incorporation of precomposed material, as "favorites," and as making use of famous opera themes. Like Beethoven, Dussek employed the idea of a "Grand" style but, unlike Beethoven, he was less able to risk alienating prospective buyers: hence he wrote compositions advertised as "for piano with additional keys," and then immediately qualified them with the phrase, "arranged likewise for those without"—the level of grandness presumably being adjustable to the consumer's home piano. Similarly, he composed pieces "for harp or piano" (enabling him to capitalize on two markets, as the harp was popular among young women in Britain) and pieces "for piano with violin obbligato," which could be sold to a pianist, a violinist, or both. From the perspective of the emerging Viennese ideology of musical seriousness and master composers, Dussek may have compromised his reputation as a potential master through his essentially exoteric appeal and through the more loosely stipulated conditions for the performance of the works.

Dussek thus had far stronger ties than did Beethoven to the music business, in part because, being in London, he had no other choice. It is not only Dussek's music that evidences the importance of a popular appeal, however; his case should be viewed as representative of some of the ways musicians in general operated within London's musical worlds. When Hummel, Mozart's pupil, visited London, he too wrote variations on favorite themes such as "The Ploughboy," as did Beethoven's friend and English-based advocate, Ferdinand Ries. Conversely, during the early 1790s, Beethoven could afford to be more uncompromisingly aloof, to maintain artistic integrity (or at least an illusion of autonomy), to ignore the popular market,[7] and to write for a specific set of instruments, as opposed to the flexible stance Dussek took.[8] It was not that Beethoven did not also shrewdly attempt to cultivate attention through his style—indeed, he did just that—rather, his work was oriented to a taste for specialness and exclusiveness. It was Beethoven, not Dussek, who provided the prototypical image of the "great" composer. For Dussek it was hardly profitable to be too adamant about being serious and exclusive since, especially in these early years, he had to sell. Had Beethoven been in London at that time, it is unlikely that his particular claims could have been articulated, let alone sustained. Beethoven's Viennese pianistic rival of 1799, Joseph Wölffl, observed that a Viennese composer in London was required to orient his works to a more popular and accessible aesthetic of musical consumption. Arriving in London in 1805, he wrote to Breitkopf and Härtel, music publishers and parent company of the *Allgemeine Musikalische Zeitung*:

Since I have been here, my works have had astonishing sales and I already get sixty guineas for three sonatas; but along with all this I must write in a very easy and sometimes a very vulgar style. So much for your information, in case it should occur to one of your critics to make fun of me on account of any of my things that have appeared here. You won't believe how backward music still is here and how one has to hold oneself back in order to bring forth such shallow compositions, which do a terrific business here. (Loesser 1954, 251)[9]

BEETHOVEN'S PROSPECTIVE SUCCESS

In this and the previous two chapters, I have been concerned with the structural, cultural, and social dimensions of Beethoven's prospective success. In particular, the question I have been exploring is why Beethoven, more than his contemporaries, was well positioned for becoming a new kind of musical talent. The answer lies in Beethoven's situation in the organizational structure of the Viennese musical world and, in particular, his relation to a culturally powerful segment of music sponsors who were becoming increasingly concerned with the *idea* of great music.

The categories and models that the concerns of these patrons implied ("Handel and the Bachs and those few great men . . . who, taking these as their masters, follow resolutely in the same quest for greatness and truth" [A. Schindler 1966, 49]) structured not only the issue of how many musicians could or should be recognized as artistically worthy, but also the shape of what would be recognized as an "appropriate" artistic response. The cultural context of musical life helped to construct the ways that the artistry of a "great" (that is, self-consciously serious, aloof, and historically oriented) musician should be framed. For an artist such as Beethoven, who had unusually close ties to this controlling segment of patrons, the constraints and incentives posed by the incipient canonic ideology were intensified. One popular idea is that Beethoven subsequently "forced" his patrons to take notice of him in new ways, to accord him a new kind of respect previously unheard of: "Thanks to his genius and to his uncompromising personality, Beethoven made himself into a pure composer, and he forced the aristocracy of Vienna to support him at it, more or less on his own terms" (Kerman and Kerman 1976, 190). While not inaccurate, this view is too simple. Though Beethoven's own contribution to his subsequent recognition as a genius was crucial, his success was partly preconditioned. There was both an organizational and an ideological receptivity to the idea of the "great" musician during this time, and these factors were important parts of the matrix in which Beethoven's later recognition and stylistic development occurred.

"From Haydn's Hands": Narrative Constructions of Beethoven's Talent and Future Success

Given his connections, age, and earlier accomplishments in Bonn, Beethoven was a likely candidate for success as a Viennese musical celebrity. How were early claims of his special promise substantiated? And how was the prospective aspect of Beethoven's success (the concerns of key music patrons and the ways Beethoven was connected to these patrons) mobilized to present Beethoven, rather than some other musician, as the master composer? To answer these questions it is necessary to follow specific courses of action—to focus on Beethoven's emerging network of supporters, and, more broadly, to discover the means of producing the culture of Beethoven's success, including what was being said and done for Beethoven, by whom, and under what circumstances.

THE STORY OF "HAYDN'S HANDS"

On the eve of Beethoven's departure from Bonn, several of the composer's friends and patrons commemorated the event by inscribing greetings in an autograph album. As was the custom, many of these entries were highly sentimental, such as Eleonore von Breuning's quote from Johann Gottfried Herder ("Friendship with that which is good / Grows like the evening shadow / Till the setting sun of life") (Thayer and Forbes 1967, 1:115). One of these entries, by Count Waldstein—who, along with the elector, was responsible for Beethoven's journey to Vienna—stands out for its grandiloquence:

Dear Beethoven. You are going to Vienna in fulfillment of your long-frustrated wishes. The Genius of Mozart is still mourning and weeping the death of her pupil. She found a refuge but no occupation with the inexhaustible Haydn; through him she wishes once more to form a union with another. With the help of assiduous labour you shall receive Mozart's spirit from Haydn's hands. Your true friend, Waldstein. (Thayer and Forbes 1967, 1:115)

Along with the elector Max Franz, Waldstein was one of the most zealous Mozart supporters during the 1780s, and this entry is one of the earliest examples of Mozart's posthumous deification. Yet when it is considered today, this now famous quote is often severed from its cultural context and read instead as if it were merely prophetic—as if it did not help to *create* the phenomenon of Mozart's greatness and Beethoven's promise as heir to that greatness.

In this chapter, I try to recover that social and cultural context—the circumstances under which this particular piece of Beethoven mythology originated. My purpose is to point out that the telling and retelling of a story about Beethoven's potential was a condition of his eventual success. The anecdote provided a particular type of publicity, and it created a resource for the subsequent favorable reception of Beethoven's works; recounting the story of Beethoven's talent, in other words, was a means of dramatizing Beethoven as someone who had received approval and acceptance from a famous teacher. Waldstein's entry in Beethoven's autograph book is significant because it is the first in a series of stories told about Beethoven's relationship with Haydn. In all of these anecdotes, Beethoven is portrayed as Haydn's prodigy, as receiving "from Haydn's hands" the mantle of Mozart and, more broadly, the honorific of budding "master" composer.[1]

Briefly summarized, the "Haydn's hands" story conveys how the "father" of the Viennese tradition (indeed, Haydn was affectionately known by musicians during this period as Papa Haydn) was bequeathing his accumulated musical wisdom to the musician who was to become his heir. Significantly, during the early 1790s this story did as much for Haydn as it did for Beethoven. At that time, Haydn's reputation varied according to location. Only in London was he revered as a "great" man, though later Haydn's London reputation reflected back on his standing in Viennese society.[2] To tell a story about Beethoven receiving Mozart's spirit from Haydn's hands was also a way of constituting Haydn as great within the Viennese musical world. Simultaneously, it further articulated the notion of greatness itself within this world, a point I discuss in the conclusion to this chapter.

In addition to the Waldstein entry described earlier, there are four additional extant versions of this story. The first comes from Beethoven's teacher, Christian Gottlieb Neefe, who contributed the following to Cramer's *Magazin der Musik* in 1783: "Louis van Betthoven [*sic*] . . . of most promising talent. He plays the clavier very skillfully and with power, reads at sight very well. . . . This youthful genius is deserving of help to enable him to travel. He would surely become a second Wolfgang Amadeus Mozart were he to continue as he has begun" (Solomon 1977a, 26). This account is interesting because it was articulated early in Beethoven's career—a full decade before he came to study with Haydn. Beethoven is depicted as a "promising" and "youthful genius." Written during the height of Mozart's popularity in Vienna, this account presents Beethoven as a prodigy and promising talent, but also as a talent not yet proved. Beethoven would "surely become" a second Mozart (who was greatly admired by the Bonn court and hofkapelle) *if* he were given the proper advantages, such as training and travel.

This more modest portrait of Beethoven's abilities is partly related to Beethoven's age (he was thirteen at the time) and to the fact that during the 1780s the meaning of the term *genius* in musical discourse was being transformed. Even in northern Germany, where the language of genius was first restructured and took on its modern form, the category of genius in musical discourse of the 1780s most often referred to an individual's "spirit" or unique characteristics (as in the phrase, "the genius of Mozart"). During the early 1780s, it was still possible to speak of genius of anyone; genius was not yet an exclusionary term in musical life and did not refer to superiority, to magnitude, or to the extraordinary, superhuman and, increasingly, male ability to be creatively dominant (see, for example, Murray 1989 and Battersby 1990).

During the 1790s, the meaning of the term *genius* began to change, as is evident in the next extant version of the "Haydn's hands" story. Like Waldstein's, it also originates in Bonn. It is a letter to Charlotte Schiller from B. L. Fischenich, a professor at the University of Bonn, dated 23 January 1793:

> I am enclosing a musical setting of the Feuerfarbe and I would like to know your opinion of it. It is by a young man from here, whose musical talents are praised everywhere and whom the Elector has sent to Haydn in Vienna. He is also going to set Schiller's *Joy* with all the verses to music. I expect some-

thing perfect [from him] for, as far as I know, his ambitions are for the great
and the sublime. Haydn has hitherto reported that he would turn over grand
operas to him and would soon have to give up composing. Normally he does
not bother with such trivialities as the enclosed (song), which he only composed at the request of a lady. (Landon 1970a, 59)

In this description, the notion of Beethoven's talent is aligned with the
northern German concept of the sublime. With it, the idea that Haydn is
to "pass on" the tradition to Beethoven is elaborated through a discussion of how the "master" (Haydn) has now intimated that the pupil is
destined to surpass him. In this respect, Fischenich's version can be understood as elaborating Waldstein's observation that the spirit of Mozart
found "a refuge but no occupation" with Haydn. Haydn is, in other
words, constituted in Waldstein's and Fischenich's accounts as a medium
or vessel through which Beethoven's (implicitly superior) talent will be
cultivated.[3]

It seems unlikely that Haydn himself would echo this line of thought.
Yet, ten months later, in a rather formal letter to the Bonn elector, Max
Franz,[4] Haydn goes so far as to describe Beethoven as destined to be-
come "one of Europe's greatest composers" and observes that when this
occurs, he (Haydn) will be "proud to be able to speak of [himself] as
[Beethoven's] teacher":

Serene Electoral Highness! I humbly take the liberty of sending Your Serene
Electoral Highness some musical works . . . of my dear pupil Beethoven, with
whose care I have been graciously entrusted. I flatter myself that these pieces,
which I may recommend as evidence of his assiduity over and above his actual
studies, may be graciously accepted by Your Serene Electoral Highness. Connoisseurs and non-connoisseurs must candidly admit, from these present
pieces, that Beethoven will in time fill the position of one of Europe's greatest
composers, and I shall be proud to be able to speak of myself as his teacher.
[23 November 1793] (Landon 1959, 141)

Of the four accounts considered so far, the first three were by Bonn-
based writers (Waldstein, Neefe, Fischenich) and the fourth, by Haydn,
was addressed to the Bonn-based elector of Cologne. It would be natural, in the 1790s as today, for Bonn's culturally active residents[5] to desire
one of their local talents to succeed in the larger cultural milieu of Vienna, and to find stories about Beethoven's promise originating from his
"home town" is hardly surprising. More significant is that these stories
came to be repeated in Vienna, and that, in being retold, they imported
into Viennese musical discourse aspects of a northern German concep-

tion of "serious" music which—van Swieten's interests aside—was not yet a pervasive part of aristocratic Viennese musical life.

Haydn appears to have been the first Viennese-based writer to employ this originally Bonn-based imagery of musical greatness and of Beethoven's status as heir to such greatness. Haydn would have functioned as a culturally powerful promoter of these concepts. That he appears to have been one of the first to circulate such imagery is also significant, because a strong northern German tradition during the eighteenth century criticized Haydn for not being serious enough. Why was Haydn apparently willing to adopt such a discourse and advocate this version of Beethoven's talent?

The first extant telling of the Haydn-Beethoven story offered by a Viennese observer to Viennese recipients was published in Schönfeld's 1796 *Jahrbuch*:

> Beethoven, a musical genius, has chosen Vienna as his residence for the past two years. . . . He seems already to have entered into the inner sanctuary of music, distinguishing himself for his precision, feeling and taste; consequently his fame has risen considerably. A living proof of his true love of art lies in the fact that he has put himself in the hands of our immortal Haydn in order to be initiated into the holy secrets of the art of music. The latter great Master, during his absence, has turned him over to our great Albrechtsberger. What cannot be expected when such a great genius places himself under the guidance of such excellent masters! (Landon 1970a, 59)

Schönfeld's book was a compendium of musical personalities during the early 1790s, and this entry would have been the first extant version of the story prepared explicitly for public consumption. This account disseminated to a wider musical audience a means of constituting the Beethoven-Haydn relationship that the world of aristocratic Beethoven supporters "already knew."[6] The fact that Schönfeld's version of the "Haydn's hands" story was similar to the preceding accounts of the Haydn-Beethoven relationship would suggest that, by the middle 1790s, Schönfeld was making use of a quasi-public form of accounting for Beethoven's relation to Haydn, one that was already circulating within the relatively well-integrated Viennese aristocratic music world. While this point remains speculative, it is reasonable to suggest that, over the previous three years, there had been talk among aristocrats about Beethoven's relation to Haydn, and that this talk functioned as a means of registering Beethoven's special promise. Certainly, music loomed large as a newsworthy topic for aristocrats in both Bonn and Vienna,[7] and there would have been plenty of material for discussion: the two composers had collaborated in a public concert in 1795, and by 1796 Beethoven had dedicated his first published piano sonatas to Haydn. During the 1790s Beethoven and Haydn were, at least occasionally, programmed together at private salons.[8]

Schönfeld's report, though published in 1796, appears to have been written sometime between January 1794 and August 1795, because Schönfeld speaks of Haydn being abroad: Haydn, "during his absence, has turned [Beethoven] over" to Albrechtsberger. Written about two years after Waldstein's and Fischenich's accounts, Schönfeld's description of the Haydn-Beethoven relationship elaborates these earlier versions. Beethoven is now identified as a "musical genius" who, having "put himself" in the hands of "immortal Haydn" (and Albrechtsberger as well), is entering the "inner sanctuary" of music and continues to promise even further greatness. Equally telling here is that the space allocated in this publication to Beethoven is second only to that devoted to Haydn, and four or more times greater than that given to any other musician listed.

Discussions of Beethoven and his link to Haydn are remarkable because no other Haydn pupil—before, after, or during these years—was depicted in terms that could be said to resemble even remotely those employed to describe Beethoven's relation to Haydn.[9] The closest any other musician came to being similarly discussed appears to have been Haydn's much less grandiloquent account of his plans to help one of Mozart's sons. In a letter to Michael Puchberg in January 1792, Haydn wrote, "I wrote the poor woman [Mozart's widow] three weeks ago, and told her that when her favorite son reaches the necessary age, I shall give him composition lessons to the very best of my ability, and at no cost, so that he can, to some extent, fill his father's position" (Landon 1959, 125). Compared to those for Beethoven, Haydn's testimonials for his other pupils were far more low key. In 1800, for example, Haydn wrote the following on behalf of Johann Spech:

> I, the undersigned, acknowledge and certify that my pupil Herr Johan [sic] Spech, under my direction and supervision, has mastered advanced composition, and consequently everything which concerns the vocal and instrumental branches; I further certify that he has made sufficient progress therein to enable him to preside over any music school, not only as director but also as a teacher of pianoforte and organ. I herewith testify to this. (ibid., 174)

Only one other Haydn pupil is even mentioned in Schönfeld (the publication appeared too early for Neukomm and too late for Pleyel, who had by this time left Vienna and was concertizing in London). This is Paul Wranitzsky, of whom Schönfeld says only, "Director of Prince Lobko-witz's Kapelle, he is our premier artist on the violin. He has produced excellent students to which Mr. Schuppanzigh and Mr. Turke clearly attest" ([1796] 1976, 67–68).

It is difficult, as Walter Benjamin once put it, "to brush history against the grain" (Buck-Morss 1977, 48). Seen from the perspective of twentieth-century musicology, Beethoven's status as a talent, as discussed in versions of the "Haydn's hands" story, seems self-evident. Spech, while undoubtedly competent, appears as a less imaginative, inventive, and colorful figure. It seems only "right" (and a matter of common sense) that Beethoven received a qualitatively different and more highly articulated form of praise from his teacher. If we are willing to suspend this commonsense view, however, we can recover at least three new ways in which the emergence of the "Haydn's hands" anecdote can be explored.

First, our own evaluations of Beethoven are made in retrospect. Beethoven's identity as a genius, as we perceive it, has been clarified through a rich variety of cultural practices that have accumulated over time, beginning with the 1790s. At first, however, Beethoven's worth was contested. There were people (including Haydn himself) who had at least occasional doubts about Beethoven's claim to genius. It is too simple to explain the emergence of the "Haydn's hands" story solely as a result of the quality and promise of Beethoven's works, even if, from our present point of view, the reality of Beethoven's worth (and his contemporaries' inferiority) seems axiomatic. Second, we can ask questions about how Beethoven may have been better placed for producing the kind of work most likely to be hailed as special, and we can compare Beethoven's situation with that of Haydn's other pupils (as was done with Dussek in chapter 4). Spech, for example, had fewer resources for asserting himself as a more than merely competent musician. Third and finally, we can ask how Haydn may have been in a situation where he was constrained to contribute to the "Haydn's hands" version of Beethoven's abilities, or where it may have advanced his interests to produce effusive statements of Beethoven's worth, regardless of what he may actually have thought of his pupil.

HAYDN'S REPUTATION AND PUPILS DURING THE 1790s

After Prince Nikolaus Esterhazy died in 1790, the new prince, Paul Anton, disbanded the Esterhazy kapelle. Free to travel, Haydn made the first of his two extremely successful London visits in 1791–92. He attended the Handel commemoration in Westminster Abbey and, in July 1791, traveled to Oxford, where he received the honorary Doctor of Music degree. He then returned to Vienna, where he supplemented his pension with earnings from teaching, the proceeds of occasional benefit concerts, and lucrative publication fees. In 1794–95, he visited London again.

During the 1790s, Haydn was comfortably placed between "old" and "new" worlds, the world of aristocratic sponsorship and that of musical entrepreneurship. In 1794, after the death of Prince Paul Anton Esterhazy, the new prince, Nikolaus the younger, requested Haydn to return as kapellmeister, and Haydn reentered Esterhazy employ after his second London tour. Since the princely residences were now in Vienna and Eisenstadt (Esterháza had been given up after the elder Prince Nikolaus's death), Haydn could continue to live in a suburb of Vienna (not in the Esterhazy household) for most of the year, spending summers at Eisenstadt.

Although Haydn's reputation among his Viennese contemporaries was considerably enhanced after his two foreign concert tours, even as early as 1790 his standing in Vienna was special in comparison with his fellow musicians. At the same time, Haydn's Viennese repute was not without problems: as noted in chapter 3, musicians in Vienna—even the most renowned—did not yet command respect as autonomous professionals. By 1790 Haydn was in the peculiar position of being one of Europe's most famous musicians while at home his reputation was changing qualitatively, moving away from his previous identity as musical "servant." Haydn's Viennese fame is substantiated by his standing in the Viennese concert repertory and by the large number of his works published by Artaria. His repute was boosted by recognition abroad: even before Haydn's first visit to London, the eminent English music historian Charles Burney referred to Haydn in the concluding chapter of his *General History of Music* (London, 1789) as follows (the passage was written in 1786):

> I am now happily arrived at that part of my narrative where it is necessary to speak of HAYDN! the admirable and matchless HAYDN! from whose productions I have received more pleasure late in my life, when tired of most other Music than I ever received in the most ignorant and rapturous part of my youth, when everything was new, and the disposition to be pleased undiminished by criticism or satiety. ([1789] 1935, 958)

For a young musician during the 1790s, study with Haydn provided an excellent way of launching a career. In the final decades of his life (1790–1809), Haydn took on comparatively few students (his fees were high for those who could afford to pay). Because of the select number of pupils and the prestige this conferred, association with Haydn often provided an entrée to aristocratic circles. Even in those cases where it did not, when musicians were thrown back on their own resources for professional survival, to be identified as a pupil of Haydn was, in itself, capable of increasing the chances of future success, whether as an itinerant concert artist or as a composer in the provinces.

Two of the most successful Haydn pupils during the 1780s were the Wranitzsky brothers, Paul (1756–1808) and Anton (1761–1820). Born in Moravia, both Wranitzskys established Viennese careers. A brief examination of the features of these careers clarifies some of the typical strategies available to aspiring provincial musicians, arriving in Vienna initially unconnected to aristocrats or to aristocratic ensembles. Like Dussek, both Wranitzskys attended grammar school at a local monastery. Paul (the elder brother) then studied theology at Olomouc and, in 1776, entered the theological seminary in Vienna, where he served as choirmaster (Postolka 1980b, 539). He studied music with an unknown teacher (perhaps J. M. Kraus, kapellmeister to the Swedish court) before coming to Haydn sometime around 1783. Two years later, he was appointed music director to Count Johann Esterhazy, the brother of Haydn's patron. During the 1790s (after the Esterhazy kapelle was temporarily dissolved), Paul Wranitzsky served as leader of the orchestra at the Burgtheater and Kärthnerthor theater, the two court-controlled theaters in Vienna.

Anton read philosophy and law at Brno and arrived in Vienna in 1783, at the age of twenty-two (Beethoven's age on leaving Bonn), where he was appointed choirmaster to the Theresianisch-Savoyische Akademie in Vienna. Once in the capital, he continued musical studies with Mozart, Haydn, and Albrechtsberger. According to Milan Postolka, during the 1790s (after the Theresianisch Akademie was disbanded), Anton was employed by the younger Prince Lobkowitz, first as konzertmeister, composer, and music teacher and then, after 1797 as kapellmeister to Lobkowitz's private orchestra. When Prince Lobkowitz assumed the directorship of the Viennese court theaters, he appointed Anton Wranitzsky director of the orchestra. In 1814 Anton also became director of the orchestra at the Theater an der Wien.

Both Wranitzskys had first-rank reputations as violinists and violin teachers; perhaps the most well known of Anton Wranitzsky's pupils were Ignaz Schuppanzigh and Joseph Mayseder, who later served, respectively, as first and second violinists in the Schuppanzigh Quartet, known especially for its performances of Beethoven's works.[10] Both Wranitzskys composed many symphonies, concerti, and works for chamber ensemble; Paul was also the author of eight ballets, six singspiels, two operas, and one operetta.

One of Haydn's most successful pupils during the 1790s was Sigismund Neukomm (1778–1858). Unlike most of Haydn's pupils, Neukomm was Austrian, born in Salzburg. His father was a schoolmaster and his mother, a singer, was related to Michael Haydn (Franz Joseph's younger brother). According to Rudolph Angermüller (1980, 121), Neukomm first studied music with a Salzburg Cathedral organist and then with Michael Haydn before entering gymnasium in 1790. Going on to study philosophy and mathematics at Salzburg University, Neukomm became honorary organist at the university church and then choirmaster at the Salzburg court theater. In 1797 he went to Vienna to study with Haydn and began a period of apprenticeship that lasted seven years, during which time he supplemented his Viennese income with music teaching (one of his pupils was Mozart's son, Wolfgang Amadeus the younger). In these respects, Neukomm's background is similar to the Wranitzskys'; unlike them, however, Neukomm was unable to secure a position in a private kapelle (increasingly difficult during the end of the century) and he left Vienna in 1804 for Saint Petersburg, where he embarked on a foreign concert tour. He returned to Vienna in 1808 and visited the ailing Haydn daily. In 1809—in the company of many fellow Viennese musicians whose opportunities were impeded by the private and relatively small scale of Viennese concert life—Neukomm emigrated to Paris, where he remained for the rest of his life. In 1814, he took up the position of pianist to Prince Talleyrand and was eventually invested as Chevalier of the Légion d'honneur in 1815. During his time in Vienna, Neukomm composed intermezzi, a one-act opera, and instrumental phantasies, among, presumably, other works.

Much less is known about the Haydn pupils Franciszek Lessel (c. 1780–1838), Paul Struck (1776–1820), Johann Spech (c. 1767–1836), Peter Hänsel (1770–1831), and Francesco Tomich (1759–after 1796). Lessel, born in Poland, became a pupil of Haydn in December 1799 (see Nowak-Romanowicz 1980, 693). Unlike the Wranitzsky brothers, whose corpus of works survives only in manuscript, there are extant published versions of some of Lessel's compositions. The Viennese publications include three pianoforte sonatas (op. 2, 1800), a flute quartet (op. 3, 1806) published by Artaria, and two flute duets, also published by Artaria. Lessel went to Vienna, like Beethoven, with the distinction of having already enjoyed some aristocratic patronage (in Poland). He went to Vienna to study medicine but was accepted by Haydn as a pupil at the turn of the century. He then remained in Vienna until 1810 before returning to his native Poland, where he enjoyed a successful concert career as, his contemporaries noted, "the representative of the Haydn school in his native country" (Landon 1976–80, 4:335).

Paul Struck was born in Stralsund and studied with Albrechtsberger in 1795, then with Haydn from 1796 to 1799.[11] On the advice and recommendation of Frederik Samuel Silverstolpe (chargé d'affaires to the imperial court), he traveled to Stockholm, where he eventually became a member of the Swedish Royal Academy of Music (taking part in the first Swedish performance of Haydn's *Creation* in 1801). While in Stockholm he composed a symphony and a cantata. After a year in Florence, Struck returned in 1802 to Vienna, where he was able to make a living as a piano teacher. In 1817 and newly married, he and his wife settled in Pressburg.

Janos (Johann) Spech was born in Hungary. Biographical sources on Spech slightly contradict one another. According to the *New Grove Dictionary,* which offers one item only in its bibliography, Spech studied law for a time before becoming one of Haydn's Viennese pupils. He subsequently returned to Hungary where he worked as a civil servant in Budapest from 1800 to 1812. In 1804 he became a theater conductor and in 1809 personal composer to Baron Podmaniczy. He lived in Paris during the 1820s and 1830s. His compositional output, produced between 1805 and 1825, consists for the most part of Hungarian songs, though he also wrote three operas, numerous cantatas, and an oratorio, as well as piano sonatas, string quartets, and miscellaneous other music for ensembles. Landon, who has interviewed Spech's great-grandson (and who also cites two additional biographical articles on Spech), presents a somewhat different biographical picture. He says that Spech went to Paris after leaving Haydn and that he studied at the conservatory for four years before returning to Hungary, where he devoted his life to the reform of church music and, on the advice of friend and patron Count Leopold Nadasdy, concentrated entirely on a musical career (Landon 1976–80, 3:556n.).

Peter Hänsel was born in Silesia the same year as Beethoven. He learned violin from an uncle in Warsaw and played in Prince Potemkin's orchestra in Saint Petersburg in 1787. He studied composition with Haydn for several years, starting in 1792 (again, the same year as Beethoven),[12] and began to publish some of his work in 1798 (three years later than Beethoven). From 1802 to 1803 Hänsel lived in Paris. He then returned to Vienna and to a position—assumed in 1791—as kapellmeister to Princess Lubomirsky's orchestra. His published works consist of fifty-five string quartets, four string quintets, six string trios, and numerous other pieces for keyboard and strings (van der Straeten and Charlton 1980, 150).

Francesco (Frantisek) Tomich (Tomes), who dedicated three sonatas to Haydn in 1792, studied music at the Breslau foundation of the Barmherzige Brüder and later studied pharmacy in Vienna. While in Vienna he also studied music with Haydn, then emigrated in the early 1790s to London, where he pursued a musical career.

To be associated with Haydn was undoubtedly an asset for all of these composers, and in most cases, Haydn's pupils were eager to advertise their link to such a famous teacher. It was not uncommon for their earliest publications to be prefaced with the words "pupil of Haydn." Ostensibly, this practice provided a means of deferring to their "master"; it was a conventional way of demonstrating gratitude and respect. In addition, it endowed published works with allure and provided, in a promissory way, an insignia of quality that could preface the work. While basking in the reflected glory of the master, a "pupil of Haydn" could also export some of that glory to provincial regions, and association with Haydn could function as a means through which young and unknown composers gained exposure to aristocratic patrons, both in Vienna and abroad. Acting as Haydn's emissary, for example, Neukomm gained access to the empress dowager of Russia. She (Maria Feodorovna) in turn wrote to Haydn in 1804:

> The letter and composition which your pupil Neukomm brought me gave me much pleasure, and I remembered with joy that I had met you personally in Vienna. This, and the flattering description of me you gave to the bearer, moved me to have him play it for me at once; and I did not fail to recognize his teacher in him. I do thank you so much for the beautiful songs that you sent me . . . and I beg you to regard the enclosed remembrance [a ring] as a token of my sincere good wishes, with which I am, as always, Your ever well-disposed. (Landon 1959, 236)

Four years later, on the eve of his return to Vienna, Neukomm wrote to Haydn to describe how the Philharmonic Society in Saint Petersburg had struck a medal in Haydn's honor, which they wanted Neukomm to deliver to Haydn (Neukomm refused because he thought it more fitting for the ambassador to present it personally to Haydn). In closing, Neukomm entreated Haydn to "preserve your affection for me, which is the only thing which renders my lot an enviable one, and makes me one of the happiest inhabitants on this earth" (ibid., 247).

Access to and inclusion in aristocratic patronage networks were essential for a musician to survive at a time when the Viennese music world was still controlled by Vienna's old aristocrats and musical life was conducted primarily in private. Occupational musicians took care not to alienate potential patrons, both at home and abroad. Haydn, writing a letter of reference for Peter Hänsel to Ignaz Pleyel (then in Paris),[13] notes that Hänsel is a "charming young man of the best character and also a good violin player. . . . You will see how talented he is by examining his three new quartets. He is in the service of the Polish Princess Lubomirsky, and for that reason I suggest that you treat him kindly" (ibid., 212). Similarly, Paul Struck's own success, on his return to Sweden as a "pupil of Haydn," was bolstered when (at Silverstolpe's instigation) Albrechtsberger, Salieri, and Haydn were made honorary members of the Swedish Royal Academy in 1799. Haydn's increasing profile in that country was further enhanced along with that of his pupils. Thus Haydn was something of a musical gatekeeper to career paths, to the extent that close association with him could provide access to the upper echelons of the high culture musical world and to the networks of aristocratic patrons. Contact with Haydn would have been especially important for those pupils who were otherwise denied access to elite patrons.

THE SOCIAL CONSTRUCTION OF SKILL
AND SKILL TRANSMISSION

I have so far left unexplored the issue of what Haydn's pupils may have learned from their teacher; instead, I have focused on the secondary benefits that association with a renowned teacher such as Haydn could confer. In this respect, my discussion runs counter to conventional musical historical and biographical treatments, which accent the ways that lessons with Haydn could enhance his pupils' musical skills. Such accounts correspondingly downplay the secondary benefits of the relationship between famous teacher and promising pupil, as if these were simply ancillary to the teaching process itself. Yet, over the past decade, a growing body of research on extraordinary achievement has specified the crucial role a famous teacher plays in the production of a pupil's achievement. This research highlights how the teacher is important for reasons that extend beyond the issues of whether knowledge and skill are handed down as sets of explicit instructions, and whether it requires a "great" teacher to recognize and bring to fruition a "great" pupil's potential. Emphasis is placed on how, apart from crucial practical help (such as introductions and exposure), contact with a famous teacher exposes a pupil to the often tacit "culture of success"—how to "act the part" and how to mobilize various contacts (see, for example, Feldman 1979; Bourdieu and Passeron [1964] 1977; Lareau 1989). This approach is not meant to suggest that the "lesson content" and the quality of the interaction between pupil and teacher should be ignored. Rather, these scholars observe that what a pupil gains from lessons with a great teacher should not be conceptualized only to reinforce a preconceived view of how skill and the ability to become a "great" talent is "transmitted" from one "great" individual to another; that view tends to elide the way the description of skill and its successful transmission from teacher to student is, in several senses, a micropolitically charged issue.

Consider, for example, the following report from Silverstolpe, the Swedish diplomat, of an anonymous pupil's[14] lesson with Haydn in 1798. It suggests (if Silverstolpe was reasonably accurate in his report) that the type of criticism Haydn offered his pupil was, while clearly of a substantive nature, also rather vague:

> Once when I visited Haydn, he was just in the process of going through the work of a pupil. It was the first allegro of a symphony, in which form the young man was displaying his first essay. When Haydn cast his eye over the attempt, he found a long passage in which the wind instruments had rests, and he paid the pupil a compliment and said in a half-joking tone: "rests are the most difficult thing of all to write; you were right to remember what a big effect longer piano passages can have." The more he read, the darker became his mien. "I haven't anything to find wrong about the part writing [*Satz*]" he said; "it is correct. But the proportions are not as I would like them to be: look, here is a thought that is only half developed; it shouldn't be abandoned so quickly; and this phrase connects badly with the others. Try to give the whole a proper balance; that can't be so difficult because the main subject is good."—This was all spoken with charm, and the young man, hungry for knowledge, was—far from being hurt—full of thankful recognition. I never knew his name; perhaps he later became one of the well-known ones. (Landon 1976–80, 4:335)

One could of course question the value of this report as an ethnographic account; perhaps, for example, Silverstolpe was not sufficiently knowl-

edgeable musically to follow and be able to recall Haydn's more technical instructions (though Silverstolpe, like most diplomats, was a keen
amateur musician). Yet for anyone who has been a pupil of an established and therefore busy teacher in any field, the notion that advice is
often conveyed in broad brushstrokes—and that it is often left up to the
student to determine just what such terse advice is meant to index—is
surely not foreign. The "how to" is often alluded to and left for the pupil
to discover on his or her own, with the teacher sometimes returning to
"take credit" retrospectively for the pupils' efforts (whether that appro-
priation is justified, of course, is a potential topic for negotiation).

To tell a student, for example, that a phrase "connects badly," is not
to tell her or him how it "should" have sounded. Similarly, to ask that
the whole composition be given "proper balance" is not, practically
speaking, much help in teaching just what such a goal might entail. This
is not to say that Haydn, with his far greater experience, was not capable
of "improving" some of his pupil's early works—it is not, in other
words, to assert cynically that Haydn did not, after all, have skills to
convey. Rather shorthand instructions were naturally employed as a
practical strategy in teaching, which suggests that the tacit content assumed to be present in the "gap" between the improvements that Haydn
may have had in mind and the way he expressed himself would, of necessity, be filled in later by the student. Recognizing that such a gap between a teacher's instructions and a pupil's applications exists serves to
highlight the possibility that these gaps may be filled in creative and un-
anticipated ways—at least some of which the teacher may not have
intended.

How, for example, would we know whether "proper balance" has
been achieved? The answer is inextricably linked to the quality of accounts that can be mobilized in favor of a pupil's work and to how that
work is viewed in relation to a body of other works. In turn, these accounts are themselves linked to the relative authority ascribed to them as
"legitimate"—that is, to the ways authority itself can be accounted for.
Thus a creative attempt can be evaluated according to a variety of (potentially conflicting) grounds: Is the student's production "what Haydn
would have done"? Has it exceeded Haydn or has it fallen short? Or was
it oriented to an entirely different set of criteria? In other words, justifi-
cations and evaluative criteria have to be selected; only when the student's creative attempts are viewed against selected criteria do they become meaningful in evaluative terms—as good or poor, creative or
plodding, far from the mark or perfectly in keeping with a given ideal.

Not surprisingly, therefore, any opportunity for criteria selection raises micropolitical issues. Depending on the nature of the criteria invoked, the distribution of various resources (in this case, honors and accolades) creates a variety of consequences. In this sense, then, the examination of how a teacher recognizes a pupil's work cannot be understood in isolation from the ways that recognition relates to numerous contextual features of the teacher-pupil relationship, features often considered as external and irrelevant to the teaching process. By no means is this argument meant to suggest, however, that musical factors (those intrinsic to musical practice itself) are reducible to external issues. Rather its purpose is to recognize that—because the perception and evaluation of compositions occur partly through reference to aesthetic ideas—"purely musical" factors alone cannot form the basis for an explanation of how works are assessed.

We need to distance ourselves from the conventional cultural notion of what study with a famous teacher provides. The major problem with that concept is that it idealizes the teacher's contribution and circumvents the ways both the pupil's and the teacher's abilities are constituted through the teacher-student relationship. Evaluation of what a pupil has "learned from" a teacher (and how talented that pupil is) has a social, interpretive dimension that cannot be accounted for through musical terms alone. Moreover, a student's ability to "profit" from the criticism of a teacher is often conceived in ways that undervalue the student's ability to "fill in" or second guess a teacher or, indeed, to impute a greater amount of intent to the teacher than the teacher's actual instruction may warrant. This discussion leads to the issue of how the teacher-pupil relationship was beneficial not only to Haydn's students but also to Haydn himself.

THE TEACHER'S GAIN FROM THE PUPIL

First, as I have already noted, underneath the cultural imagery of what a pupil gains from a master (primary skills rather than secondary benefits that help to assure success, such as contacts and prestige), a teacher can allow credit for that pupil's success to accrue back to him- or herself. A teacher can appropriate credit and do so legitimately where, according to the cultural imagery of the teacher-student relationship, "credit is due." Teaching becomes a resource for enhancing a teacher's standing as one who is able to foster talent. It is a resource because it provides a view of the pedagogic relationship that highlights the teacher as the imparter of knowledge, while leaving in shadow the work of the pupil as "receiver" (and creative interpreter) of wisdom.[15]

Without the support of ethnographic access to Haydn's encounters with his pupils, this discussion must remain speculative. There were, however, concrete ways Haydn's pupils were useful to him. By the middle 1790s, Haydn was Vienna's most famous composer. He had begun to be recognized as one of Vienna's cultural treasures, an identity that was intensified after his two trips to London. After receiving an honorary doctorate in music from Oxford in 1791, Haydn was officially described as a composer of whom "his Fatherland can be proud . . . a great creative and ever productive genius."[16] As the cultural climate of aristocratic music patronage grew more receptive to the notion of musical "greatness," however, Haydn, rather than resting on the laurels of previous successes, actively engaged in expanding and to some extent redefining his reputation. For this project, his pupils were extremely useful as support personnel.

During the 1790s Haydn was increasingly recognized as not only a public and popular composer (he was involved in numerous charity concerts, for example) but also a great composer, foreshadowing the sort of reputation that Beethoven's success continued and expanded. Haydn's renown as a serious composer derived primarily from his work for the Gesellschaft der Associierten Cavaliere, the large-scale oratorios *The Creation* and *The Seasons*. During the last decade of the eighteenth century and the first decade of the nineteenth, Haydn was actively concertizing, composing prolifically (especially after 1792, in styles that were new for him), and making arrangements for travel and business. His students (particularly those who could not afford to pay the hundred-ducat fee) provided a variety of support services, which relieved him of many tedious but necessary chores—the sorts of chores through which international standing was maintained and through which it could be advanced.

Both Wranitzskys and Neukomm, for instance, acted as Haydn's assistants, arranging some of the master's larger works for smaller ensembles.[17] Neukomm helped Haydn in an even more substantial way by assisting with the arrangements of the national airs, nearly four hundred in all (written between sometime before 1792 and 1805), a lucrative commission for Haydn from the Scottish publisher George Thomson. Thomson advertised these airs as having been arranged "by Haydn"; yet, according to Silverstolpe, who became friendly with Neukomm between 1804 and 1808, Neukomm revealed that he had written accompaniments for seventy Scottish songs (Landon 1959, 216). In April 1803, Haydn wrote to Neukomm: "Dearest Friend, Your servant Jos. Haydn urgently requests you to do the enclosed two Songs as soon as possible, and to tell my servant on which day he may come and get them—I hope perhaps the day after tomorrow" (ibid.).

Like the Renaissance artists who painted only the most important sections of a work (such as the faces of figures) and left the completion of background sections to their assistants (Baxandall 1972, 20–23) (or like contemporary academics who lend their names to papers "coauthored" by research assistants), Haydn was able to spread the wealth that his name could generate by contracting out some of his commissions and other tasks.[18] A sense of the organization of such collaborations can be gleaned from a letter to Haydn's eventual biographer, Georg August Griesinger.[19] Haydn says: "As far as the arrangement of the *Seasons* for quartet or quintet is concerned, I think that Herr Wranizky, at Prince Lobkowitz, should receive the preference, not only because of his fine arrangement of the Creation, but also because I am sure that he will not make use of it to further his own ends" (see Landon 1959, 191). Neukomm and Paul Wranitzsky also served as conductors for performances of Haydn's works during the late 1790s and early 1800s, thereby allowing Haydn's music to be performed under conditions that would assure high quality without placing too many performance demands on the composer.

Thus it was important for Haydn to have pupils who could function as support personnel and who could also attest to (and advertise) the importance of their teacher, both at home and abroad. The relationship Haydn enjoyed with his various students during the 1790s was symbiotic. For the pupils, most of whom came to Haydn without strong pre-existing aristocratic sponsorship, there was much to be gained from the appellation "pupil of Haydn"; for Haydn, pupils helped him maintain and expand a reputation by publicly acknowledging him as their "master," by acting as his emissary, by exporting his music and style to provincial areas, and by assisting him with some of the more mundane aspects of composition.

BEETHOVEN AND HAYDN

Although study with a famous teacher is capable of enhancing a pupil's chances of future success it may also, under some circumstances, limit how far a student can go. Being known as the pupil of a famous teacher guarantees recognition, but it may also mean that the student's reputation will never equal or surpass the master's. Indeed, one reason Lessel, Neukomm, Hänsel, Struck, and Spech became recognized as "Beethoven's lesser contemporaries" may have been that they played the role of devoted pupil too well—they were drawn too far in to playing supporting roles in the larger project of expanding Haydn's own reputation. Beethoven managed to avoid precisely this predicament. In the remainder of the chapter, I consider how Beethoven's relationship with Haydn compared with that between Haydn and his other pupils.

In certain respects Beethoven's initial position as "pupil of Haydn" differed little from the experience of these contemporaries. In 1793 Beethoven was a young and, in Vienna, relatively unknown musician who had achieved some amount of distinction in a culturally important but distant north German town. As his Bonn teacher Neefe observed (quoted earlier), one way of looking at Beethoven's journey to Vienna was that Beethoven had been recommended to Haydn to gain further mastery in composition and, more important, the imprimatur of Vienna's most famous living composer.

Yet the nature of Beethoven's tie to Haydn was qualitatively different: Beethoven was the only Haydn pupil ever to be praised as "heir" to the Mozart-Haydn tradition and as Haydn's greatest prodigy.[20] In the Fischenich letter Haydn is said to endorse this view, and Haydn himself told the Bonn elector that he would be proud to be known as Beethoven's teacher. At the same time, the relationship between Beethoven and Haydn appears to have been more complicated and characterized by far more ambiguity than that between Haydn and any of his other pupils. Landon has described the relationship as "ambivalent and even morbid," as having begun under a shadow "as cloudy as was Haydn and Mozart's sunny" (1976–80, 3:204), and he has emphasized the "ambiguity with which their intercourse was clouded almost from the beginning" (ibid., 4:61).

The traditional version of the "Haydn's hands" story suggests, as the earlier quotations from Beethoven's contemporaries describe it, that Haydn took on Beethoven because of the younger composer's unusual promise as the Viennese musical heir, and that the younger was "initiated" into the "holy secrets" of music (to use Schönfeld's words) while the elder was a proud and admiring teacher. In at least one version of the story (the Fischenich letter), Haydn is depicted as a teacher who recognized the possibility that his pupil would eventually surpass him. In keeping with this narrative, Beethoven could be understood as paying homage to Haydn by collaborating with him in public concerts (where he improvised on some of Haydn's themes [Solomon 1977a, 74]) and by dedicating his first published piano sonatas (op. 2) to his teacher, a conventional form of tribute. Considering the components of the story's "plot," we can outline the narrative as follows (1) Haydn was at the height of his fame, enjoying (via his international entrepreneurial ventures in London and engagements at Vienna salons) more attention than any of his contemporaries. (2) Haydn consented to take Beethoven as a pupil ("with whose care," as Haydn writes, he had been "graciously entrusted") because of Beethoven's extraordinary promise ("Beethoven will in time fill the position of one of Europe's greatest composers"); (3) in an environment of mutual respect (Beethoven "has put himself in the hands of our immortal Haydn," Schönfeld notes, and accordingly, Haydn says he will "be proud to be able to speak of myself as his teacher"), (4) the tradition was passed from an established to a budding genius ("to be initiated into the holy secrets of the art of music"). (5) As the pupil's experience increased, so did the master's conviction of the pupil's ability ("Haydn has . . . reported that he . . . would soon have to give up composing" [Fischenich]).

These components add up to an admirable and charming story, and for the most part this anecdote continues to be told by current Beethoven scholars, who accept it even in the face of contradictory evidence. As these elements are examined more closely, however, we find that not one of them can be accepted without qualification. There are numerous contradictions that have to be manipulated to present this story as a whole, and these contradictions suggest that the reality of the relationship is far less mythological, indeed, far less conventionally satisfying as a "good" (that is, dramatic and unambiguous) narrative.

According to Haydn's contemporary biographer Griesinger (1968, 63), Haydn "used to praise Pleyel, Neukomm and Lessel as his best and most grateful pupils." While there is no direct evidence to suggest that, during the early years of their relationship, Haydn's opinion of Beethoven was low (which seems unlikely), there is also not enough persuasive evidence to show that Haydn had clearly singled out Beethoven as the best or most talented pupil he had ever encountered. To the contrary, as Beethoven's reputation grew, Haydn seems to have grown increasingly *less* confident in the quality of his work. According to Giuseppe Carpani, Haydn's contemporary and biographer who was also acquainted with Beethoven, "Haydn was asked once by one of my friends what he thought of this young composer. The old man replied in all sincerity, 'his first works pleased me quite a bit, but I confess that I do not understand the latest ones. It seems to me that he always writes fantasies.'" (that is, in free form, improvisational style).[21] To be sure, Carpani is not, as James Webster has observed (1984, 27), the most reliable of sources, but Solomon notes: "No single one of these reports can be confirmed by documentary evidence. But the sheer number of these recollections—and the total absence of reports of praise by Haydn for any of Beethoven's compositions following the Septet and The Creatures of Prometheus—makes it rather probable that Haydn was unable or unwilling to comprehend Beethoven's greater achievements" (1977a, 77).

One obstacle to a richer sociological understanding of what Haydn may have thought of Beethoven's work is the commonsense assumption that Haydn had some kind of clearly formulated and coherent opinion about how Beethoven compared with other musicians who were his pupils—that "opinion" has an existence independent of the changing circumstances under which it is elicited. This commonsense assumption, when it is conjoined to the strong pro-Beethoven bias of much of mainstream musicology, often results in the failure to consider the circumstances in which Haydn's accounts of Beethoven's talent were produced. We can, however, bracket belief in Beethoven's transcendent ability and recognize instead that Haydn's accounts of Beethoven's ability, like all accounts, must be understood in the context of how, when, where, and for whom they were produced. Then it is possible to recover a sense of the Haydn-Beethoven relationship outside of its conventional narrative frame and to see it as characterized by ambiguity, contradiction, and ambivalence, and as extremely difficult (if not impossible) to summarize definitely. Once we begin to consider such issues, the case for Beethoven as Haydn's favorite seems far less clear.

First, given Beethoven's origins in a major electoral kapelle, Haydn could have refused only with difficulty to take Beethoven on as a student. As the contemporary composer Johann Schenk observes in his memoirs, "In 1792, His Imperial Highness, Archduke Maximilian, Elector of Cologne was pleased to send his protegé Louis van Beethoven to Vienna in order that he might study musical composition with Joseph Haydn" (1951, 272). Similarly, the "mutual respect" between the two musicians was not always present in private, nor was "the tradition" always conceived as having been adequately transmitted. In 1795, for example, when Haydn wanted Beethoven to put "pupil of Haydn" at the top of his first publication (op. 1), Beethoven refused because, as he told his friend Ferdinand Ries, he had "never learned anything from [Haydn]" (Wegeler and Ries 1987, 75). Certainly Beethoven was concerned with making a good impression on Haydn and depicting himself to his teacher as talented and industrious. One way Beethoven seems to have accomplished this was through covert help with his "homework" from the senior (but less celebrated) composer Johann Schenk:

> Towards the end of July [actually it was early in 1793—see Thayer and Forbes 1967, 1:142] the Abbé Gelinek informed me that he had made the acquaintance of a young man who displayed a rare virtuosity on the pianoforte, such as he had not heard since Mozart. At the same time he explained that Beethoven had begun to study counterpoint with Haydn more than six months before, but was still at work on the first exercise. He also said that His Excellency Baron von Swieten had warmly recommended the study of counterpoint to him and often inquired how far he had progressed in his studies. On Beethoven's writing desk I came across a few phrases of the first exercise in counterpoint. After a cursory examination it was clear to me that in every tonality (short as these were) there were several mistakes. This tended to bear out the truth of Gelinek's above-mentioned remarks. Since I was now convinced that my pupil was ignorant of the primary rules of counterpoint, I gave him the universally known text-book by Joseph Fux, *Gradus ad Parnassum,* so that he might obtain a summary of the subsequent exercises. Joseph Haydn, who had returned to Vienna from London towards the end of the previous year, was engaged in harnessing his Muse to the composition of great new masterpieces. Taken up with these important endeavors it was clear that Haydn could not easily occupy himself with teaching grammar. Now I was seriously anxious to be of assistance to one so eager to acquire knowledge. Before I began to teach him, however, I pointed out to him that our work together must forever remain a secret. In this regard, I ordered him to copy out once again every passage which I had corrected in my own hand, so that every time that Haydn examined it he would not notice the work of a strange hand. (Landon 1970a, 60–61)

Schenk may well have thought that this secret association would be of benefit to himself as well as to Beethoven, insofar as some of Beethoven's obvious and increasing cachet might rub off on him (Schenk was not nearly so close to the music aristocrats). But the association would clearly have been advantageous to Beethoven also, to the extent that it could enable him to demonstrate to Haydn a greater degree of competence.

In an essay that considers the Beethoven-Haydn relationship in detail and casts it in a favorable light (tending to discredit Schenk's account), Webster has suggested that Schenk's story was fabricated and that Schenk "doubtless saw no harm in puffing up his relationship with the great man into something more rewarding personally and, in its dupe-like role for Haydn, more titillating" (1984, 12). At least some of the circumstantial evidence Webster presents does cast doubt on some of Schenk's statements (for example, that the manuscripts studied by Gustav Nottebohm [1873] reveal numerous errors in spite of this supposed help and that Schenk's claim that Beethoven was inexperienced at throughbass is contradicted both by Neefe's commendation of Beethoven's skills and by the fact that Beethoven held keyboard positions at the Bonn court). Moreover, as Webster observes, Schenk seems to have been an enemy of Haydn (though Webster also notes that the sources for this claim are as untrustworthy as Schenk's own account), which, "if it should be accurate . . . would go some distance toward explaining the animus that would have led Schenk to fabricate his story about Haydn and Beethoven"(14). But if Schenk felt animosity toward Haydn, could not this animosity have been served just as well by covert tutoring as through a fabricated account of tutoring?

It does seem plausible that Beethoven studied secretly with Schenk. We know, at any rate, that Beethoven attempted to mislead Haydn about his ability and productivity in at least one other way. He brought Haydn several examples of his "recent" compositions, including a quintet (lost), an eight-part *parthie* (later published as op. 103), an oboe concerto (lost), a fugue (WoO unknown), and some piano variations (unknown). All of these works (except perhaps the fugue) had been composed some years previously, while Beethoven was still in Bonn; unfortunately for Beethoven, these were the works that Haydn enclosed in his 23 November 1793 letter to Maximilian ("as evidence of his assiduity over and above his actual studies"). Maximilian's rather chilly reply bears quoting in brief:

> The music of young Beethoven which you sent me I received with your letter. Since, however, this music, with the exception of the fugue, was composed and performed here in Bonn before he departed on his second journey to Vienna, I cannot regard it as progress made in Vienna. . . . I am wondering therefore whether he had not better come back here in order to resume his work. For I very much doubt that he has made any important progress in composition and in the development of his musical taste during his present stay [in an earlier draft of this letter Maximilian says, more harshly, "for I very much doubt if he can have learnt anything from you"; see Landon 1959, 143 n.] and I hear that, as in the case of his first journey to Vienna he will bring back nothing but debts. (Thayer and Forbes 1967, 1:145)

This mishap benefited neither teacher nor student. Whether Haydn contemplated bringing Beethoven along with him on his second London trip (some scholars, such as Landon [1976–80, vol. 3], have suggested that Haydn may have considered the possibility), he went without Beethoven and, in his absence, "turned him over to our great Albrechtsberger" (Schönfeld's *Jahrbuch*).

While Haydn was alive, the "mutual respect" depicted in the "Haydn's hands" story was often preempted by rivalry. Indeed, as we have seen, it seems that as Beethoven's career progressed, Haydn admired his former pupil's music less and less. We can periodize roughly the quality of their relationship as follows: (1) From 1793 to around 1796 they were involved in acting out various versions of the "Haydn's hands" account of their talents, with Haydn recognized as the "master" and Beethoven as the "disciple." (2) From about 1796 to around 1803 the two composers behaved openly like rivals, during which time their reputations were on a more equal footing, Beethoven coming into his own as a stylistically innovative composer. (3) After 1803, Beethoven and Haydn again colluded in promoting the story (at the 1809 performance of Haydn's *Creation,* Beethoven knelt down and kissed the hands of the master). As later reported in the *Allgemeine Musikalische Zeitung,* in 1803 Haydn reversed their roles, respectfully asking Beethoven for some artistic "advice." (4) After Haydn's death in 1809 (and when Haydn was thus no longer a rival), Beethoven publicly professed admiration for Haydn's genius and publicized his close ties to his former teacher.

The reality of the Beethoven-Haydn relationship is hard to summarize; it was characterized by contradictions that the clearer and more dramatic "Haydn's hands" narrative tends to elide. These contradictions have been explored by contemporary scholars, such as Solomon (1977a), who attempts to specify the diverse motives that informed Haydn's and Beethoven's interactions. He considers that Haydn may have been jealous of Beethoven's easier access to aristocrats but rejects this notion because Haydn was also helpful to Beethoven by introducing him to important aristocrats. Solomon also suggests that Beethoven was angry with Haydn for criticizing his compositions. So far, however, music scholars have not considered the Haydn-Beethoven relationship in the context of the changing occupational and cultural climate of musical life in late eighteenth-century Vienna. We can reach a deeper understanding of why Haydn colluded in the production of the "Haydn's hands" narrative by examining how, within this changing Viennese climate, the two musicians could be of help to each other—in ways that differed qualitatively from the mutual aid that characterized Haydn's relationship with his other pupils. This approach provides a way to accept the contradictions of the composers' relationship without having to resolve these contradictions in favor of one or the other of the alternatives that Haydn and Beethoven scholars have presented. It accounts for the production and dissemination of the "Haydn's hands" story without suppressing the numerous tensions with which it is riddled.

Beethoven, unlike other Haydn pupils, did not arrange or conduct his teacher's music. Although he did improvise on a theme by Haydn when he was a featured artist in Haydn's 1795 benefit concert (allowing him to demonstrate his improvisatory skill, for which he was rapidly becoming renowned), the remainder of his contribution to that concert consisted of performing his own works. Nor did he help Haydn with the numerous Scottish airs (indeed, Beethoven was subsequently invited by George Thomson to write accompaniments under his own name, a lucrative project during the 1810s). Moreover, as observed earlier, Beethoven refused to attach the phrase "pupil of Haydn" to his earliest publications (though he did dedicate his first published piano sonatas, op. 2, to his teacher—a less deferential gesture). One might wonder, therefore, what Beethoven could "do" for Haydn: if Beethoven avoided many of the more conventional forms of service a pupil could provide to a teacher, what practical benefit could Haydn derive from teaching Beethoven? One might suggest that Haydn agreed to tutor Beethoven simply because he had a genuine belief in Beethoven's talent, but this explanation bypasses too much material that is of interest.

An association with Beethoven could, in fact, benefit Haydn, and to understand the reasons requires looking once again into Haydn's own status and aspirations during the 1790s and into Beethoven's social background. I have already discussed the ways Haydn was actively engaged in furthering and redefining the quality of his reputation. Even so, though the status of the Viennese musician was changing during these years, it was still held in check by the aristocratic practice of treating musicians as domestic servants. This practice had an effect on the social innovations Haydn was able to accomplish.

Ideological conceptions of the musician's role changed as the notion of "great" music was elaborated and disseminated during the late 1790s and early 1800s. A major catalyst for this change was Beethoven himself and the quality of his reception. It is important to recognize that although Haydn was, in comparison to his fellow musicians, quite comfortably situated between the old (patronal) and new (quasi-freelance) forms of music sponsorship, in Vienna he was still closer to the old than the new. The Viennese did not begin to honor Haydn as a national celebrity until after he was awarded the doctorate of music at Oxford in 1791. Karl Geringer has suggested that, to many Viennese during the 1790s, Haydn was still known primarily as the musical servant of Prince Ester- hazy rather than a figure in his own right (1946, 85–86).

While this view tends to overstate the case, it seems clear that, espe- cially as Beethoven's own star ascended, Haydn risked being conceived (by strong Beethoven supporters, at least) as a musical exponent of the old regime, of music "in service to" aristocratic festivities and ceremo- nies. This notion colored Haydn's reception up until the twentieth century: his work—including the highly innovative, dark, and emotive works of the 1770s—became decontextualized and perceived (unfairly) as benign and anachronistic. To suggest, however, that all of Vienna came to perceive Haydn as old-fashioned and Beethoven as the "wave of the future" would be far too simplistic. Haydn was, after all, an established international figure, whereas Beethoven was a young upstart and a *pianist*-composer at the beginning of his career. Yet, unlike Beethoven, Haydn had spent nearly a lifetime under the older system of patronage, and, in addition, the Esterhazy family maintained a conservative ap- proach to both musical-occupational issues and stylistic changes. Even as late as 1802, according to Landon, Haydn was treated openly as a servant, as extant communications from Prince Nikolaus II to Haydn suggest. In 1801, for example, Esterhazy wrote: "To Herr Kapellmeister Haydn: I urge you to bear in mind that the members of the band must appear at all times with their uniforms clean and neat, and with pow- dered wigs. Disobedience will result in the offender being dismissed from the band. Eisenstadt, 26th September 1801" (Landon 1959, 191). And in 1802:

> To Kapellmeister Haydn: [speaking of Fuchs, a new assistant kapell- meister] . . . Just as the said Assistant Kapellmeister is now entrusted with the direction of the orchestra and church music in your absence, so the leader Luigi Tomasini is to assume the direction of the chamber music. Together with you, both of them, according to these circumstances, are to ensure that all the individual members of the band show the proper obedience; whereby I insist that there will be no case of insubordination, and that the various duties be performed in an exemplary manner; this includes personal appear- ance, care of uniforms, and other tokens of good behavior. . . . I have ob- served, not without displeasure, obvious proof of negligence of duty among certain members of the band: in future, a monetary punishment will be levied on any member of the band who absents himself from the [church] service. (ibid., 207)

Landon has commented on how "the difference between [Haydn's] position in London and that in Vienna and Eisenstadt will have been forc-
ibly made clear to him almost every day" (1976–80, 3:195). Thus, despite Haydn's celebrity late in his career, even then this fame was
qualified by his former position as musical "servant."

Haydn was on the verge of a new kind of celebrity during the 1790s,
and this potential dictated a partial transformation of his previous reputation. Beethoven, on the other hand, was distinctly poised for this new
kind of fame from the start of his career, at a time when the possibility
of the older type of success (as a kapellmeister/servant) became increasingly unlikely. In contrast to Haydn, whose repute accumulated gradually over a long and increasingly international career, Beethoven's success
had a prospective dimension: Beethoven was primed for success even before the start of his Viennese career. Moreover, unlike Haydn, Beethoven
could follow a career path that ran closer to the perimeter of (and in
some respects entered) the circle of aristocratic patrons. As I discuss in
the following chapter, even at the outset of his career, Beethoven was
much closer to his aristocratic backers than Haydn ever was, including
during the final years of his career. Nevertheless, Haydn could also be of
help to Beethoven. While Beethoven's familiarity with aristocrats during
his first two years was probably deeper than Haydn's, it was also nar-
rower; Beethoven needed to widen the extent of his support. So Haydn
was helpful to Beethoven in the concrete sense of being able to broaden
the base of aristocratic contacts. Beethoven spent the summer of 1793 at
Eisenstadt with Haydn, and, according to Landon (1976–80, 3:219),
Prince Esterhazy was later an early subscriber to Beethoven's Piano Trios
op. 1. It was also through Haydn that Beethoven was introduced to
Countess Thun and the Erdödy family. Finally, the association with
Haydn provided a pretext for discussion of Beethoven's special talent—
the "Haydn's hands" story.

Beethoven's social connections to aristocratic patronage, unlike those
of Neukomm, Lessel, Struck, and Spech (Hänsel had connections to
Prince Potemkin's kapelle in Saint Petersburg)—none of whom were
from backgrounds that gave them proximity to important aristocrats
(including Haydn himself, the son of a wheelwright)—were established
long before he arrived in Vienna to study with Haydn. Whereas most of
Haydn's other pupils were entirely dependent on their teacher for introductions and recommendations, Beethoven was already backed by key
aristocrats. In comparison with Haydn's other pupils, therefore, Beetho-

ven was less reliant on Haydn for making his way in the world of aristocratic musical life. Beethoven's aspirations were, however, qualitatively
different from those of Haydn's other pupils; Beethoven was far more
ambitious. To be viewed as Mozart's legitimate heir, Beethoven needed
Haydn's help, and in ways that extended beyond compositional training.

Solomon (1977a) has observed in passing that perhaps Beethoven did
not recognize Haydn's assistance because he did not want to remain
known as a "pupil of Haydn" all his life. It does seem the case that Beethoven was strategically conscious of how he could enhance his status as
an "important" musician; his letters and conversation books suggest a
meticulous attention to self-portrayal as an autonomous, ideologically
committed artist, as do his activities in the concert world (see the following chapters). Beethoven was in a position that allowed him to take some
initiative in his self-presentation and in his relationship with his teacher.
Unlike Haydn's other pupils, he had the social capital that made creative
independence possible, permitting him to purchase some independence
from Haydn. From the start of his career, there was a group of elite
aristocrats—some of whom were Vienna's music controllers—interested
in observing and underwriting Beethoven's progress. The Beethoven-
Haydn relationship had, from its inception, a high degree of visibility. It
provided a public arena, a means for both musicians to enhance their
profiles. This context reveals what Haydn had to gain from a connection
with Beethoven.

Association with the "rising" Beethoven—that is, with a young musician whose success was expected, at least by an initial cluster of prominent aristocrats—provided Haydn the means for a new kind of success.
This connection with Beethoven, especially as he was so swiftly taken up
by some of Vienna's musical princes, was an opportunity for Haydn to
come closer to or gain more status in relation to these music aristocrats.
Collaborating or playing along with the "Haydn's hands" story, as this
story became increasingly public, could be useful to both musicians even
if the private reality of their relationship was more complex. This is by
no means to suggest that Haydn and/or Beethoven were acting in a cal-
culating and conscious manner—for instance, that Haydn was privately
hostile to Beethoven and his music, but that he praised it in public for
purely instrumental reasons. Rather, it is to call for a more naturalistic
imagery of how decisions are made and stances taken toward individuals
and works, one which recognizes individuals as often indecisive and ambivalent, and where ideals and practical circumstances are inextricably
and interactively related.[22] Thus whatever Haydn may have thought of

Beethoven, he could hardly contradict any imagery of Beethoven as his prodigy that was projected onto their relationship by such august patrons as van Swieten, Waldstein, Lichnowsky, and Lobkowitz.

NARRATIVE AND ITS USES

Rather than attempting to determine Haydn's and Beethoven's opinions of each other, I look instead at how the two participants entered or were drawn into a cultural structure, a narrative historical account of people and events, and consider this account's effects—its impact on the organization of Vienna's music world. The "Haydn's hands" story helped to create certain entitlements and had implications for the allocation of resources, such as attention, time, and space in publications. Like a turn in conversation that establishes a concrete platform for initiating or shaping certain courses of action, a story provides a platform for depictive, representational work.[23]

Analysts of conversation describe how a story provides a way of organizing the statuses and relations between teller(s), addressed recipient(s), principle character(s), and nonaddressed recipient(s) by aligning them and clarifying their identities both substantively and in relation to each other. As a prerequisite to the work that telling accomplishes, however, it is necessary to "get the floor," that is, to mobilize the attention of addressed and nonaddressed recipients. Getting the floor is achieved through the pretext of providing something of value, something worth listening to, such as news, drama, comedy, and so on. The promise of a story worth telling is thus a pretext for the opportunity to advance a claim or series of claims about the way(s) reality is to be represented. To be able to tell a story or write a history, and to have established an entitlement to a venue, to listeners, and ideally to some means of reproducing that story over time, is to possess a resource for the classification and framing of what comes to pass as the "real" or "correct" version of events.[24]

"Stories" should be understood as providing resources for organizing the perception of an ongoing, often ambiguous present that lends itself to a plethora of interpretations. "Good" stories provide their recipients with what Melvin Pollner (1987) and Hugh Mehan (Grimshaw 1990, 160–77) have referred to as "incorrigible propositions"—sacred principles to which further ad hoc, practical sense-making processes ("documentary practices") become subservient. In Beethoven's case, once a valid claim was established for the "Haydn's hands" version of Beethoven's talent, the chances increased that perception of Beethoven would occur in ways that helped to substantiate, flatter, and elaborate that claim.[25] The issue of who can mobilize resources necessary to empower and privilege particular accounts (and in which contexts) is crucial. Pretexts for gaining access to a story-telling venue (a floor) are key, and these pretexts will themselves be perceived to have greater and lesser degrees of value, which will in turn have an impact on the quality of the venue and thus on the conditions under which reception occurs.

Telling the "Haydn's hands" story was useful in a number of respects. First, it established a high-profile platform—a legitimate pretext for attention—on which entitlements to future claims about Beethoven could be dramatized. In addition, because this story contained prophetic dimensions, it helped to organize perception and expectations about the musical future. The association with Haydn was a resource in two senses: it established a venue and it inaugurated a clarification of Beethoven as someone special, as someone of whom "great things" were expected. Second, the "Haydn hands" story was a vehicle for the creation of a qualitatively different type of publicity. The narrative organized the music field (tellers, principle characters, addressed and nonaddressed recipients) according to new and more hierarchical lines. It highlighted the notion of a definitive and self-conscious tradition of "greatness": Mozart, Haydn, and Beethoven could be opposed in this discourse to the more workaday, ordinary musicians who came to be constituted as their lesser contemporaries. Although the narrative cleverly described the value of Mozart as if it had remained constant over time, we have seen (in chapter 2) that the notion of Mozart's "greatness" (as opposed to his popularity) was an emerging and evolving phenomenon during the 1790s. The conceptual resource of Mozart's spirit—awaiting an heir—was constructed and mobilized in the service of this larger story line. The "Haydn's hands" narrative helped to transform Mozart's reputation, it also affected Haydn's status, and, most important for the purposes of this study, it helped to structure the ways Beethoven was perceived.

Thus the "Haydn's hands" narrative provided a means to dramatize the worth of both composers. It could enhance their reputations and distance them from the older, more traditional image of musician-as-servant; it could also more closely align them with the newer image of musician-as-celebrity. It is important to emphasize that Viennese-based musicians did not have at their disposal as many ways of dramatizing themselves as independent or as celebrities as did their English counterparts (or even as did Haydn when he performed in London). Within the scope of aristocratic receptivity, this drama of "Mozart's spirit from Haydn's hands" was one route to enhanced reputation that was not impeded by Vienna's more traditional organizational structure. Playing such parts worked to the composers' mutual advantage in that it let them appropriate more attention, repertory, and repute for themselves as independent musicians. The ideas of "master" and "heir" tended, in theory at least, to contribute to the further inflation of the musical enterprise by dramatizing it as a serious undertaking.

Certainly, the association with Haydn enhanced the description of Beethoven in Schönfeld's *Jahrbuch* because it was a medium through which discussions of his special qualities could be broadcast. Simultaneously, it resulted in the allocation of even more space in that publication to Haydn because, within the entry for Beethoven, Schönfeld discusses the link between teacher and pupil (the entry for "Josef Haiden" was already two-and-a-third pages long, as compared to Beethoven's single page and the more typical fifth or less of a page accorded to most others). Both musicians benefited from the interaction between the categories of Haydn's greatness and Beethoven's promise. At the same time, they were also, within the scene's various performances, involved in negotiating their respective roles, and it is here that the breaches in their performances often occurred.

My intention is not to debunk Beethoven and Haydn by suggesting that their actions were instrumentally careerist. On the contrary, I am attempting to describe how actors trying to accomplish constructive work of any kind are caught in a web of circumstances, including their own understandings of these circumstances. In Vienna, the idea of the canonic tradition (Bach, Handel, Mozart, Haydn), and with it the notion of the extraordinary composer and the new practices of concert behavior, comprised an available route away from the framework of servant-composers; it was useful as a response against the more traditional conception of the musician's role. It was a vehicle with which musicians such as Haydn and Beethoven could negotiate identities different from those linked to musician-as-lackey. I am not, in other words, suggesting that Beethoven pursued the new line of conduct for purely egotistical reasons—for recognition in and of itself. What I am suggesting is that, given Beethoven's position in Vienna and the circumstances surrounding his arrival there, this was one way of making the most of a quasi-freelance, quasi-private musical organizational setting, of creating a "space" in which to work. In a sense, Beethoven was "pulled" by available cultural and structural resources as much as he "pushed" with them.

Haydn's association with Beethoven was an opportunity to "tell about" musical events in ways that highlighted Haydn's distinctive role as greatest living exponent and bearer of the newly constructed tradition. In the short term, this was good for Haydn's reputation; by lending his existing clout to the prefiguration of Beethoven's greatness in terms of his promise, Haydn could enhance his own greatness. In the long term, however, once Beethoven's reputation began to grow (and Beethoven's antagonism toward Haydn with it), Haydn risked being constructed in the role of father to a younger and more advanced version of the "great" tradition. The nickname "Papa," which began as an endearment, began to highlight how Haydn, though venerable, was past his prime. Although this line of thinking was not fully elaborated until later in the nineteenth century, these 1790s stories about Beethoven and Haydn were seminal for this later development.

The "Haydn's hands" story had short- and long-term benefits for Beethoven, as well. It was initially useful because it aligned him with Haydn and established his entitlement to publicity: Beethoven became "the man to watch" (what Mozart reportedly said after Beethoven reportedly played for him, an entirely fabricated story about Beethoven that circulated later in Beethoven's career). In the long run the anecdote contributed to the restructuring of the musical field. It fostered modern conceptions of musical hierarchy and serious musical "stars" or "geniuses." The "Haydn's hands" story can be understood as providing a "pre-text" for action or a guide for how to regard Beethoven in relation to other musicians. In sum, it provided Beethoven with a resource—being aligned with the unimpeachable Haydn—and, equally important, it created a space for talk about Beethoven and, implicitly, for talk about others who did not have access to that resource—those who were not recognized as Haydn's "heir." At the same time, the story of "Haydn's hands" transformed that space; it helped to create new and more imposing hierarchies in the field within which artistic reception occurred.

CHAPTER 6

Beethoven in the Salons

The "Haydn's hands" story provided a pretext for considerations of Beethoven as a musician of exceptional promise. The next issues are how this "promise" was converted into evidence of Beethoven's worth and what Beethoven was able to achieve during his first decade in Vienna; to what extent Beethoven's achievements were collaboratively produced; and how Beethoven's increasing legitimacy was linked to, as Landon puts it, his ability to become "a force in music" (1977, 71).

BEETHOVEN AND PRINCE LICHNOWSKY

According to Carl Czerny (1791–1857),[1] one of Beethoven's few pupils: "It has repeatedly been said in foreign lands that Beethoven was not respected in Vienna and was suppressed. The truth is that already as a youth he received all manner of support from our high aristocracy and enjoyed as much care and respect as ever fell to the lot of a young artist" (Thayer and Forbes 1967, 1:444). During the early years of his Viennese career, Beethoven's most significant patrons were Prince Karl Lichnowsky (1756–1814) and Lichnowsky's wife, Princess Christiane (née Thun). The Lichnowskys were old nobility, positioned near the top of the multitiered, rigid structure of the Viennese aristocracy (Landon 1988, 24). In the music world they were also recognized as one of Vienna's foremost patronal families. Both Lichnowsky and his mother-in-law, Countess von Thun, had been important patrons of Mozart during the composer's later (and less economically secure) years. When Lichnowsky made a required visit to the Prussian court in Berlin in the spring of 1789 (as a landowner in Silesia it was necessary to make occasional visits [Schenk 1959, 406]), he took Mozart with him, stopping off in Prague, Leipzig, and Potsdam along the way.

Princess Lichnowsky was influential in social circles. In her autobiography, Countess Lulu von Thurheim (never a particular friend of the Lichnowskys) described the princess as able "with a gesture, with a scornful smile or merely by means of a slightly disparaging remark, [to] destroy someone socially. . . . This defect was derived, moreover, from the evil spirits of the coteries who had dominated Vienna in her youth and whose motto was *nul n'aura de l'esprit hors nous et nos amis* (no one will have wit but us and our friends)" (Landon 1970a, 67).[2] Princess Lichnowsky's influence would have been of use in promoting Beethoven, and Czerny, for one, believed that Prince Lichnowsky "induced the entire nobility to support [Beethoven]" (Czerny 1956, 309).

Allowing for exaggeration, what did Czerny mean by this? While music consumption and patronage were de rigueur for aristocrats during these years, the activity was pursued with various degrees of enthusiasm and energy. Some aristocrats, though they regularly attended musical events, were not particularly active in either evaluating or shaping taste. Count Zinzendorf,[3] for example, who attended numerous public and private concerts in Vienna during the years 1761 (when he arrived in Vienna after his university studies) to 1813 (the year of his death), rarely criticizes the musical life in which he participated.

On the other hand, some aristocrats—Baron van Swieten, for example—had highly formulated opinions and played active roles in shaping musical life. We have already heard from Schönfeld, for example, that concert audiences during the early to middle 1790s turned to van Swieten for cues about the "correct" opinion of the music. It would be premature, at this early stage in a burgeoning of eighteenth-century Viennese archival studies (and at a time when many of the results of this research remain unpublished), to attempt more than a sketch of the range of opinions and practices of aristocratic patrons. It does seem fair to suggest, however, that during the 1790s the Viennese musical field was characterized by a relatively consolidated structure of patronage, and that this structure was constituted by the participation but partial indifference of most patrons, who consciously or de facto delegated the right to govern musical affairs to their more musically enthusiastic peers. The number of Viennese music patrons was small in comparison both with the Viennese population and with London, and the patronage structure was hierarchical. As a result, the high culture Viennese music world was particularly conducive to aesthetic entrepreneurship.

How Beethoven initially met Prince Lichnowsky is unclear; possibly they were introduced by Lichnowsky's mother-in-law, Countess von Thun, whom Beethoven met through Haydn early in 1793. Alternatively, Beethoven may have met Lichnowsky through van Swieten (since Lichnowsky was one of the members of van Swieten's Sunday morning concert group during the early 1790s) or Haydn. It is also possible that Beethoven and Lichnowsky became acquainted only after Beethoven moved, several months after arriving in Vienna, to number 45 Alserstrasse (Beethoven rented a room in the ground-floor flat occupied by a printer named Strauss).[4] At this time, the Lichnowskys owned the building and resided on one of the higher (and more desirable) floors. Shortly after Beethoven moved in with Strauss, Lichnowsky invited the composer to live as his guest, and Beethoven remained with the Lichnowskys until at least May 1795.[5]

Because of the Lichnowskys' social position, simply residing with the family was an enormous advantage for a young musician. More practically, it meant that Beethoven, who was at least ostensibly treated as a member of the family rather than as a musical servant, was able to take meals with the family, though he often did not. He was also living rent-free. Thus, at this time, and the only such time in his life, Beethoven was materially well provided and able to enjoy the security of the traditional musician-patron relationship. Simultaneously, he was able to pursue a quasi-freelance career. Small as it appears, this economic advantage was, as Moore (1987) has shown, large in relation to the conditions faced by many of Beethoven's contemporaries; economically, Beethoven's first decade in Vienna was his most secure.

Close contact with the Lichnowskys provided musical benefits as well. As in Bonn, Beethoven was exposed to the numerous musicians who came to play for Lichnowsky salons. At this time, Lichnowsky hosted Friday morning concerts of quartet music, for which he engaged the violinists Ignaz Schuppanzigh (considered to be Vienna's leading violinist) and Louis Sina (a pupil of the composer Emanuel Aloys Förster who arrived in Vienna in 1794 and who deeply admired Beethoven's music), the violist Franz Weiss, and the cellist Anton Kraft. By 1794 Beethoven was studying violin with Schuppanzigh three times a week. This association later helped Beethoven introduce his own compositions for strings; Schuppanzigh worked closely with Beethoven and, as Czerny notes, "employed all his artistry to show the public the greatness and

beauty of Beethoven's works. And indeed, there was no one better qualified than Schuppanzigh to penetrate to the core and spirit of these compositions and his friendship was useful to Beethoven" (1956, 310). Not
all Viennese-based composers had the good fortune to work intimately
with respected and highly skilled performers. This collaboration resulted
in Beethoven's works being performed at a high standard and, even more
crucial, being performed at all. Beethoven also benefited from the suggestions these musicians offered for improving his works. Wegeler, for
example, writes: "Once when I was there . . . Kraft, the famous cellist,
pointed out to him that he should mark a passage in the final of the third
trio, Opus 1, with *sulla corda* G and that in the second of these trios the
finale, which Beethoven had marked 4/4, should be changed to 2/4"
(1987, 32).

Beethoven was situated at the center of the Lichnowsky circle, connected with some of the finest musicians in Vienna, and relieved for a
time of the need to pay for meals and rent. In return, during the next few
years, from around 1793 to 1795, he participated in Lichnowsky's private concerts (and others as well—certainly van Swieten's Sunday morning sessions). He became established within the world of aristocratic salons as a major figure.[6]

This acceptance, crucial to the launching of any musician, was especially important in Beethoven's case. From the start of his career, Beethoven was known as a unique sort of pianist. More than that of his
contemporaries, Beethoven's style was recognized during the 1790s as
unconventional, a quality evaluated in varying ways. That his different
style came to be praised should be seen in the context of the management
of Beethoven's reception: through careful presentation, Beethoven's characteristic and often controversial approach could be framed to flatter
and protect it from misapprehension. Who Beethoven was paired with,
on what sort of territory, and for which audiences were all important
factors in the reception of his work as worthy, and this was especially the
case during his early career, when building up an "official" record of his
success was key. As this record was compiled, it became a base on which
further and even larger-scale success could be mounted.

THE INITIAL CLARIFICATION OF BEETHOVEN'S
DIFFERENT PIANISTIC IDENTITY

During the early 1790s, while Beethoven was becoming established as a
first-rank pianist, he improvised often, and it was on his ability as an

improvisational pianist that his initial reputation was built. Through these improvisations, moreover, Beethoven's differences from his contemporaries were clarified and increasingly hailed as evidence of his ability (see Table 12 for a list of Beethoven's most significant contemporary piano rivals).[7]

One early (and perhaps the first) official performance through which Beethoven's distinctive style came to be known was the pianistic contest in 1793 between Beethoven and the Abbé Joseph Gelinek.[8] Judging from the discussions of this piano duel among members of the Viennese music community, the event helped define Beethoven, early on in his Viennese career, as being in opposition to the lighter and more generally popular pianistic approach, which Gelinek represented. Such duels provided object lessons in taste and fashion, and their outcomes had implications for patrons as well as performers.

Gelinek was born in Bohemia in 1758. He was much appreciated by Mozart, who knew him in Prague (Czerny 1956, 303n.), and was known primarily as the composer of piano variations, one of the most popular forms among dilettantes.[9] Because of his prodigious output—including at least a few spurious pieces by other (anonymous) composers, which his contemporaries came to attribute to him or perhaps more accurately which he allowed his name to absorb—Gelinek was known as the "variation-smith."

In general, these variations were relatively easy to play, simple in texture, and idiomatically predictable—so much so that they later inspired the composer Carl Maria von Weber to caricature Gelinek in verse with the following: "No theme on earth escaped your genius airy / The simplest one of all—yourself—you never vary" (trans. Thayer and Forbes 1967, 1:139). Gelinek embodied the quintessential late eighteenth-century, quasi-commercial composer, oriented to the amateur market and to exoteric values, the opposite of what Beethoven came to represent.

Not surprisingly, discussion in Vienna of the Beethoven-Gelinek "duel" appears to have contributed to the foundation of an initial record of Beethoven's success. Czerny recalls it as follows:

> I still remember how one day Gelinek told my father that he was invited to a party that evening where he was to oppose a foreign virtuoso in a pianistic duel. "I'll fix him," Gelinek added. [Landon's translation reads, "I'll make mincemeat out of him," 1970a, 110]. Next day my father asked Gelinek about the outcome of the battle. Gelinek looked quite crestfallen and said: "Yesterday was a day I'll remember! That young fellow must be in league with

TABLE 12
BEETHOVEN'S PIANISTIC CONTEMPORARIES
IN VIENNA AND LONDON, 1790 – 1810

Vienna

Leopold Kozeluch: 1752 (Velvary, Bohemia) to 1818 (Vienna). Anti-Beethoven and earlier anti-Mozartian. Entrepreneurial (owned a music publishing business after 1785).

Wolfgang Amadeus Mozart: 1756 (Salzburg) to 1791 (Vienna). Abhored Muzio Clementi, thought the Abbé Vogler sloppy. "Dueled" with Clementi in 1780 at imperial palace under Joseph.

The Abbé Joseph Gelinek: 1758 (Bohemia) to 1825 (Vienna). Esterhazy's house chaplain after 1795; intrigued against Beethoven's Mass in C in 1807.

Joseph Wölffl: 1772 (Salzburg) to 1812 (London). Studied under Leopold Mozart. "Dueled" with Beethoven at Baron Wetzlar's (new nobility) in 1799. See *Allgemeine Musikalische Zeitung* article on difference between Wölffl and Beethoven, 1799.

Johann Nepomuk Hummel: 1778 (Pressburg) to 1837 (Weimar). Last major exponent of Mozartian manner.

Carl Czerny: 1791 (Vienna) to 1857 (Vienna). Studied with Beethoven. His father was a keyboardist at whose house a musical circle gathered, which included Beethoven and Gelinek.

Ignaz Moscheles: 1794 (Prague) to 1870 (Leipzig). Student of F. D. Weber. Came to Vienna in 1806 to study with Salieri and Albrechtsberger. For a time part of the "anti-Beethoven clique," which included these two teachers and Louis Spohr, among others. Settled in London in 1821.

London

Muzio Clementi: 1746 (Rome) to 1832 (Warwickshire). Influenced by C. P. E. Bach. According to Liszt, Clementi never raised his hands as high as Beethoven. Known for anti-Mozartian, legato style. Publisher and piano manufacturer.

Jan Ladislav Dussek: 1760 (Caslav, Bohemia) to 1812 (St. Germain-en-Laye). Reputedly the first to turn the piano sideways. In London until early 1800s as a publisher. Known in Paris as "le beau Dussek."

John Cramer: 1771 (Mannheim) to 1858 (London). Pupil of Clementi and Friedrik Abel. Publisher. Beethoven called him the "contra-subject." Likened to Mozart for his graceful playing; known as "glorious John."

John Field: 1782 (Dublin) to 1837 (Moscow). Composer of nocturnes.

Sources: Landon 1976–80; Thayer and Forbes 1967; Morrow 1989.

the devil. I've never heard anybody play like that! I gave him a theme to improvise on, and I assure you I've never even heard Mozart improvise so admirably. Then he played some of his own compositions which are marvelous—really wonderful—and he manages difficulties and effects at the keyboard that we never even dreamed of." "I say, what's his name?" asked my father with some astonishment. "He is a small, ugly, swarthy young fellow, and seems to have a willful disposition," answered Gelinek; "Prince Lichnowsky brought him to Vienna from Germany to let him study composition with Haydn, Albrechtsberger, and Salieri, and his name is Beethoven." (1956, 304)

Johann Schenk, Beethoven's "secret" tutor, reports that "towards the end of July the Abbé Gelinek informed me that he had made the acquaintance of a young man who displayed a rare virtuosity on the pianoforte, such as he had not observed since Mozart" (Landon 1970a, 60). There are several points of interest here. First, whatever Gelinek thought of Beethoven is less relevant in this context than the ways his conversations with Czerny senior and Schenk were converted subsequently into topics in their own right—material for further discussion within the music world. Once again, we see that Beethoven's reputation can be conceived of as the accumulation of a repertoire of recorded, publicized stories about his talent. His growing fame was a function of an increasing public stock of knowledge about his worth; that "stock of knowledge" consisted of a body of accumulated tales, images, and other representative materials concerning Beethoven, which became resources for putting together talk about the composer and his work. Beethoven's "good publicity," was, whether intended as such, a way of configuring a particular social space, of framing or providing conceptualizations of the objects and individuals who furnished the space of Vienna's high cultural music world in ways that were accommodating to Beethoven.

In telling the story of Beethoven's talent, Gelinek positioned himself as subordinate to Beethoven (as a less talented but admiring colleague); thus Gelinek testified to and helped to publicize a favorable view of Beethoven's talent by aligning his own abilities as inferior to Beethoven's. In the stories about Beethoven and Gelinek, the latter's talent was appropriated as an "indicator" of Beethoven's "greater" ability. In the process, the fundamental discontinuity of their respective styles (light and dilettante-oriented versus complex and unconventional) was downplayed as these styles were vertically ranked with respect to each other.

The choice of Gelinek as Beethoven's first dueling partner could hardly have been better for distinguishing Beethoven's pianistic style from that of his Viennese contemporaries. By 1793, Gelinek's works would have been perceived as pleasing but predictable, and Gelinek would have provided a foil for Beethoven's different and somewhat shocking style, allowing it to be received as new and exciting. The Gelinek-Beethoven occasion provided an early aristocratic-public forum for the reconsideration of musical taste in ways that worked to Beethoven's advantage.

Some of the flavor of how different Beethoven's improvisations sounded to Viennese ears at this time (particularly to Gelinek and Schenk) is conveyed in Schenk's autobiography, written near the end of his life and long after Beethoven had become an established name:

> A day was fixed on which I was supposed to meet Beethoven in Gelinek's living quarters and to hear him play the piano. On that day I saw and heard for the first time that now so famous composer. After the usual polite phrases were exchanged, he expressed a desire to play a fantasy [i.e., improvisation] on the piano and asked me to listen to it. After a few chords and somewhat casual figures which he produced nonchalantly, this creative genius gradually unveiled the profound and sensitive image of his soul. The beauty of the manifold motifs, interwoven so clearly with utter loveliness, compelled my attention and I let myself be carried away by this delightful impression. Surrendering himself completely to his imagination, he gradually departed from the magic of his sounds and, to express violent passion, he threw himself into discordant scales with the glowing fire of youth. (1951, 273–74)

Schenk's romantic rhetoric aside, the message is that Beethoven, unlike Gelinek, was not a delicate pianist. Other contemporary reports suggest that Beethoven's playing was characterized by a heavy touch (Thayer says that this may have been because Beethoven was also an organist)[10] and that his extemporaneous playing was oriented to the goal of emotional expression. Beethoven's compositions, even early on, are characterized by a thickness of texture and complexity uncommon in 1790s Vienna. As Solomon suggests (1977a, 58), Beethoven's pianism was clearly opposed to the sweet, delicate, and "cloying" variety of earlier musicians.

The study of artistic reception is an often undeservedly peripheral area within musicology (though not within sociology). In musicology, artistic reception is frequently conflated with considerations of repertory or with a musician's financial status, which are then construed as indicators of whether a musician's works were "popular." Certainly, if a musician appeared often on concert programs or did comparatively well with sales, we can infer popularity. But such studies leave much unexplained; they tell us little, for example, about factions within music worlds, about constituencies for and against a musician, and they tell us nothing at all about the phenomenology of music reception.

As discussed in chapter 2, although extant repertory data shows Beethoven was frequently programmed (in comparison with other musicians between 1791 and 1810), his works were most often performed at aristocratically controlled venues. It is therefore inappropriate to describe Beethoven as a "popular" composer (that is, appealing to all social strata equally) on the basis of his status in the repertory.

In this study, I am interested in the responses of Beethoven's contemporaries to his works, as these responses occurred in a social context. I am not interested, however, in evaluating these responses from a musical-analytical standpoint (for example, how initial listeners may have been "mistaken" in their assessments of his work). That kind of enterprise is historically imperialistic, because it makes the responses of previous others subservient to our own, later responses, which are inappropriately projected backward in time. Because an appreciation of how Beethoven's music was perceived by his contemporaries is crucial to the arguments advanced here, it is worth pausing to consider some of the tacit assumptions of conventional musical analysis. By so doing, we can further appreciate some of the ways music analysis has functioned as a resource for the creation and maintenance of the musical canon. To this end, the following section consists of a theoretical excursus—necessary for outlining why a consideration of reception issues is essential to any sociological understanding of music.

EXCURSUS: APPROACHING THE STUDY OF RECEPTION

I begin with an example from one of the best and most respected works in the field: Charles Rosen, in his otherwise excellent book on the classical style has suggested that, in the Hammerklavier Sonata of 1817–18, we can see how "the emancipation of piano music from the demands of the amateur musician was made official with a consequent loss of responsibility and a greater freedom for the imagination" (1972, 404). Statements such as this, which attempts to assess stylistic "turning points" in a composer's body of works, are problematic from a sociological point of view because music analysis is formulated, and only makes sense within, specific historical and cultural contexts. It is formulated, moreover, with reference to specific agendas, explicit and implicit—a point that has not yet been incorporated into collective musicological discourse. "Turning points" in a composer's corpus of works will vary according to the categories of analysis brought to bear on that work. An appreciation of the ways that analytical categories help to structure the perception of musical material has several important implications for our understanding of the reception of Beethoven's work.

From the vantage point of the late twentieth century (and faced with a relatively finite corpus of works by Beethoven),[11] it has become conventional to view the piano sonatas of the 1790s as still within a "classical" mold and as still oriented to the demands of the amateur musician. It is also conventional to view the "break" with classicism as occurring later in Beethoven's compositional development. While assumptions such as these are persuasive and in accord with both common sense and late twentieth-century music-analytical perspectives, they also tend to close off potentially fruitful lines of historical research. First, they implicitly treat classicism and musical "emancipation . . . from the demands of the amateur" as objective developments that can be accurately dated, rather than as historically specific, symbolic constructions or ways of conceptualizing music history.[12] Second, these assumptions tend to imply, fallaciously, that for any point in the history of Beethoven reception our twentieth-century analytical categories are appropriate—that we share a culture with aristocratic and/or upper middle-class members of the late eighteenth-century Viennese music world (indeed, the notion that there is one history, rather than a multiplicity of narrative accounts from time to time and place to place throughout the period, is itself a resource in constructing this assumption).[13]

From a late twentieth-century point of view, we may assume that the formal "distance" between the Sonatas op. 2 and the music of not only Mozart or Haydn, but also Gelinek is "smaller" or less significant than that between op. 2 and the Hammerklavier. While this evaluation may seem accurate to us, it is wrong to assume, without attempting to verify, that a hypothetical listener in 1795 would perceive Beethoven's early works as not very different from works by Mozart. To do so would mean that we impute to the 1790s listener our own retrospective frame of reference; we assume that the 1790s listener would hear op. 2 as we do— in light of subsequent music by Beethoven, and by other nineteenth- and twentieth-century composers. The source of our error here lies in failing to consider (and this is always a problem with historical research) the relativity of reception, the ways in which listeners' responses are constructed with reference to the categories of analysis and evaluation available to them as conceptual resources (or instruments for organizing perception) within their contexts of reception.[14]

In other words, how were these pieces experienced, not by twentieth-century analysts, but by members of the Viennese concert and salon audiences? Because music analysis is typically antihistoricist, it has not yet incorporated the ways that categories of analysis are often imposed on works and how this imposition precludes consideration of the inappropriateness of music-analytical categories when applied to specific contexts of hearing. With respect to the various "turning points" or radical departures in Beethoven's work, we need to consider that what we may perceive as a comparatively "small" distance (between Mozart and Beethoven in the 1790s) may have been perceived by contemporaries as much larger (see DeNora n.d.a.).

This musical issue is part of a wider and more fundamental concern with cultural relativity, multiple realities, and the social construction of the object. Music scholarship often concerns itself with the topic of meaning and symbolic reality, but until recently there has been an absence of bridges between musicology and the human sciences; this gap has helped to sustain an implicit form of naive positivism within music analysis and criticism. This is a polemical claim. By the term *naive positivism*, I mean modes of explanation that postulate categories of analysis as historically transcendent. Naive positivist modes of accounting in music analysis can be most easily spotted when analysts turn their attention to the issue of music's social meanings, especially the forms of analysis that "read" musical texts as if the referents of these texts were "in" the text rather than socially and culturally constructed through the interaction of text and recipient (and as if the act of writing about music were not part and parcel of the meaning construction process). Once we realize, however, the importance of contexts of reception, we can begin to consider conventional musicological positions more critically and rethink the claims that music and its social meanings are an appropriate concern for analysis. I am reminded of the ongoing debate in musicology, often the topic for panels at scholarly meetings, between "formalists" and those who focus on music's "content." From the sociologist's point of view, both positions have merits and flaws.

On the one hand, formalists criticize interpretive forms of music analysis as unsystematic and subjective, and as importing unacknowledged assumptions into their analysis in ways that conflate the analyst's "personal" understanding of musical structure and content with a more "rigorous," analytically derived form of explication. Some examples of recent and well-known attempts to deal with music's ideological "content" illustrate the nature of formalist critique.

In his reading of sexual politics in Mozart's operas, Charles Ford has suggested that Mozart's music embodies a version of the feminine as musically subservient, as an "empty though plentitudinous [sic] space" within which male desire and will can be projected (1991, 136). Musically, this configuration of the male-female dichotomy is embodied through the dichotomy of forward-thrusting dominant modulation and musically static harmonic ambiguity. Referring to Dorabella's and Fiordiligi's duet in scene 2 of *Così fan tutte* for example, Ford suggests: "The fact that such harmonic and moral determination is inauthentic for Enlightened femininity is registered by their minor mode, by the improperly resolved leading notes in the bass part, and by the lack of a clear melodic middleground. This muddled, un-Enlightened harmony represents the women's moral instability and irrationality" (146). Ford's account focuses on how music and gender are "mapped" onto and therefore mutually constitute each other. If we assume for the moment that Ford's analytical conclusions would be shared by other musicologists,[15] Ford's interpretive claims are secured through the ways that musical material is allocated by gender.

Analyses of music's social and ideological content are compelling when they focus on the ways music is mapped onto other social phenomena. Analyses of musical content are less successful, and consequently more susceptible to formalist critique, when they are applied to instrumental music. At its best, Susan McClary's work employs a strategy similar to Ford's. In her analyses of *Carmen* (1991; 1992), McClary details the ways Georges Bizet employed musical material to construct gender, character, and operatic plot. McClary is on less secure ground, however, when she suggests that Beethoven's symphonic works are about masculine domination, as in this discussion of the Adagio movement of the Ninth Symphony:

> If the first two movements are monomaniacal, the Adagio is dialogic. It stands strangely aloof from the striving narrative of the other movements: perched as it is on the never-never-land degree of flat-six, it may be arcadian recollection, the imaginary sublime, or a dream of utopia. It offers the image of a world in which pleasure is attainable without thrusting desire, where tenderness and vulnerability are virtues rather than fatal flaws. But it can never be reality, as its infinite regress through a spiral of flat-six relationships indicates. And its seductive lure must finally be resisted. The return to the real world at the outset of the final movement quashes the alterity of the Adagio with star-

tling violence—violence that might seem excessive, if we did not understand culturally that to linger in that pleasureable, semiotically and structurally feminine zone would be an act of intolerable transgression. (1991, 128–29)

Admittedly, this sort of music writing can be seductive. McClary has advanced the vocabulary of feminist music appreciation and criticism by providing new and often imaginative categories for the configuration of musical experience. Yet her work treats musical compositions as if they are simply "waiting to be read"—that is, as if their meanings are located outside of situated contexts of reception. This analytic discourse reifies the relationship between music and extramusical phenomena in a way that bypasses exploration of how musical texts come to possess social connotations and how these connotations are initially established, elaborated, and consolidated over time.[16] Moreover, as individual writers' personally and culturally situated responses, readings of musical texts risk being inappropriately inflated into generalizations that other historical actors, past, present, and future, may or may not share. Analytical readings within the growing cultural studies field often tell us as much if not more about the social contexts of their own production and about their writers than about the music itself (thus they become material for historians of music history).[17] While the analysis of music's content is interesting and, as is the case with the preceding two quotations, often illuminating as a form of criticism, hagiography, and music appreciation, it can be argued that it is not ultimately analytical.[18] Interpretive readings of music do not properly attempt to investigate the issue of whether their analytical and responsive categories are shared by others in various temporal and spatial contexts. John Cage once made this point: "Does not a mountain unintentionally evoke in us a sense of wonder? Otters along a stream a sense of mirth? Night in the woods a sense of fear? . . . These responses to nature are mine and will not necessarily correspond with another's" (1961, 10).

While Cage may overstate the case for an individualistic conception of how reception occurs, his general point is that any reading of musical content and meaning is best understood as a form of cultural politics, of claims on the relation between the status, content, and structure of music. A flaw in most approaches to music's social "content" is that analytic claims are derived from the interaction between one interpretive "reader" (the analyst) and the music text(s) in question. What historical actors/listeners may have had to say and the various identities imputed to the text by its recipients (at any time in the text's history of reception) remain conspicuously absent. Analysis of music's content is thus fraught with methodological and theoretical problems; as a result, many music scholars become, whether explicitly or implicitly, formalists by default, avoiding the question of music and ideology altogether.

Although formalist modes of analysis may seem "safer," they bring their own set of problems. The most obvious issue (and the objection most often launched against them) is that formalist insights are about nothing beyond the musical text itself. All questions about music's social meanings and social force are forfeited in favor of music as, at worst, a "windowless monad" or, at best, referring to other musical texts. Beyond this objection are others that revolve around the issue of whether formalist modes of analysis are, in fact, any less subjective than their more interpretive counterparts. Formalists often like to depict themselves as "purely" technical, as if analytic techniques can be developed independent of values and assumptions about the musical text and its relations to cultural and social factors. While music scholars have so far left this position uncriticized, it is one familiar to and easily undermined by sociologists of science and technology.[19]

The problem, then, is how to address the issue of music's social meaning in ways that, first, are capable of distinguishing between the analyst's readings/responses to music, others' responses, and selective constructions of the musical object, and second, do not sacrifice the issue of music's social content in favor of a pseudoscientific formalist position. One response to this problem, as I have already suggested in part, can be found in the theory and methodology of reception studies. In addition to posing our own interpretations of how music articulates with social phenomena, we can try to follow specific, historically located respondents as they make sense of the music. We can explore how music's social meanings are constructed and mobilized by others—the ways that actors help to construct meaningful contexts for and in the music. While reception history is never capable of providing an undistorted view of a past musical culture (what could?), it at least has the virtue of admitting voices apart from the music analyst's own.

Returning to Beethoven, we need to appreciate the accounts his listeners offered about their responses to his music, not as a window to these respondents' cultural or psychological makeup, but as a way of exploring the uses of that music in context, of exploring the definition of the music's social impact by specific individuals within a specific context.[20] Attempting to describe Beethoven's music in the terms available to his contemporaries does constrain the range of our analysis. We need to stay close to what the recipients of Beethoven's music during this period had to say, and we need to operate within the limits that this model imposes. To this end, the following section is devoted to a consideration of the categories and conceptions available to these listeners.

BEETHOVEN'S PERCEIVED MUSICAL DIFFERENCES

The remainder of this chapter addresses the extant reports of how Beethoven's contemporaries responded to his music. Several differences between Beethoven and his contemporaries were observed during the 1790s: (1) Beethoven's music was increasingly perceived as thicker textured, (2) the piano music was discussed as less inclined to scale patterns, (3) the melodies were perceived as more ambiguously structured and less periodic, (4) the harmonies were perceived as more adventurous and ambiguous, (5) the dynamic range was perceived as greater (with sudden changes and sforzandos more common), and (6) some of the compositions were noted as lengthier than those of his predecessors and contemporaries. From the perspective of his contemporaries, the "departure" from the amateur tradition, which Rosen perceives as having occurred at the time of the Hammerklavier Sonata (1817–18) as quoted earlier, can be construed as occurring far earlier in Beethoven's career—as early as 1795. From our late twentieth-century vantage point, this may not seem like much of a departure at all. But the closer we approach the habits and modes of music apprehension relevant to 1790s Vienna, the more this break appears to be magnified. Haydn and Beethoven scholars have noted this before; for instance, Landon has observed:

> The *Sturm und Drang* manner of op. 1, no. 3 is continued and refined in the great F minor Sonata with which the set [the Piano Sonatas op. 2] opens. The same atmosphere of intellectual density that we noted with regard to the slow movements of op. 1 prevails to even greater extent in the new set. . . . Haydn will also have been impressed by the technical level of the piano part, for which the composer occasionally provided the fingering: the semiquaver octaves in triplets in op. 2, no. 1, set a new standard in piano technique, and there are other passages equally startling to the amateur. "One day," reports Frau von Bernhard[21] . . . "Streicher[22] put some things by Beethoven in front of her [Frau von Bernhard speaks of herself in the third person here, a narrative convention of the period]; they were the Piano Sonatas, Op. 2, which had just appeared at Artaria's. He told her that there are new things in them which the ladies do not wish to play, because they are incomprehensible and too difficult; would she like to learn them?" (1976–80, 4:67)

While we may perceive continuity between Beethoven's early works and the works of his predecessors, and although Beethoven and his patrons helped to convince others that this continuity really existed ("Mozart's spirit from Haydn's hands"), we cannot afford to ignore the differences that Beethoven's contemporaries said they perceived in his music. The issue should not revolve around whether Beethoven's works were continuous with Mozart's or Haydn's, but rather how this issue was itself politicized—how particular interpretations of Beethoven's work and the relation of his compositions to those of his predecessors were constructed and publicized.

Beethoven's style and the empirical characteristics of his pianism, as these were recognized by his Viennese contemporaries, were considered unconventional, far more so than the music of most of his contemporaries. Beethoven's music, especially during the early years of his Viennese career, fell outside conventional boundaries of musical worth. This difference provided a potential resource for Beethoven. To the extent that the acceptance of his works had implications for the way music recognized as more conventional was received, Beethoven could become a "force" within the Viennese music world. He could be forceful in the sense that the different aesthetic to which his work was oriented could challenge more conventional notions of musical value in direct proportion to the amount of praise his works received. Conversely, the difference of Beethoven's approach was simultaneously a potential liability, insofar as the possibility of a "safe," routine form of success was denied; from the point of view of his contemporaries, his controversial and different music implied new criteria of value, and if these new criteria were not developed, then Beethoven's music was placed in a weak position. If, on the other hand, they were developed and disseminated, then Beethoven's music was empowered for reconfiguring the music-evaluative space. For his work to succeed, Beethoven's perceived differences required protection from misapprehension, and the construction of a different evaluative framework. With this in mind, I examine in further detail some of the obstacles to Beethoven's evaluation as "great" during the mid-1790s, focusing in particular on the reception of Beethoven's pianistic style.

Beethoven was known initially as a keyboard virtuoso and, later in the 1790s, as a pianist-composer. During this period, his compositional experiments were often worked out at the keyboard. As Douglas Johnson has observed (1982, 18), music for piano served as a "practice genre" for Beethoven during these years. On a similar point, William Newman has suggested that "more than any other category of his music [the sonatas] give a rounded view of his styles and forms throughout his creative periods. Furthermore, unlike the keyboard sonatas of Haydn and Mozart, they have generally been ranked among the most important works in the total production of their creator" (1963, 507).

BEETHOVEN'S "DIFFERENCES" AS CULTURAL RESOURCE AND AS LIABILITY

In the early nineteenth century, Carl Czerny—Beethoven's pupil from the later 1790s and subsequently a virtuoso pianist-composer in his own right—outlined the differences between what he refers to as Mozart's versus Beethoven's respective "schools":

> Mozart's clear and markedly brilliant playing [is] based more on staccato than legato . . . [this] manner, which was so excellently perfected by Hummel, was more suited to the German Fortepianos which combine a delicate and shallow touch with a great clarity and thus are best adapted for general use and for use by children. . . . Beethoven, who appeared around 1790, drew entirely new and daring passages from the Fortepiano by use of the pedal, by an exceptionally characteristic way of playing, particularly distinguished by a strict legato of the chords and thus created a new type of singing tone and many hitherto unimagined effects. His playing did not possess that clean and brilliant elegance [the term brilliant playing was generally used to describe the rapid flow of notes] of certain other pianists. On the other hand, it was spirited . . . and, especially in the adagio, very full of feeling.[23]

In making a distinction here between Mozart's and Beethoven's respective pianistic "schools," Czerny adhered to a concept of Mozart in keeping with the ways Mozart's contemporaries understood his pianistic work, a conception firmly grounded in the empirical characteristics of that work (as opposed to ideas about what the work may have represented or been associated with). As Czerny puts it, the Mozartian school is characterized by "complete mastery over all difficulties; the utmost velocity; delicacy and grace in the manifold decorations; the most perfect clarity calculated to a nicety for every type of ambience and a proper declamation which can be appreciated by everyone, combined with elegance and good taste" (trans. Landon 1970a, 132).

Czerny observed that during the early 1800s, the "general public completely condemned Beethoven's works" (1956, 305), arguing that it was Johann Nepomuk Hummel (1778–1837), Mozart's pupil (and whom Mozart considered to be his pianistic heir), who was the general (nonconnoisseur) favorite:

It was quite natural . . . that the general public preferred [Hummel] as a pianist and soon the two masters formed parties which opposed one another with bitter enmity. Hummel's partisans accused Beethoven of mistreating the piano, of lacking all cleanness and clarity, of creating nothing but confused noise the way he used the pedal and finally of writing willful, unnatural, unmelodic compositions, which were irregular besides. On the other hand, the Beethovenites maintained that Hummel lacked all genuine imagination, that his playing was as monotonous as a hurdy-gurdy, that the position of his fingers reminded them of spiders and that his compositions were nothing more than arrangements of motifs by Mozart and Haydn. (ibid., 309)

According to Czerny, Beethoven explained his differences from Mozart as follows:

In later years Beethoven also told me that he had often heard Mozart play and that, since in his day the invention of the Fortepiano was as yet in its infancy, Mozart had become used to playing in a manner suited to the more customary harpsichords, which was not at all suited to the Fortepiano. Afterward I made the acquaintance of several people who had studied with Mozart and found that their way of playing fully bore out this observation. (Landon 1970a, 52)

Certainly, this interpretation allowed Beethoven to contrast his own approach with that of the earlier master (and thereby emphasize his novelty) while allowing him to explain his differences by interpreting them in his favor. That is, Beethoven implied that Mozart—had he been exposed to subsequent and "more advanced" piano technology—would have done what Beethoven himself did.

It is not clear whether Beethoven ever heard Mozart play at all.[24] If we judge from the views expressed by Beethoven's contemporaries, however, Czerny's description of the differences between Mozart and Beethoven seems to be representative of the conceptions among the musical public at large. In the 1790s, then, the fundamentally "Mozartian" categories according to which musical worth was recognized were resistant to the recognition of Beethoven's talent. There was as yet little vocabulary for discussing Beethoven's "greatness." Within an aesthetic that celebrated lightness, grace, delicacy, and cleanliness, the "force" of Beethoven's art was difficult to sustain and disseminate.[25] As the composer Johann Wenzel Tomaschek observes:

I admired his brilliant and powerful playing but I did not over-look his often daring leaps from one motive to another, whereby the organic connection and a gradual development of ideas is lacking. . . . Not infrequently, the unsuspecting listener is jolted violently out of his state of joyful transports. The most important thing in composition for him seems to be the unusual and original. (Landon 1970a, 104)

We turn now to a more workaday (and more widely disseminated) source on what constituted "good" pianism and therefore "good" musicianship in late eighteenth-century Vienna. Here we encounter a strikingly similar dichotomy, only this time with no names attached and in a more polemic context.

Andreas Streicher's pamphlet "Notes on the Playing, Tuning and Maintenance of the Fortepiano manufactured in Vienna by [Nannette Streicher, Geburt] Stein Written exclusively for the owners of these instruments" was a sort of owner's manual for the instrument,[26] written in the middle or late 1790s and used until around 1802. It had a relatively short life because Streicher abandoned it when the pro-Beethoven position gathered weight (see Hood 1986) and as Beethoven himself began a campaign for piano reform. The book was composed of chapters on the mechanics of the Viennese action, on execution, and on tuning, repair, and general maintenance. Of interest to us is the second chapter, where Streicher explicitly advocates a pianistic ideal. For didactic purposes, he asks the reader to imagine "a true musical artist who is now playing the fortepiano publicly or socially":

> As he runs his fingers over the keys, the very first notes which escape his fingers are *so light, solid, neat and so naturally beautiful* that no one is even aware of the artistry . . . *the action of the fingers themselves is extremely quiet* . . . how light is his quick staccato, how quiet the hand and how rounded the tone, however brief the note. . . . He has learned to subordinate his feelings to the limits of the instrument and, through a correct knowledge of mechanical treatment . . . is . . . capable of making us feel what he himself feels. (trans. de Silva, in Streicher 1984, emphasis original)[27]

By way of contrast, Streicher next turns to the "player who is unworthy of imitation but who will serve to illustrate mistakes which should be avoided":

> A player of whom it is reputed, "he plays extraordinarily such as you have never heard" . . . operates in a fiery manner and handles his instrument like someone bent on revenge, someone who has his arch-enemy in his hands and, with sadistic pleasure, wants to torture him to death. . . . He *pounds so hard* that suddenly the maltreated strings are put out of tune; several fly in the direction of bystanders who hurriedly retreat to safety in order to protect their eyes. . . . But why . . . does the player have such an obstinate instrument that it will only obey his fingers and not his gesticulations? . . . His playing resembles a script which has been smeared before the ink is dried. (ibid., emphasis original)

One could infer from this conception of good musicianship that Beethoven's alternative approach was undesirable, perhaps even ridiculous. It was also relatively easy, around 1795, to "read" Mozart in ways that made him difficult for Beethoven supporters to appropriate as anticipating Beethoven. Yet Mozart's position in the emerging pantheon of great or master composers was unimpeachable and, if a strong link could be forged between Beethoven and Mozart, Beethoven's reputation could be secured. One possibility was for Beethoven to emulate, in a conscious way, the Mozartian model. There may be some evidence that he did attempt to do this (see also Solomon 1977a), yet it would have been difficult, because Beethoven's pianistic habits differed considerably from Mozart's, as did the stylistic climate in which he had been trained.

Of course, difference can, under suitable conditions, be constructed as novelty and, even better, as innovation.[28] Thayer suggests that by 1795 (the year of Beethoven's public debut[29] in Vienna at one of the Burgtheater's Tonkünstler Society concerts),[30] the name "Beethoven" had a strong attraction for the public at large, "which as yet had no opportunity to learn his great powers except by report" (1967, 1:173). The fact that Beethoven had already been marked as successful in the private world of aristocratic salons (where the preliminary and necessary "record" of his acceptance had been established), combined with his reportedly different style, would have made him even more interesting to those members of the musical public located outside but oriented to this private aristocratic world.

Landon has observed that some of Beethoven's early works are characterized by a "muscle flexing," unlike Haydn "even at his loudest and certainly not like the feline subtleties of Mozart" (1976–80, 4:58–59). Far from attempting to discourage Beethoven from pursuing an unfamiliar and distinctive approach, his closest supporters, particularly Prince Lichnowsky, apparently encouraged Beethoven to innovate and they did so from the start. Franz Gerhard Wegeler[31] reports, for example, that

> the Prince was a great lover and connoisseur of music. He played the piano, and by studying Beethoven's works and playing them more or less well, he tried to prove to Beethoven that he did not need to change anything in his style of composition, even though the difficulties of his works were often pointed out to him. (Wegeler and Ries 1987, 32)

By the early 1800s, Beethoven was the first musician to be known as a composer, not a pianist-composer. A turning point in this transition occurred when Beethoven's first instrumental works were published, the

Trios op. 1. "The instant and striking success of Beethoven as a virtuoso," Thayer observes, "by no means filled up the measure of his ambition. He aspired to the higher position of composer, and to obtain this
more was needed than the performance of variations however excellent.
To this end, he selected the three Trios afterwards published as opus 1,
and brought them to perform at the house of Prince Lichnowsky
[c. 1794–95], to whom they were dedicated" (1967, 1:164).

Once again, the circumstances surrounding the reception of these
works suggest that Beethoven's early supporters were aware that Beethoven's differences required a supportive frame. According to some contemporary accounts, the Trios op. 1 may have been the source of a minor
quarrel between Beethoven and Haydn. As Ferdinand Ries[32] reports:

> Beethoven's three trios (opus 1) were to be introduced to the music world in
> a soirée at Prince Lichnowsky's. Most of Vienna's artists and music lovers had
> been invited, above all Haydn, whose opinion was anxiously awaited by ev-
> eryone. The trios were played and caused a tremendous stir. Haydn, too, said
> many fine things about them but advised Beethoven not to publish the third
> one in C minor. This astonished Beethoven since he considered it the best . . .
> I must admit that I did not really believe Beethoven when he told me this. I
> therefore later took the opportunity to ask Haydn himself about it. His an-
> swer confirmed Beethoven's story in that he said he had not imagined that this
> trio would be so quickly and easily understood nor so favorably received by
> the public. (Wegeler and Ries 1987, 74)

As Thayer (1967, 1:165) points out, Ries's story is confusing, because
it implies that Haydn heard these works before they were published.
Haydn left for London on 19 January 1794 and was away until September 1795. The performance would need to have taken place before January if the trio were still in manuscript stage. Landon (1976–80, 4:61–
63), however, has suggested (on the basis of evidence from Gustav
Nottebohm, which shows that opp. 1:2 and 1:3 were still being
sketched in 1794, in which case they would not have been ready for performance) that Haydn may have heard the works performed after they
had been published, and that Haydn may have told Beethoven in retrospect that the third and final trio of the set was too complex for most
dilettantes. In this case, Haydn would have been offering advice at a time
when it could no longer be of any use, that is, when criticism could only
detract from their success.

Not surprisingly, Haydn scholars have tended to dismiss Ries's account as either wrong or fabricated. Landon rejects the possibility that
Haydn may have commented unfavorably on the published trios and

concludes that the story must be false. He suggests that Haydn may have heard the pieces in much earlier versions, perhaps performed informally for a select group. More recently, Webster (1984, 10) has suggested that Ries's dubious chronology tends to discredit the entire story. Why, though, would Ries wish to fabricate such a story? The dates in Ries's account (recorded some time after the event) may have been recalled incorrectly, but this does not necessarily mean that the gist of the anecdote—that Haydn had some doubts about the third and most adventurous of the trios—was inaccurate. In light of the discussion of the Haydn-Beethoven relationship presented in chapter 5, Haydn may well have offered a less than wholehearted commendation of one of Beethoven's more characteristic and ambitious early works.

It seems reasonable that Haydn may have criticized the work for the difficulties it posed to listeners. Given the descriptions by Beethoven's contemporaries of these new works and the fact that Haydn was personally concerned with reaching and pleasing his audience and its tastes (Schroeder 1990), it would not be surprising if Haydn had reservations about Beethoven's work. Haydn would perhaps have been especially concerned about a work that was intended to serve as Beethoven's passport to recognition as a composer. As for problems with the chronology of when Haydn could have offered this criticism, it is possible that he heard and commented on the works while they were still evolving in manuscript form and that Beethoven subsequently revised the works before publishing them, a possibility Landon also suggests.

Whatever the case, Haydn scholars need not be defensive about the fact that Haydn may have voiced misgivings about Beethoven's works. Haydn's reservations should not be viewed as a sign of weakness (such as petty jealousy) or as a lack of vision—an inability to perceive Beethoven's "advances" in the musical field. Whereas during the 1790s Beethoven was oriented to the tastes of a select musical interest group, Haydn was oriented to a wider and more inclusive notion of the "musical public," a notion still as firmly anchored to the concerns of the general listener as to those of the connoisseur. Correspondingly, Haydn was concerned with the conventional eighteenth-century notion of pleasing the musical public, and he was oriented to this notion much more explicitly than was Beethoven. This mindset surfaces most clearly when we consider Haydn's approach when he was in London, where he (like Beethoven) was self-consciously trying to innovate. Mrs. Charlotte Papendiek (whose observations of London musical life during this period are invaluable) says, for example, that Haydn intended to compose his London symphonies "after he had had ample opportunity of studying the taste of the English. He was determined that his first production should both amuse and please the musical public and rivet him in their favor" (quoted in Schroeder 1985, 60). Perhaps one reason Haydn is often undeservedly slighted by scholars (and listeners) today is that he was both a craftsman and a professional; innovative as he may have been during the 1790s, Haydn did not attempt, as Beethoven clearly did, to endow that craft with mystery and to eschew general public approval in favor of approval from the connoisseur. One area for further study would trace the ways that Haydn was posthumously depicted, via reports of his opinions about Beethoven, as an anachronistic emblem of the old-world role of the musician: bewigged, in livery, and overly keen to please his patrons—as if concern with public taste involved, of necessity, artistic compromise. Such a study would surely provide insight into the nineteenth-century bifurcation of music as entertainment and music as edification.

In any case, on the basis of extant reports of how Beethoven's contemporaries (including Haydn) talked about his work, we can conclude that Beethoven required careful presentation to his public, especially at the initial stages of his career. From the outset Lichnowsky seemed to recognize that Beethoven's style, even in its early manifestations, would be an acquired taste, and he was instrumental in fostering a taste for Beethoven. One way this liking was cultivated was through supportive but limited presentations of Beethoven's early compositions, rather than his improvisations. Within the protective envelope of Lichnowsky's salons, Beethoven's works were never subjected to random listener responses. Instead, Lichnowsky helped Beethoven present his work in frameworks within which it could "make sense" and be understood as worthy. One contemporary observer (possibly Nikolaus Zmeskall)[33] notes that Beethoven's often idiosyncratic works were met with actively sympathetic hearings: "Hearers not only accustomed themselves to the striking and original qualities of the master but grasped his spirit and strove for the *high privilege* of understanding him" (Thayer and Forbes 1967, 1:164; emphasis added).

PRINCE LICHNOWSKY'S ENTREPRENEURIAL STRATEGIES

In 1795, when Beethoven published the trios with Artaria on a subscription basis, Lichnowsky again played a supportive role. The terms of Beethoven's contract with Artaria have puzzled scholars and have been interpreted in several ways.[34] The contract stipulates that Artaria should receive an advance payment, possibly from Beethoven himself (perhaps 122 florins [see MacArdle and Misch 1957, 17).[35] This was not an uncommon practice at the time, because it allowed a new and relatively unknown composer to assure that his publisher would at least recoup the printing cost. Prince Lichnowsky may have secretly underwritten this cost without telling Beethoven. Solomon takes up an argument presented by Ludwig Nohl (1864, 2:59) by suggesting that Lichnowsky was attempting to conceal his gift in order to avoid rejection (1977a, 63), which is plausible given other examples of the composer's reputed pride and aversion to the more visibly "patronizing" methods of support. But MacArdle and Misch have argued that "this could hardly have been unbeknownst to Beethoven unless he was content to believe that the publisher had waived the initial payment so definitely called for in the contract. The explanation may be merely that Nohl's information was third hand after a lapse of more than seventy years" (1957, 17).

Whatever the case, Artaria, having received an advance fee, provided Beethoven with printed copies of the work, which Beethoven could then sell (keeping all profit). To insure that Beethoven would find a market for these copies (his publisher retained ownership of the plates), the publishers agreed not to sell any copies of the work in Vienna for two months, though they could sell it abroad. Finally, the contract states that Beethoven was to enclose a list of subscribers, those who had agreed in advance to purchase a copy or copies of the work (the subscription list was Beethoven's insurance of recovering the initial investment of 122 florins).[36] According to the contract, this list was to be printed along with the work and included with subscribers' copies. This list, however, though printed, was never included (it could not have been printed by Artaria anyway because the company had no facilities for typesetting [see MacArdle and Misch 1957, 17 n. 2]).[37]

Emerging from this muddle is the fact that Lichnowsky underwrote the success of Beethoven's first publication in at least one way and possibly two. First, he subscribed to 20 copies and, if we count the additional subscriptions by members of his family, between them the Lichnowskys and the Thuns (his wife's family) accounted for 21 percent (53) of the 249 copies (see Table 13).[38] Second, it is possible that it was Lichnowsky who provided the initial sum of 122 florins and that Beethoven was indeed aware of this, though he may have acted as if he were not.

TABLE 13

SUBSCRIBERS WHO TOOK TWO OR MORE COPIES OF BEETHOVEN'S OP. 1[a]

The Lichnowsky Family
  Prince Lichnowsky (20)
  Princess Lichnowsky (née Thun) (3)
  Count Maurice Lichnowsky (2)
  Countess Henriette Lichnowsky (2)
  Countess Halberg (née Lichnowsky) (2)
  Countess Maria Wilhelmine von Thun (née Uhlfeld—Prince Lichnowsky's mother-in-law (2)
  Countess Maria Anna von Thun (née Kollowrath—perhaps married to Countess Maria Wilhelmine's oldest son) (22, for Prague)

Others
  Herr de Lischka (12)
  Count de Taasse (10)
  Prince Schwarzenberg (4) and Princess Schwarzenberg (3)

  Count Appony (6)
  Prince Lobkowitz (6)
  Herr Siche (6, for Troppau)
  Baron de Stroganof (6)

  Baron Joseph Podmaniczky (4)

  Count Browne (2) and Countess Browne (1)
  Count Joseph Erdödy (3)
  Prince Nikolaus Esterhazy (3)
  Prince Grassalkowitz (3)
  Countess Kinsky (3)
  Count Razumovsky (2) and Countess Razumovsky (née Thun) (1)
  Mme. de Rieq (3)
  Baron van Swieten (3)
  Baron Wetzlar (3)
  Count Wrbna (3)

  Herr Joseph Breindel (2)
  Count Czernin (2)
  Countess Dalton (2)
  Countess Fries (2)
  Countess Hazfeld (2)
  Mdlles. de Kurzbeck (2)
  Lord Longford (2)
  Herr Mentzl (2)
  Mr. Saunders (2)
  Lord Templetown (2)

---

[a]There were also 89 individuals who took single subscriptions; the complete list can be found in Landon 1970a, 64–65. There were 117 subscribers and 249 total subscriptions.

This subsidy could contribute to the illusion that Beethoven's ties to the music public were more extensive than they actually were—that his reputation was greater than it actually was—and perhaps (if the fact of Beethoven's or Lichnowsky's initial downpayment was not publicized) that it was Artaria who was willing to "speculate" on Beethoven. This invention could be used to imply that Beethoven was a composer whom publishers considered to be a worthy investment. Underwriting of the publication costs was a way Beethoven could be made to look like an already successful published composer. Once again, we see how the dramatization of Beethoven as corresponding to a preconceived imagery of success—in this case the achievement of a highly successful first publication—was part of the frame within which Beethoven could be constructed as worthy. It provided, in other words, an additional piece of the evidence of Beethoven's talent to which supporters could point. Thus the dramatizations of already existing success, public acceptance, and achievement were in fact preconditions to the success that they were meant to index, and, in this case, the dramatization that Beethoven was "ready" and deserved to be published contributed to his success. Conversely, the 288 florins that Beethoven earned from sales of op. 1 could function as proof of his (tacitly assumed) worthiness in the first place. In the circumstances surrounding Beethoven's first publication, we can glimpse the often tautological process of constructing the bases of perceived talent and success.

Beethoven's second major achievement as a composer came in November 1795, when he was chosen to write dance music for the annual ball at the Redoutensaal, in aid of the Gesellschaft der bildenen Künstler (Society of Visual Artists). An invitation to compose for this event was understood as an acknowledgment of already proven reputation, not a means of launching a new composer.[39] In previous years, those who had done so were Haydn in 1792, Kozeluch in 1793, Dittersdorf and Eybler in 1794—in other words, well-established and frequently performed Viennese composers.

Successful reception of the commissioned works was more or less guaranteed because of the prestige of the event. In 1795, Beethoven was asked to compose music for the smaller of the two rooms and Franz Süssmayr for the larger. This invitation was clearly a coup for Beethoven, who, as Thayer points out (1967, 1:177), had, in the way of serious compositions, only the op. 1 publications to his credit (Landon speculates that Beethoven was chosen because Haydn put in a word for him [see 1976–80, 4:56]). It was an unparalleled way of getting further ex-

posure to an aristocratic audience, since the aristocrats who attended
would have included individuals and families outside Beethoven's current circle of patrons.

Beethoven's reputation was further enhanced by his trip to Prague in
1796. In February of that year (after a three-year apprenticeship under
Haydn and, covertly, under Schenk), Lichnowsky took Beethoven with
him to Prague, as he had done for Mozart in 1789,[40] introducing him to
the local nobility. Traveling with a musician during the eighteenth century was a means for diplomacy and cultural exchange; it provided a
pretext for contact with foreign nobility and a reason for socializing under the guise of introducing the musician to new and curious publics.

From Prague, Beethoven wrote to his brother: "My art is winning me
friends and renown and what more do I want? And this time I shall make
a good deal of money" (Anderson 1961, 1 : 16).[41] A quick survey of Beethoven's letters during these first three years of his Viennese career reveals the composer's gradually increasing confidence in his powers and
future career. Two years before, Beethoven was describing his pianistic
competitors and "enemies" and was possessively committing to print his
extemporaneous piano pieces in order to protect "the peculiarities of my
style," as he called them (ibid., 9), from being plagiarized by another
composer.

Lichnowsky returned from Prague to Vienna, and Beethoven, who
had initially intended to go no further afield but who was no doubt encouraged by the success he enjoyed in Prague, carried on to Dresden,
Leipzig, and Berlin, where he impressed King Friedrich Wilhelm II. Beethoven arrived in Berlin on his own, but he would no doubt have been
welcome as a musical acquaintance of Prince Lichnowsky. As several
scholars have noted, Friedrich Wilhelm was pleased by the inclusion of
the Cello Sonatas op. 5. A cellist himself, Friedrich Wilhelm would no
doubt have been equally pleased by the unconventionally prominent part
Beethoven had given to the cello. As Solomon (1977a, 99) has suggested,
the king may also have noted with pleasure Beethoven's choice of theme
in the cello variations, which he could read as a reflection on himself as
a great leader (the variations are based on Handel's "See the conqu'ing
hero comes"). Approval was expressed with the gift of a gold snuffbox
filled with louis d'ors, a present that, as Beethoven was proud to tell his
friends, was not the ordinary snuffbox presented to musicians but rather
the more valuable kind usually offered only to visiting diplomats.

When he returned from his tour to Vienna, his reputation was clearly
enhanced by reports of foreign success; Beethoven was beginning to pos-

sess a history, a record of success and acclaim. This record was an important part of the rhetorical framework within which the composer was increasingly being presented as an authoritative figure. From 1796 on, Beethoven could be introduced as the composer who had experienced wide acclaim abroad and who had particularly pleased the King of Prussia. Thus Beethoven attained the aura of independently achieved public success, when in fact this success was framed partly by the strong ties between his patron and key figures abroad. It is worth recalling here that, in comparison with Dussek's situation, Beethoven's reception abroad was eased by his Viennese connections. Though Dussek did have aristocratic patrons who might have been able to help him, they were not as active as Lichnowsky. The years Dussek spent with Louis Ferdinand in the early nineteenth century, for example, were (when the two were not on the battlefield) spent mostly at home, and thus offered Dussek little exposure.

Beethoven's reputation as a first-rank musician and, to some extent, composer was initially consolidated in 1796. During the next few years, as Moore (1987) has shown, Beethoven's economic situation was better than it ever would be again. Thayer observes that "the change in his pecuniary condition might have thrown a more equitable temperament than his off its balance. Three years ago he anxiously noted down the few kreutzers occasionally spent for coffee or chocolate 'fur Haidn und mich'; now he was keeping his own servant [provided by Prince Lichnowsky] and a horse [a gift from Count Browne]" (1967, 1:180).

One may wonder whether any composer, once "plugged into" the supportive patronage network that surrounded Beethoven, would have been able to achieve such historically unprecedented success. This view, however, overlooks the fact that Beethoven was not a passive object around which his patrons constituted a frame of greatness. Beethoven's initial and subsequent status during the early nineteenth century was inextricably linked to his own entrepreneurial contributions, both musical and social. This is not to say, however, that there were not composers who might have been capable of garnering a similar sort of reputation. Some, I think, were better suited for the part than others (Gelinek less so than Dussek or Wölffl, for instance). It is interesting to consider what our modern musical evaluative standards would look like if a different composer had been inserted into the supportive frame that surrounded Beethoven: consider the Irish-born composer John Field (1782–1837), whose prophetically Chopinesque nocturnes provided a contemporary alternative to Beethoven's forceful approach. As I observed in the preface, I see Beethoven's reputation as the product of an interaction between his own efforts, his social circumstances, and the efforts of others.

Beethoven independently carried out innovations in the realm of the music listening setting and within the composer-patron relationship. These innovations helped to prepare his listeners (including his closest aristocratic supporters) to receive his new and increasingly unconventional musical works. Simultaneously, they reassured his listeners that it was worth reinvesting their initial support in ways that would sponsor even more sustained forays into uncharted and increasingly complicated musical terrain. I examine next some of the ways Beethoven was active in restructuring aesthetic categories and music listening conventions to align them more closely with his own approach and characteristics.

BEETHOVEN AS SOCIAL ENTREPRENEUR

From the start of his career, Beethoven actively conditioned his patrons' behavior toward him. He worked to construct an image of himself as a self-determining composer. Some of the strategies he employed in attempting to renegotiate the traditional composer-patron relationship became resources for subsequent generations of composers (such as Liszt, Berlioz, and Wagner) in their own attempts to elaborate on the imagery of "great artist." In Beethoven's career, we see an early stage in the process through which the occupation of composer came to be aligned with charismatic and, eventually, professional ideology (in the sense that the functions of evaluation and setting standards moved from the patron's to the composer's province).

Ironically, perhaps, a key resource for Beethoven was the traditional conception of privilege, namely, that some individuals (that is, nobles) were more worthy than others. Contrary to the received, mythical image of Beethoven's political engagement, Beethoven was not involved in abolishing this conception. Rather, he was involved in hollowing it out, disconnecting the conception of privilege from its traditional content so that it could accommodate or be transferred to other, nonhereditary (though not unascribed) types of nobility: nobility of spirit, of character, or of talent. Beethoven's efforts to redress the quality of the musician-patron relationship were clearly dependent in part on the extraordinary amount of credit he brought with him and had acquired as a stylistically different yet highly celebrated musician within aristocratic circles. These efforts were also due, in part, to the peculiar advantage served by what Solomon calls Beethoven's "nobility pretense."

It was assumed, among at least the more distant members of Beethoven's public, that the prefix *van* in his name was, like the German prefix *von,* an insignia of nobility. This duplicity was maintained until 1818, when, during the final litigations over the custody of his nephew, Beethoven accidentally disclosed that his nephew was not of noble birth. This revelation led the court to inquire into the composer's own origins and Beethoven was forced to concede that the Dutch prefix *van* was not identical to the German *von* (see Solomon 1975a, 1975b; Thayer and Forbes 1967, 2:704); understandably, there is still popular confusion today, and scholars sometimes refer to Beethoven as Ludwig *von* [see, for example, Becker 1982, 136). As Solomon observes, there was "surely no *economic* necessity involved in this deception. Haydn had risen to the rank of a national composer despite his humble origins, and without benefit of a nobility patent. It was not necessary for Beethoven to pretend to nobility in order to gain entrée as a musician and composer to the homes and salons of the nobility, for these were open to those of less than noble rank" (1977a, 88; emphasis added).

Solomon's point is well taken, but the "psychological" reasons he offers for why Beethoven perpetuated the pretense are less convincing as a complete explanation. Solomon argues that the nobility pretense indicated a psychological necessity for acceptance: "Central to the nobility pretense is the need for acceptance by those in command of society: the leaders and shapers, the royalty and nobility. That Beethoven felt he had to pretend nobility in order to obtain such acceptance may be a poignant indication of the depth of this need in him" (1977a, 87). Equally, the pretense signaled a need for fulfillment of Beethoven's "family romance"—namely, Beethoven's fantasy that he was the natural son of a king of Prussia (ibid., 5): "Through the pretense, he sought transcendence of his parentage and his humble origins; through it he could, perhaps, pursue his quest for a mythical, noble father to replace the mediocre court tenor who had begotten him. The nobility pretense, then, may well have been a fantasy through which Beethoven 'lived out' his Family Romance" (ibid., 89).

From a sociological point of view, the problem with Solomon's explanation is that it confines the inquiry to the psychological motives or origins of Beethoven's duplicity, and in so doing, deflects attention away from the social effects or consequences the nobility pretense facilitated. Specifically, the *van/von* confusion seems to have served as a practical resource in Beethoven's attempt to renegotiate his status vis-à-vis his patrons. Solomon is undoubtedly correct in arguing that the nobility pretense addressed no economic necessity and that Beethoven did not need to feign nobility to be as successful as Haydn, for example. However, Beethoven was oriented to a type of success that differed qualitatively from Haydn's. On the strength of Beethoven's nobility pretense (and also because of weakened patronage authority brought about through the diffusion of patronage), Beethoven was able to innovate socially and, in so doing, redefine the patron-composer relationship. Into this framework fit some of the more "bizarre" aspects of Beethoven's comportment and conduct, which can be perceived as strategic attempts to redefine the musician-patron relationship—to create a shift in the basis of musical-critical authority from its origins in the institution of nobility to the nascent institution of the autonomous music world, and to the expertise of composers and other musicians (see also Moore 1987).

Frau von Bernhard's recollection, for instance, of Haydn, Salieri, and Beethoven waiting in a corridor of Lichnowsky's home, the former two dressed in the old fashion (silk hose, buckled shoes, and wigs), the latter in Rhenish costume, "almost ill-dressed" and wigless, depicts one way Beethoven carried out these social innovations (Landon 1970a, 64). Similarly, Beethoven's increasing dislike of performing when requested (Thayer and Forbes 1967, 1:172) and his not uncommon refusals to perform (which seem more than once to have reduced certain of his more enthusiastic aristocratic supporters to begging him to play) can be understood as attempts to control the conditions of where and when he would perform. As his reputation increased, Beethoven was especially strict about the type of attitude with which his playing ought to be heard. Ries tells of an incident in 1802 when he and Beethoven were performing the Marches op. 45 at Count Browne's:

> Young Count P—, sitting in the doorway leading to the next room, spoke so loud and so continuously to a pretty woman, that Beethoven, after several efforts had been made to secure quiet [these efforts were made by other audience members, since Beethoven and Ries seem to have been playing] suddenly took my hands from the keys in the middle of the music, jumped up and said very loudly, "I will not play for such swine!" All efforts to get him to return to the pianoforte were in vain; he would not even allow me to play the sonata. So the music came to an end in the midst of general ill humor. (quoted in Thayer and Forbes 1967, 1:307–8)

These strategies reveal Beethoven's attempt to demarcate his salon performances as special events and to reform music listening etiquette. Beethoven increased the stakes of music consumption by trying to formalize the music listening situation, redefining it as one in which ritualistically solemn devotion to the performance was the appropriate form of audience conduct. He was, in other words, realigning his relationship to his listeners to evoke audience responses quantitatively greater and qualitatively different from the behavior typical of his time.

As other scholars have previously discussed,[42] "appropriate" late eighteenth-century audience conduct at secular music events included a wide range of behaviors that are not typically found at modern high culture music events: participants could talk, move about the room or hall, eat and drink, play card games and other games of chance, and (in the privacy of opera boxes) meet with courtesans and lovers. This variety of conduct was progressively narrowed during the nineteenth century. The transformation of the concert setting both occurred through and was reflected in seating arrangements, architecture, music programming practices, and, of course, the musical forms themselves.

Beethoven was one of the first musicians to campaign consciously for a reform of the conditions of musical reception in Vienna. His ability to have such an impact on the concert setting was linked to the fact that, unlike his fellow Viennese musicians, he had considerable social resources at his disposal. Singled out for support by Lichnowsky and van Swieten, Beethoven could also trade on the cultural capital that the "Haydn's hands" story provided. Chapter 8 describes the extent to which Beethoven's attempts to structure the Viennese musical field and thereby assure his authoritative place within it extended to the technological instruments of musical life as well. First, however, it is necessary to return to the question of just how far, by the end of the eighteenth century, Beethoven's reputation extended. In the following chapter, I examine the social boundaries of the new taste for Beethoven and, more broadly, the newly emerging connoisseur aesthetic.

CHAPTER 7

The Beethoven-Wölffl Piano Duel: Aesthetic Debates and Social Boundaries

"Whoever sees Beethoven for the first time," wrote Carl Friedrich, Baron Kübeck von Kubau in 1797, "and knows nothing about him would surely take him for a malicious, ill-natured, quarrelsome drunkard who has no feeling for music. . . . On the other hand, he who sees him for the first time surrounded by his fame and his glory, will surely see musical talent in every feature of an ugly face" (Landon 1970a, 71). The so-called ugly face of Beethoven's music needed to be seen from flattering perspectives. By 1799 those ways of seeing were fairly well established, at least within the private world of exclusive aristocratic salons.

But what happened when those boundaries were transgressed—when Beethoven's music was presented outside the shelter of its aristocratic context? If his reputation were to continue to grow, new publics would have to engage in sympathetic readings of his music and talent. Yet there was no guarantee that this process would occur automatically. Indeed, Beethoven's network of success was constructed in the face of opposition or, at the least, skepticism. Moreover, as Beethoven's style changed—as it became more explicitly oriented to the "Grand" tradition during the decade between 1795 and 1805—reception of Beethoven's work appears to have become increasingly polarized, judging from extant contemporary reports. In the middle 1790s, however, conflict over Beethoven's music had not yet heightened into opposing camps. In fact, while the range of responses to Beethoven certainly varied during these years, it seems unlikely that any coherent position against Beethoven would have been articulated.

During the 1790s, Beethoven and his patrons were still involved in building his reputation. It is important not to exaggerate Beethoven's stature during the 1790s—during these years Haydn was still a much more prominent figure. Yet as Beethoven's image was projected within the context of small-scale aristocratic salons, it was correspondingly magnified. There, under the right circumstances, Beethoven could indeed appear as the "hero of music," if only to the most earnest of the Beethoven devotees. Within these settings, few resources would have been available for registering dissent against the composer. During the 1790s, Beethoven was shielded from hostile and destructive reception. The support generated for him became a resource, both for itself (that is, it gained momentum as it became increasingly documented: it could be referenced as its own justification) and for the development of his own style and manner of interacting with his patrons and audience. Support generated for Beethoven helped to frame and further enhance his special status as a unique kind of musician and the image of the composer available for private consumption: Beethoven "surrounded by his fame and his glory" was, of course, Beethoven at his most attractive.

Beethoven's public image, as projected from the salons outward to the musical public, was built around his more conventional qualities. Based almost entirely on his music publications and on reports of his powers, rather than on his piano performances (which would have been unavailable to most music consumers), the imagery of Beethoven would have appeared somewhat different from his fiery salon personality. On the basis of contemporaries' reports during these years, Beethoven's more radical departures from musical convention appear to have occurred in his piano improvisations instead of in his published works. This should not come as a surprise; published works would be disseminated to broader audiences and therefore would need to appeal to less specialized tastes. In addition, publishers had an interest in the burgeoning sheet music market, where musical convention and playability (that is, dilettante values) would have functioned as constraints. Beethoven's published output during the 1790s tends to reflect these conditions to the extent that there are many sets of piano variations, which were considered to be a lighter, more popular genre, more accessible and easily adapted for domestic use (though some of these works were criticized for being overly learned). The Beethoven accessible to the musical public at large was a more conventional musician.

It would be inaccurate to speak of open conflict over Beethoven's music during the 1790s. There had been no trial—no publicly observed means of testing, debating, and discussing Beethoven's abilities in comparison with other musicians. Apart from Beethoven's 1793 duel with the Abbé Gelinek, who was a fairly weak opponent, Beethoven had not been compared explicitly with a rival. In 1799, however, this circumstance changed.

"It was now no longer the case," Thayer tells us, "that Beethoven was without a rival as pianoforte virtuoso. He had a competitor fully worthy of his powers; one who divided about equally with him the suffrages of the leaders in the Vienna musical circles. In fact the excellencies peculiar to the two were such and so different, that it depended upon the taste of the auditor to which he accorded the praise of superiority" (1967, 1: 204). The new rival was Joseph Wölffl, whom Beethoven met in March 1799 at the home of Baron Raimund Wetzlar, where they engaged in a piano duel.

This contest has not yet been considered extensively by Beethoven scholars. Yet it represents much more than an interesting excursion into the colorful backwaters of late eighteenth-century Viennese musical life. It should be counted as an important and underexamined "moment"— a point at which some of the characteristic aspects of eighteenth-century aesthetic controversy coalesce. Consideration of this moment also provides a further entrée into the otherwise elusive topic of the interrelation of social networks and networks of musical taste during this period. We know much and are currently learning more about public concert life in Vienna,[1] but the study of private musical life necessitates the use of oblique forms of evidence and of speculation.

From the beginning of his account of the Beethoven-Wölffl duel, Thayer clearly politicizes the contest. This approach is conspicuously absent from his description, four chapters earlier, of Beethoven's 1793 encounter with Gelinek. Thayer's characterization of the contest with Wölffl does not appear to exaggerate its political dimension. Rather, his account reflects the descriptive categories found in extant contemporary accounts of the event. The Theater an der Wien conductor, Ignaz von Seyfried, for example, offers the following description:

> Beethoven had already attracted attention to himself by several compositions and was rated a first-class pianist in Vienna when he was confronted by a rival in the closing years of the last century. Thereupon there was, in a way, a revival of the old Parisian feud of the Gluckists and Piccinists, and the many friends of art in the Imperial City arrayed themselves in two parties. (trans. Thayer and Forbes 1967, 1:206)

At the point of the Wölffl-Beethoven duel, Beethoven's style, as depicted by his contemporaries, emerged for the first time as part of a platform, as a style in opposition to other approaches and, in particular, to
a more dilettante ideology. Seyfried speaks of the Gluckists and Piccinists, the first time this earlier Parisian aesthetic controversy was invoked
to describe differences of opinion concerning Beethoven's works. It pre-
figured the manner of debate surrounding Beethoven's style. Simultaneously, the Beethoven-Wölffl comparison helped to clarify further Beethoven's artistic identity within the Viennese musical world.

THE SOCIAL ROLE OF THE PIANO DUEL

As I have illustrated throughout the preceding chapters, during the eighteenth century making music was a socially loaded endeavor. Musical
patronage and social hierarchy were mutually constitutive: the consumption and sponsorship of music (at least in socially conspicuous forms)
was embarked on for musical and social reasons. Through these activities, individuals and groups could constitute and signify their standing
with respect to others: they could imitate, attempt to align themselves
with, compete with, or try to impress those individuals they regarded as
standing above, alongside, or below them in terms of prestige. It is within
this context that I discuss the role of the piano contest.

At their most basic level, piano contests appear to have been like
sporting events. They provided not only "good music," but also the
drama of combat. They additionally offered forums in which rival musical styles, both compositional and pianistic, could be compared. One of
the most detailed descriptions of a piano duel comes from Mozart, who
reported his contest with Clementi at the imperial court in a letter to his
father:

> After we had stood on ceremony long enough, the Emperor declared that
> Clementi ought to begin. . . . He improvised and then played a sonata. The
> Emperor then turned to me: "Allons, fire away!" I improvised and played
> variations. The Grand Duchess produced some sonatas by Paisiello . . . of
> which I had to play the Allegros and Clementi the Andantes and Rondos. We
> then selected a theme from them and developed it on two pianofortes. (An-
> derson 1938, 793, letter 441)

The emperor "declared" that Clementi ought to begin, he turned to
Mozart and said, "fire away" (more closely translated from the German,
drauf los, as "take it away"), the two musicians competed according to
a specified format, and each had a turn at developing a theme (improvi-

sation). That the piano contest was conceived as a kind of sporting event is indicated by the competitive format and the commanding language employed for its characterization.

Mozart's contest occurred in 1783. Although the organization of musical life changed considerably over the next two decades, the piano duel—both its format and its role as a kind of musical sporting event—seems to have remained stable, to judge by descriptions of Beethoven's own pianistic encounters. Seyfried's description of the Beethoven-Wölffl contest sixteen years later refers to the "combats of the two athletes" and describes the ways this combat "offered an indescribable artistic treat to the numerous and thoroughly select gathering" (Thayer and Forbes 1967, 1:206–7). Like Mozart and Clementi, Beethoven and Wölffl also took turns demonstrating their improvisatory skills. "Sometimes," Seyfried tells us, "they would seat themselves at two pianofortes and improvise alternately on themes which they gave each other" (ibid.).

This athletic imagery can also be found in reports of Beethoven's other piano duels. For example, as was noted in the previous chapter, Czerny reports Gelinek to have said of his upcoming match with Beethoven, "I'll fix him" or "I'll make mincemeat out of him" (Landon's translation). Similarly, the composer Johann Tomaschek describes the Beethoven-Steibelt duel of 1800 by observing that Steibelt was "knocked on the head by the pianist Beethoven" (Thayer and Forbes 1967, 1:257). Of the same event, Ferdinand Ries referred to how, the first time that Beethoven and Steibelt competed, the latter had "felt sure of his victory," but the second time he "left the room before Beethoven finished, and would never again meet him and, indeed, made it a condition that Beethoven should not be invited before accepting an offer" (ibid.).

Taking account of the social position of the virtuoso through the 1790s—and more broadly, the social position of the occupational musician as servant—it seems that competing virtuosi occupied a place not unlike that of tennis players, wrestlers, boxers, or even race horses, in the sense that they were virtuoso practitioners pitted against each other in controlled contexts, for the purpose of entertaining spectators. In this respect, the piano duel was not qualitatively different from other forms of entertainment based around competition and combat.

At the same time, the piano contest was more than a sporting event. It was also a forum for aesthetic and stylistic debate. We know, for instance, that Mozart described Clementi to his father as having "not a farthing's worth of taste of feeling" (Anderson 1938, 2:792). In his autobiography, Dittersdorf reconstructs his meeting with Emperor Joseph, where Dittersdorf portrays himself and the emperor as in agreement that Clementi is "art—or artifice—alone," whereas Mozart combines "art with *taste*" (Dittersdorf [1896] 1970, 227; emphasis added).

Thus the piano contest was a place where pianistic athletes were tested, where reputations were raised and lowered, where musical fashions were put on display, and where different types of taste could be compared and pitted against each other. In addition, it was a place where the identities of patrons could be asserted, reaffirmed, and undercut. It must not be forgotten that the musical combatants were by no means "free agents" on the musical playing field. Like modern professional athletes, they had backers who would naturally be interested in seeing their representatives win.

The cluster of issues implicated in the Clementi-Mozart duel included, among other things, an international dimension of competition. Mozart was clearly playing for Vienna, empire, and "enlightened" Josephian reform. Because the duel was organized as part of the festivities to honor visiting foreign nobility (the Russian Grand Duke Paul, later Tsar Paul II, and Maria Feodorovna, who was born Princess of Würtemberg), the competition served as a forum for the display of the respective merits of native and foreign talent. Indeed, the emperor refers to Clementi as "the holy Catholic Church" (that is, Rome); in this case, the competition was friendly, featuring two quite different but equally matched players, representatives of two culturally divergent but equally matched European powers.

Like certain modern sporting or artistically competitive events, the piano contest could place a variety of issues at stake. It is important to enquire into how, in any given musical contest, lines of competition and stakes were drawn. Was there, for example, a social distribution of support for one or the other contestant, and, to the extent that spectators to these events may have constituted "opposing sides," what may have been at stake for each? In Beethoven's three known piano duels—the first with Gelinek in 1793, the second with Wölffl in 1799, and the third with Steibelt in 1800—these lines were not drawn between European powers, but there were issues at stake apart from the personal reputations of each musician.

WÖLFFL'S AND BEETHOVEN'S RESPECTIVE CAREERS

The contest took place at Baron Raimund Wetzlar von Plankenstern's villa in Vienna in 1799. Wetzlar was the elder son of Karl Abraham

Wetzlar. Karl Abraham was a wealthy Jew, originally from Offenbach, who came to Vienna in the 1760s as a court agent (Braunbehrens 1989). At a time when Jews were barred from business life, the elder Wetzlar appears to have received a special permit to conduct business in Vienna. After converting to Catholicism in 1777, he began to acquire residential property. He was ennobled in 1788. By the middle 1790s, the Wetzlar sons were fully assimilated into upper middle-class/second-society Viennese life. Raimund Wetzlar had earlier been Mozart's friend and patron (and godfather to Mozart's first child, Raimund Leopold).

In a number of respects, Wölffl seems to have been far better matched to Beethoven than was either Gelinek or Steibelt. He was nearly Beethoven's age, born on 24 December 1773 in Salzburg. He had appeared publicly as a violinist around 1780 and began a career as a chorister at Salzburg Cathedral in 1783, remaining until 1786. He received his first musical training from Leopold Mozart and Michael Haydn, traveling, on his father's advice, to Vienna to study with Mozart in 1790 (whether he actually studied with Mozart remains unclear, though he and Mozart were friends). From 1791 to 1795 he worked as a house composer for Count Orinsky in Warsaw and as a piano teacher of young Polish noblemen. He then returned to Vienna and worked as a composer and pianist. In 1798 he married the singer Therese Klemm. He competed with Beethoven in 1799 and later that year left Vienna to tour Brno, Prague, Dresden, Leipzig, Berlin, and Hamburg. He arrived in Paris in 1801, where he remained until 1805. He finally settled in London and died on 21 May 1812.

Wölffl's public Viennese career during the 1790s exceeded Beethoven's. His two heroic-comic operas, *Der Höllenberg* (*The Mountain of Hell*) and *Der Kopf ohne Mann* (*The Head without the Man*) premiered at the Theater auf der Wieden (which, at this point, a decade before it was taken over by the GAC, was a mixed-class venue) on 21 November 1795 and in 1798, respectively. While in Vienna, he also composed a singspiel, a musical pastische performed at the Theater auf der Wieden in 1798, and a third opera in 1799, *Das trojanische Pferd*. He also published prolifically: during his Viennese years, his output consists of a "Grand concerto militaire" (1799), nine string quartets, three piano trios (1798), eight piano sonatas (1786, 1797, 1798), three sonatas for violin and piano (1796), and twelve songs with piano accompaniment (1799). Morrow's Viennese public concert calendar (1989) shows that his music appeared on at least three public concert programs: first at the Burgtheater (when Josepha Auernhammer performed one of Wölffl's piano concertos), second at the Kärthnerthor theater along with works by Haydn and Süssmayr, and third at a Tonkünstler Society concert. Wölffl's 1796 entry in the Schönfeld *Jahrbuch,* though much briefer and far less grandiloquent than Beethoven's, is still highly complimentary: "What a piano player. He sightreads anything put in front of him with unbelievable accuracy and demonstrates himself admirably through his compositions. His opera *Der Höllenberg* has brought much honor upon him."

In short, by March 1799, Wölffl was fairly well established in Vienna. Indeed, if we take his operas into consideration, he seems to have enjoyed as much if not more of a public career than Beethoven, who had not yet produced a large-scale work. On the other hand, Beethoven had stronger ties to important aristocrats and, increasingly, to the resource of being known as Haydn's protégé. For Wölffl, a triumph over Beethoven could have led to further support from Vienna's old aristocrats and thus enhanced access to privately supplied support and prestige. For Beethoven, a triumph over Wölffl would have provided a means to a broader public and to the public world of music consumption outside the salons.

VIENNESE RECEPTION OF BEETHOVEN AND WÖLFFL

Wölffl was well matched to Beethoven not only in age and pianistic skill; he was also recognized as stylistically very different from Beethoven. The differences between the two pianists tended to heighten the significance of their competition. Tomaschek gives a lengthy description of Wölffl's playing:

> [In March 1799] Wölffl came to Prague. His fame as an extraordinary pianist, which had been spread abroad through various newspapers, made all the music-lovers in the city curious as to his artistic ability. Whosoever wished to see him or speak to him had to look for him at the *Blaue Weintraube,* where he was busy all day long around the billiard-table. . . . The concert took place in a theater where a large audience was assembled. Wölffl played a Concerto of his own composition with unparalleled cleanliness and precision, which—on account of the immense stretch of his hands—no one else could perform. Then he played Mozart's Fantasia in F Minor published in Breitkopf's edition for four hands, exactly as it is printed without leaving out a single note. . . . As I said, he played this piece of music without any mishaps. Then he improvised, weaving in the theme *Wenns Lieserl macht,* and brought the concert to an end with several very beautiful and brilliant variations. A hearty applause was granted to this (in his own way) unique virtuoso. He is a pianist, six feet tall, whose fingers, monstrously long, can encompass a thirteenth without

any strain and moreover, so thin that all his clothes flap on him like a scarecrow. Yet he overcomes difficulties which, for other pianists, would be impossibilities, with a somewhat weak but pleasant touch, and does not lose the quiet composure of his body. He often plays whole sections in a moderately fast tempo with only one finger, as in the Andante of the Mozart Fantasia, where he binds together the section in which the tenor voice goes on for a long time in semiquavers. Such a pianist can certainly be regarded as unique in his own way. (Landon 1970a, 104–5)

This description differs considerably from the qualities Tomaschek perceived in Beethoven, whose pianism he described as being "brilliant and powerful" but which he suggested "not infrequently" jolted the unsuspecting listener "violently out of his state of joyful transports" (ibid.).

It seems fair to say, therefore, that to debate the respective "skills" of these two musicians was inevitably to debate aesthetics. To force their quite differently oriented efforts into a single context of winner and loser meant that the aesthetic that flattered each was placed at stake. Ignaz von Seyfried's account of the duel makes this clear.

Seyfried would have witnessed the duel when he was twenty-three years old: at the time Beethoven was twenty-nine and Wölffl twenty-seven. Seyfried's account, however, was published thirty years later. Seyfried's retrospective accounts of Beethoven are often problematic, as many scholars have observed, though Solomon describes Seyfried as reliable for personal observances. In this case, there are grounds for accepting him as a reliable witness. First, Seyfried came from an aristocratic background; he would have been able to move freely either in or on the fringes of the aristocratic worlds in which Beethoven circulated. Second, he was a musician himself—one of the Theater an der Wien conductors from March 1797 (which meant he had contact with Wölffl, as well, when the latter's opera was performed there). Third (and most relevant to this case), Seyfried's account of how Beethoven and Wölffl were received tends to parallel that offered in the other extant description of the pianists' duel.

Seyfried begins by elaborating on the differences that characterized Beethoven's and Wölffl's styles:

Beethoven had already attracted attention to himself by several compositions and was rated a first-class pianist in Vienna when he was confronted by a rival in the closing years of the last century. Thereupon there was, in a way, a revival of the old Parisian feud of the Gluckists and Piccinists,[2] and the many friends of art in the Imperial City arrayed themselves in two parties. At the head of Beethoven's admirers stood the amiable Prince Lichnowsky; among the most zealous patrons of Wölffl was the broadly cultured Baron Raymond

von Wetzlar. . . . There the interesting combats of the two athletes not infrequently offered an indescribable artistic treat to the numerous and thoroughly
select gathering. Each brought forward the latest product of his mind. Now
one and anon the other gave free rein to his glowing fancy [i.e., they impro-
vised]; sometimes they would seat themselves at two pianofortes and improvise alternately on themes which they gave each other, and thus created many
a four-hand Capriccio which if it could have been put upon paper at the moment would surely have bidden defiance to time. It would have been difficult
perhaps impossible, to award the palm of victory to either one of the gladiators in respect of technical skill. Nature had been a particularly kind mother
to Wölffl in bestowing upon him a gigantic hand which could span a tenth as
easily as other hands compass an octave, and permitted him to play passages
of double notes in these intervals with the rapidity of lightning. *In his improvisations even then Beethoven did not deny his tendency toward the mysterious and gloomy* [Seyfried goes on to describe Beethoven in highly romantic
terms; though this section strengthens the argument I present, I have omitted
it since it is atypical of the period]. . . . *It was the mystical Sanscrit language
whose hieroglyphs can be read only by the initiated. Wölffl, on the contrary,
trained in the school of Mozart, was always equable; never superficial but
always clear and thus more accessible to the multitude. He used art only as a
means to an end, never to exhibit his acquirements. He always enlisted the
interest of his hearers and inevitably compelled them to follow the progres-
sion of his well-ordered ideas. Whoever has heard Hummel will know what
is meant by this.* (trans. Thayer and Forbes 1967, 1:206–7; emphasis added)

The controversy is characterized as revolving around three axes. First,
Beethoven's mysteriousness and gloominess are contrasted with Wölffl's
agility and clarity. Second, Beethoven's exclusiveness is compared with
Wölffl's accessibility, which Seyfried likens to Hummel's; Beethoven's
pianistic approach is like "the mystical Sanscrit language whose hieroglyphs can be read only by the initiated," whereas Wölffl is "more accessible to the multitude." Third, Seyfried distinguishes Wölffl by comparing him with Mozart, and, harking back to Wölffl's accessibility, by
reminding the reader that Wölffl, "trained in the school of Mozart,
was always equable; never superficial but always clear and thus more
accessible."

Seyfried seems to suggest that Wölffl was the more popular of the two
musicians, while Beethoven was more appealing to connoisseurs. As Seyfried depicts them, Beethoven and Wölffl represent different and almost
nonoverlapping conceptions of music and its audience: on the one hand,
the musical experience was accessible to only a few; on the other, music
could be considered as pleasing and openly available to the average listener. This is evidence of the already existing demarcation between

popular and serious music (and between *Kenner* and *Liebhaber*) being widened and underlined in the debate over Beethoven's and Wölffl's respective skills.

An account of the contest offered in a letter to the *Allgemeine Musikalische Zeitung* draws the comparison between Beethoven and Wölffl more or less according to the same lines.

> Opinion is divided here touching the merits of the two [Beethoven and Wölffl]; yet it would seem as if the majority were on the side of the latter [Wölffl]. I shall try to set forth the peculiarities of each without taking part in the controversy. Beethoven's playing is extremely brilliant but has less delicacy and occasionally he is guilty of indistinctness. He shows himself to the greatest advantage in improvisation, and here, indeed, it is most extraordinary with what lightness and yet firmness in the succession of ideas Beethoven not only varies a theme given him on the spur of the moment by figuration (with which many a virtuoso makes his fortune—and wind) but really develops it. Since the death of Mozart, who in this respect is for me still the non plus ultra, I have never enjoyed this kind of pleasure in the degree in which it is provided by Beethoven. In this Wölffl fails to reach him. But W. has advantages in that he, sound in musical learning and dignified in his compositions, plays passages which seem impossible with an ease, precision and clearness which cause amazement (of course he is helped here by the large structure of his hands) and that his interpretation is always, especially in Adagios, so pleasing and insinuating that one can not only admire it but also enjoy. . . . That Wölffl likewise enjoys an advantage because of his amiable bearing, contrast with the somewhat haughty pose of Beethoven, is very natural. (May 1799; trans. Thayer and Forbes 1967, 1:205)

The anonymous writer suggests that Beethoven's playing is "brilliant but has less delicacy and is occasionally guilty of indistinctness," whereas Wölffl is able to play difficult passages with "ease, precision and clearness." This description is akin to Seyfried's discussion of Beethoven's "gloomy" aspect versus Wölffl's equability and lightness. Wölffl is further described as providing interpretations "so pleasing and insinuating that one can not only admire it but also enjoy." His "amiable bearing" (as compared to Beethoven's "haughty pose") is identified as making him the preferable candidate. The writer suggests, in line with Seyfried, that Wölffl is the more accessible of the two and that "it would seem as if the majority were on the side of the latter [Wölffl]" because of this. Where this account differs markedly from Seyfried's, however, is in the way it likens Beethoven's pianism to Mozart's through Beethoven's ability to "really develop" a theme, which gives Beethoven the advantage over Wölffl.

One highly interesting feature of these two accounts is that Mozart is invoked, for different reasons, to describe the playing of both Beethoven and Wölffl. In the second account the characteristic feature of Mozart is that he could really develop a theme—a concern of a connoisseur; in the first account, Seyfried's, Wölffl is distinguished for his Mozartian clarity, equability, and accessibility.

By the autumn of 1792 Mozart (who had died the year before) had become a symbol of Vienna's musical greatness. The concept of Mozart's "spirit" provided a conceptual mantle under which the greatness of a subsequent composer could be lodged. That Beethoven should become that composer, however, is significant, because the qualities for which Beethoven was subsequently hailed (difficulty, complexity, seriousness) were, among Beethoven's contemporaries, usually perceived as antithetical to the shape of Mozart's talent. (Indeed, Mozart's music was sometimes criticized during the middle to late 1780s, when he wrote more self-consciously difficult works.) Mozart's and Beethoven's respective approaches to the piano were perceived as quite different by their contemporaries during the early and middle 1790s.

How can we characterize the range of issues at stake in the Beethoven-Wölffl duel? In addition to the implications the context had for the reputations of the two composers, the contest provided not only a forum in which different pianistic approaches were debated, but also one where the relation between connoisseur and dilettante values was subject to debate.

Both musicians obviously represented novel approaches to the piano. Wölffl's piano music was not always written with the amateur performer in mind. Wölffl was a showman, and at least some of his pieces were written with virtuosic display in mind. In 1800, an *Allgemeine Musikalische Zeitung* reviewer emphasized that "Herr W's works in fact turn out to have exaggerated difficulties for those who perform them and are approached with a certain amount of circumspection, and thus we mention that these Sonatas are easily played by any pianist with at least some training" (see Landon 1976–80, 4:592).

But there was a difference between pianistic virtuosity and emotionality, and between pleasingness and obscurity. From the point of view of the contemporary listener, as portrayed in these two accounts, Wölffl's virtuosity was never experienced as "learned" music. Similarly, it was, as far as can be inferred from extant documents, never perceived as excessively difficult, disorderly, or unpleasant. If we consider contemporary descriptions of responses to Beethoven's works, however, we find that a different and far more controversial picture emerges.

EARLY VIENNESE RECEPTION OF BEETHOVEN

In the same year that Beethoven dueled with Wölffl, an *Allgemeine Musikalische Zeitung* reviewer wrote that Beethoven was "wildly piling up ideas and grouping them in a somewhat bizarre manner so that not seldom an obscure artifice or an artificial obscurity is produced that becomes a detriment rather than a benefit to the total effect" (quoted in Newman 1963, 512). I explore in chapter 8 the vicissitudes of Beethoven's music as reviewed in the *Allgemeine Musikalische Zeitung*. For now, however, this review can serve as an index of the kind of critical response to Beethoven before 1801—responses shared by at least some well-known Viennese musicians.

The pianist Ignaz Moscheles (1794–1870), for example, recalled that sometime around 1804 he had heard of Beethoven, who "wrote the most extraordinary stuff, which no one could either play or understand; a Baroque music in conflict with all the rules" (Landon 1970a, 100). Moscheles brought a copy of op. 13, the "Pathétique" Sonata of 1798, to his teacher F. D. Weber (who thought Beethoven's compositions "hare brained"). Weber "warned against playing or studying eccentric productions . . . before I had developed a style based on more respectable models" (ibid.). These views were, it seems, shared by others. At a later date, the Abbé Gelinek said Beethoven's compositions were "lacking in internal coherency and not infrequently they were overloaded" (Thayer and Forbes 1967, 1:248). Leopold Kozeluch (see Newman 1963, 557) reportedly threw a copy of the C Minor Trio (possibly op. 1, no. 3) at the feet of his fellow composer Dolezalek after the latter (a Beethoven enthusiast)[3] attempted to play it for him (Thayer and Forbes 1967, 1:259). Kozeluch and Haydn apparently agreed that this trio was unusual—"We would have done that differently," Dolezalek reports they said to each other. Dolezalek, moreover, reported that Haydn never fully reconciled himself to Beethoven's compositions (ibid.). There are several stories of hostility to Beethoven's music on the part of the different musicians called on to perform it. The string players who first read through op. 59, no. 1 (the first of the "Razumovsky" string quartets) were convinced that the repeated note played by the cello in the opening of the second movement was intended as a musical joke at their expense. There appears to have been considerable animosity among musicians, toward Beethoven and his music.

This controversy took on a more definite shape and became more heated over time. We can begin to piece together a sense of how various publics responded to his works during these early years in his career. When Beethoven's ballet *The Creatures of Prometheus* was performed in 1801, the incident was identified by contemporary observers as Vienna's "Guerre des Buffons,"[4] though in this case the dispute was as much if not more about rival ballet masters as it was about Beethoven's music. Beethoven's supporters hailed the ballet (and the junior ballet master's choreography) for its more natural, expressive style, while opponents (and, it seems, defenders of older tastes, and of the more senior ballet master) thought the ballet ungraceful and inharmonious. The latter seem to have been in the majority at the performance attended by Haydn's friend Carl Rosenbaum (one month after the opening performance on 28 March)[5] for he noted in an entry on 27 April 1801 that, "at the end, the ballet was more hissed down than applauded" (Rosenbaum 1968, 92). According to the dramatist von Collin (for whose play *Coriolan* Beethoven wrote miscellaneous music), not even the most important affair of state would have aroused "more violent divisions of opinion than the battle did at that time over the respective superiority of the two ballet masters. Friends of the theatre divided themselves completely into two parties, who regarded each other with hatred and contumely on account of their differences of opinion" (Landon 1970a, 139).

Opinion was further polarized over the issue of the Third Symphony ("Eroica") in 1805. Two times the size of any Haydn or Mozart symphony, the work was criticized on first performance for "losing itself in anarchy" and for being "shrill and bizarre" (Wallace 1986, 15). An anonymous *Allgemeine Musikalische Zeitung* critic writing of the second performance suggested that the work would "gain immensely (it lasts a full hour) if Beethoven would decide to shorten it and introduce into the whole more light, clarity and unity. . . . But if, as now, its coherence escapes even the most attentive ear after repeated hearings, it must appear peculiar even to the unprejudiced listener. Moreover, there were very few people who liked the symphony" (ibid.). Rosenbaum, meanwhile (whom the musicologist Else Radant Landon has described as an Everyman of Viennese musical taste), considered that the symphony was not what one would have expected from someone with Beethoven's reputation.

In the responses to the "Eroica" we see again the issues first identified in the Beethoven-Wölffl controversy: difficult, disorderly, and startling versus accessible, orderly, and pleasant; expressive and self-consciously profound versus rapid, light, bright, and entertaining. In April 1805, a writer (possibly the dramatist August von Kotzebue, who collaborated with Beethoven in "The Ruins of Athens") outlined the ways that the "Eroica" was received:

> Beethoven's most special friends contend this particular symphony is a masterpiece, that it is exactly the true style for music of the highest type and that if it does not please now it is because the public is not sufficiently cultivated in the arts to comprehend these higher spheres of beauty; but after a couple of thousand years its effect will not be lessened. The other party absolutely denies any artistic merit to this work. They claim that it reveals the symptoms of an evidently unbridled attempt at distinction and peculiarity, but that neither beauty, true sublimity nor power have anywhere been achieved either by means of unusual modulations, by violent transitions or by the juxtaposition of the most heterogeneous elements. . . . the creation of something beautiful and sublime, not the production of something merely unusual and fantastic, is the true expression of genius. . . . The third, very small party stand in the middle. They concede that there are many beautiful things in the symphony, but admit that the continuity often appears to be completely confused and that the endless duration of this longest and perhaps most difficult of all symphonies is tiring even for the expert; for a mere amateur it is unbearable. . . . One fears . . . that if Beethoven continues along this road, he and the public will make a bad journey. Music could easily reach a state where everyone who has not been vouchsafed a thorough knowledge of the rules and difficulties of the art will derive absolutely no pleasure from it. (Landon 1970a, 153–54)

In its discussion of Beethoven as viewed by his supporters, this passage articulates one of the most sociologically and historically interesting themes within Beethoven research. It is one of the earliest observances, by one of Beethoven's contemporaries, of an emerging discourse of "serious" music.

In 1799, the *Allgemeine Musikalische Zeitung* writer suggested (as did Seyfried retrospectively) that the Wölffl-Beethoven contest ended in a draw; Seyfried says that "it would have been difficult perhaps impossible, to award the palm of victory to either one of the gladiators" and the journal writer notes that opinion was divided, but suggests that probably the majority were on Wölffl's side. Over the next five years (the period between this report on Beethoven and Wölffl and the report on Beethoven's Third Symphony), the basic shape of the Beethoven-Wölffl debate was brought into increasingly higher relief and with it, so too were the social divisions of Vienna's music world. The rising profile of this aesthetic controversy simultaneously helps to specify the social dis-

tribution of musical taste during these years. Moreover, the aesthetic debates surrounding the Beethoven-Wölffl duel provided a medium for the
clarification of social differences among Vienna's music patrons. These
differences can be mapped by tracing out Beethoven's and Wölffl's respective support networks.

VIENNESE MUSICAL CONSTITUENCIES IN 1799

The starting point for such a project is clear enough, at least at face
value. As Seyfried tells us, Prince Lichnowsky stood "at the head of Beethoven's admirers," while Baron Wetzlar was "among the most zealous
patrons of Wölffl."

By 1799, Beethoven's network of supporters included Vienna's major
old aristocratic patrons. Documentary evidence confirms that he was acquainted with and/or supported by the following aristocrats: Prince and
Princess Lichnowsky, Countess von Thun (the prince's mother-in-law),
Baron Nikolaus Zmeskall, Baron van Swieten, Prince Nikolaus Esterhazy, Count and Countess Browne-Camus, prince Lobkowitz the elder,
Countess Brunsvik, Count and Countess Moritz Lichnowsky, Countess
Keglevics (later Princess Odescalchi), and Baron Gleichenstein. By this
time, he was probably also acquainted with Prince Lobkowitz the
younger, Prince Schwarzenberg, Princess Liechtenstein (not a Beethoven
enthusiast), Countess Guicciardi, and Prince Kinsky.

Between 1793 and 1805, Beethoven performed or had his compositions performed at the homes of Prince Lichnowsky, Nikolaus Zmeskall,
Baron van Swieten, Prince Esterhazy, Prince Lobkowitz the elder, and,
later on, Princess Odescalchi, Prince Lobkowitz the younger, and Prince
Schwarzenberg. His aristocratic piano pupils included Princess Liechtenstein, Giulietta Guicciardi, the daughters of Therese von Brunsvick (with
whom he was intimate enough to use the *du* form of address), and
Countess Josephine de Clary.

These lists are, of course, provisional. They include only those aristocrats who had frequent, personal contact with Beethoven, those individuals or families, moreover, who helped to support Beethoven materially.
But it is also through these people that Beethoven would have been introduced and exposed to wider audiences, audiences whose enthusiasm for
Beethoven would, naturally, have varied. Nikolaus Zmeskall, for example, according to the music journalist Ignaz von Mosel's 1843 memoirs, "gave the most interesting morning concerts to which the élite of

the art world thronged" (Landon 1970a, 97). Through salons such as these, Beethoven's works were disseminated.

Within the Beethoven literature, there have been oblique references to the "mingling" of all classes who came together under the banner of "great art" and a common love for Beethoven's music. A similar picture has been most recently offered by Volkmar Braunbehrens (1989) in his discussion of Mozart's Vienna. Yet we cannot necessarily extrapolate from the social character of salon life in the 1780s to that of the late 1790s. Mozart's Vienna was not, as far as music organization, the same as Beethoven's, fifteen years later, when nearly all the hauskapellen had been disbanded. Yet there has been a tradition within Beethoven scholarship to presuppose a high degree of unrestricted social movement in salon life and to confuse the democratic rhetoric employed by Beethoven (and, in some cases his patrons) with the circumstances of the society within which Beethoven worked. The imagery of Beethoven as a middle-class composer may have been fostered by Beethoven's relations with his supporters later in his career, when the social composition of his constituency was indeed broader. Both Beethoven and Anton Schindler, for example, would have been interested in portraying Beethoven consumption as characterized by a fairly wide social base during the middle and latter parts of his career. By that time many of his initial circle of aristocratic patrons had died and Beethoven's need to earn his living by his pen became more pressing. Schindler may have projected back onto Beethoven's early career a social openness of salon life and a universality that, during the 1790s and early 1800s, Beethoven did not actually enjoy.[6]

One way to sample the more concrete circumstances of 1790s salon life is to work on a case-by-case basis, asking whether particular members of the upper middle class would have attended the private salons at which Beethoven performed. Such a project is beyond the resources of this study, but it will no doubt be developed by future scholars (see Moore n.d.b.). I address here the issues of social restrictions in the Beethoven salon forums, whether Beethoven was closely connected to any members of the upper middle class, and the contact between Baron Wetzlar and Beethoven's circle.

Wetzlar was musically active as a patron and dilettante, and he was wealthy.[7] He was also singled out by Seyfried as "one of the most zealous" of Wölffl's supporters. Wetzlar would have been a likely person to be found in Vienna's higher aristocratic salon world, if this world did indeed admit second-aristocratic and/or professional-class participation and if the tastes for Beethoven and for Wölffl were not socially exclusive. If the salons where Beethoven performed were open to upper middle-class and second-society audiences, it seems likely that Wetzlar and probably members of his family would have come into contact with Beethoven eventually and that there would have been Wetzlars present at some of Beethoven's private performances.

We know that Wetzlar attended a private concert held during the 1780s at the Auernhammers' (a middle-class family—the daughter Josepha was an accomplished pianist and Mozart pupil), to which Mozart had invited Countess von Thun, and that Baron van Swieten was also present on this occasion. Wetzlar also took part in Mozart's private ball in 1783, the guest list of which, according to Deutsch (1965, 212), included a Dr. Gilowsky and some of Mozart's professional middle-class colleagues: the Adambergers, the Stephanies, and the Langes. A decade and a half later (and after Mozart's death), did Wetzlar continue to come into contact with Countess von Thun or her son-in-law, Prince Lichnowsky? Landon has suggested that the high aristocratic salons—the ones at which Beethoven and Haydn participated regularly—were "socially very exclusive affairs" (1976–80, 4:338). If he is right, then Beethoven would probably not have come across the Wetzlar family in the course of private concertizing. One source of evidence in favor of this claim is found in a letter Beethoven wrote in May 1803. By this time, Beethoven was reaching the first high point in his career: he had emerged as a composer of large-scale symphonic works, he was about to begin an opera, and he had just had his successful benefit concert a month before at the Theater an der Wien. If the Wetzlar family had been attending private Beethoven salons in the preceding years, it seems likely that, by this time, they would have become acquainted with Beethoven.

The letter is to Count Wetzlar's brother, Alexander Wetzlar, also a musical sponsor. Beethoven writes to recommend George Polgreen Bridgetower, the famous London-based violinist, who was then on a concert tour of Germany and Austria.

> Although we have never spoken to one another, yet I have not the slightest hesitation in introducing to you the bearer of this letter, Herr Brischdower [*sic*], a very able virtuoso and an absolute master of his instrument—He not only performs his own concertos but is also an excellent quartet player. I earnestly hope that you will obtain for him a wider circle of acquaintances. He has already had a favourable impression on *Lobkowitz* and *Fries* and all the other distinguished lovers of music—
>
> It would not be at all a bad thing, I think, if you were to take him some evening to *Therese Schönfeld,* at whose house, I am told, many friends as-

semble, or if you even invited him to your house—I know that you too will thank me for having procured you this acquaintance—. (Anderson 1961, 90)

The letter raises several issues that require further examination, and it allows us to speculate on the ways that Wetzlar's and Beethoven's social circles may have been distinct. First, we learn that Beethoven has never spoken to Alexander Wetzlar. His wording, as opposed to "we have never met" or "you don't know me but," suggests that he had come across Wetzlar but never been introduced, and that he had thus had little contact with the extended Wetzlar family. Second, Beethoven asks Wetzlar, a man to whom, he says, he had never spoken, to take Bridgetower along to Therese Schönfeld's. At the very least, this suggests that Beethoven himself was distanced from or was not acquainted with the Schönfeld salon, and it may also suggest that Beethoven had no other closer acquaintance of whom he could ask this favor. If this was the case, it implies that there was a musical circle to which Alexander Wetzlar belonged that did not overlap or did not overlap significantly with that in which Beethoven and his patrons moved.

It is not possible to say whether the same held for Alexander's brother Raimund, Wölffl's patron and host of the Beethoven-Wölffl duel. If Raimund were a regular attendant at the high aristocratic salons in which Beethoven performed, it seems reasonable that Beethoven would have approached him—if only to request him to ask Alexander, his brother, to meet Bridgetower. If Beethoven did this and was told by Raimund to contact Alexander on his own, it seems likely that Beethoven would have mentioned this in his letter.

The third issue this letter raises revolves around the fact that Beethoven tells Alexander Wetzlar of how Bridgetower "has already made an impression" on Lobkowitz, Fries, and "all the other distinguished lovers of music." The significant aspect here is that he tells this to Wetzlar as if it were news, which implies that Wetzlar was denied access to that group of "distinguished music lovers" who had heard Bridgetower first (and to whom Beethoven has access). The fact, moreover, that this mention seems to be intended to impress Wetzlar is itself interesting, as it suggests that the names Lobkowitz and Fries[8] would have been impressive to Wetzlar (in which case he would have "looked up" to but been distanced from them). Assuming that the reverse of this situation never occurred—that Wetzlar never wrote to Beethoven to suggest that a musician be introduced upward, as it were, having already impressed bourgeois families—Beethoven's words point to a trickle-down character of musical taste and its dissemination in Vienna of the 1790s. Those individuals on the periphery or outside of circles of aristocratic music consumption may have been receptive to the musicians and music that the core circle had previously endorsed.

To observe this receptivity is by no means to undercut the argument that these same upper middle-class and second-society patrons tried to compete with aristocrats by proposing a rival pianistic candidate in Wölffl. Rather it is to suggest that proximity to the exclusive circles around Beethoven was desirable and was pursued through various means according to the resources available, including imitating musicians recommended by the elite, and also through cultivating and putting forward challengers. All of these cultural-political practices would have helped to position social outsiders closer to the officially recognized, aristocratically sponsored, and, therefore, legitimate forms of late eighteenth- and early nineteenth-century musical culture, whether to move closer to what already counted as part of that culture, or, conversely, to move that culture closer to where those outsiders currently stood.

As we saw in chapter 2, the Gesellschaft der Associierten Cavaliere concerts, run by Baron van Swieten and explicitly devoted to "great" music, were programmed with increasingly wider dissemination in mind, and the circumstances surrounding the dissemination of the "Eroica" Symphony also suggest a trickle-down model of musical taste among aristocrats old and new and the general public. The piece had three "premiers"—one for each of the three kinds of high culture musical public. The first performance was at a private concert, held at the home of Prince Lobkowitz the younger, in 1804 (see Morrow 1989, 403). A semipublic premier was held at Baron Würth's later in the same year (ibid., 387), and the public premier took place at the Theater an der Wien on 7 April 1805 (see Morrow 1987, 330).

It seems likely, then, that Beethoven was not on speaking terms with either Wetzlar, that he would have had no or limited contact with the Schönfeld salon, and that the Wetzlars, at least Alexander Wetzlar, attended a salon that was socially distant from the circles in which Beethoven ordinarily moved.

The issue of Therese Schönfeld's identity is complicated by the fact that there were several Schönfeld families in Vienna, and also because there were two Johann von Schönfelds, both of whom were living in Vienna during the 1790s (this point is often overlooked by music historians—including myself, see DeNora 1991, 327). The first of these men we have met before: Johann Ferdinand, the Ritter von Schönfeld, author and publisher of the *Jahrbuch der Tonkünst von Wien und Prag* (1796). As he is described by Constantin Wurzbach (1856–91, 152–56), this Schönfeld was an industrialist and collector of art objects purchased from churches and monasteries during the years of Joseph II's church reforms. In Vienna, he was a publisher and sold books in his shop in the Kärthnerthor theater. His son Ignaz, Ritter von Schönfeld, was born in 1780. Unfortunately, the Christian name of Johann Ferdinand's wife is unknown. Was she the Therese to whom Beethoven referred?

We do know that Therese was not the wife of the second Johann Schönfeld, the Count Johann Hilmar, Saxon ambassador to Vienna. He was married to Ursula Margereta, née Countess Fries. She is listed in the Ritter von Schönfeld's *Jahrbuch* as a piano pupil of Kozeluch. She was also most likely the singer to whom Count Zinzendorf referred in his diary on 4 April 1799 (Landon 1976–80, 4:546).

There are other Schönfelds as well. Next to the entry for Countess Schönfeld, the *Jahrbuch* lists a Fraulein Nanette Schönfeld, "daughter of . . . Hrn. v. Schönfeld from Truowa." There were also some Jewish Schönfelds, three brothers, all officers in the infantry regiment of the Austrian army. One of these, Franz Thomas, born in 1753, was killed during the Terror in Paris in 1793.[9]

On the basis of the evidence available so far, it seems most likely that the salon to which Beethoven asked Wetzlar to bring Bridgetower was not an aristocratic one. First, there were no members of the Count von Schönfeld's family with the Christian name Therese. Second, the Count von Schönfeld and his family would have moved with ease in the salon worlds in which Beethoven circulated; Ursula was a Fries, and Count Fries was, by 1803, a prominent member of Beethoven's world, mixing easily with people like Prince Lobkowitz the younger, who had become one of Beethoven's closest patrons.

Unless we discover that the Christian name of Johann Ferdinand Schönfeld's wife was *not* Therese, I suggest that the salon to which Beethoven referred was hosted by this Schönfeld family. My reasoning is as follows: Beethoven speaks of Therese's as a place where, he is told, "many friends assemble." This implies that Therese is a fairly regular salon hostess. The only regular salons hosted by a Schönfeld that are listed in the *Jahrbuch* are those of Schönfeld's own household ("Hrn. von Schönfeld aus Prag"). This salon is listed in company with second-society ones: Hrn. v. Henikstein, Hrn. Hofrath von Greiner, Fraulein von Martines.

If Therese was indeed the wife of Johann Ferdinand Schönfeld, then there is evidence that Alexander Wetzlar moved in middle-class circles distinct from the aristocratic milieu in which Beethoven moved.[10] This detail would support the picture other scholars have elaborated of the continuing rigidity of social boundaries in Viennese musical life—of separate but often parallel spheres of musical activity in the late eighteenth and early nineteenth centuries.[11]

This information also helps us piece together a more detailed portrait of Schönfeld as a music consumer/patron and the ways his own support of music was related to aristocratic activities and tastes. Beethoven tells Wetzlar that he hopes the latter "will obtain for [Bridgetower] a wider circle of acquaintances." The Schönfeld salon would function as a conduit to broader taste, a gateway for Bridgetower's exposure to the wider (and more middle-class) world of the music consuming public.[12] In this regard, Schönfeld can be understood as a disseminator of aristocratic taste, which sheds further light on the status and social role of the *Jahrbuch:* in addition to listing prominent musicians in Vienna, it may also have functioned as a kind of guide to musical fashion, listing, rather like a social column, the luminaries of Viennese musical society from a point of view which celebrated that society's upper echelons and their musical values. We have already seen this aspect in Schönfeld's discussion of Beethoven and his expected "greatness," having placed himself in the hands of such excellent teachers (Haydn and Albrechtsberger). Moreover, if Beethoven was socially distanced from Schönfeld's salon and vice versa, which does appear to be the case, then we can see the Schönfeld salon as receptive to but lagging behind aristocratic taste.

To put Wölffl forward as Beethoven's rival, therefore, may have provided a second-society entrée into the high-status game of musical contests and helped to substantiate the Wetzlars as partisans of a musical aesthetic distinct from that associated with Beethoven. Wölffl can be understood, in other words, as a representative of an at least partly separate musical constituency, and the serious music ideology as represented by Beethoven can be further clarified as the property of Vienna's old and highest aristocracy. The Beethoven-Wölffl duel may have served as a vehicle through which two different social networks were distinguished.

The Beethoven-Wölffl piano contest marks an important moment in music history. We can see perhaps the earliest emergence of the nineteenth-century ideology of serious music as a debatable issue and as in contrast to more conventional dilettante values. Simultaneously, it further enhanced Beethoven's emerging reputation as a highly original, specialist's composer. The duel features both of these issues at a time when

they were still equivocal, before either the notion of serious music or
Beethoven's reputation was fully institutionalized as a dominant part of
elite musical culture. While these issues clearly require further exploration, it seems clear at this point that study of the circumstances of the
Beethoven-Wölffl duel illuminate the ways that support for Beethoven
was linked to the emergence of a serious music aesthetic and to the further definition of a serious music public. Through the pursuit of what
was recognized as his esoteric style, Beethoven's patrons were able to
redefine themselves as princes—not merely of society but also of taste.
Within the high culture music world, the Beethoven-Wölffl duel placed
at stake relations between an upwardly aspiring middle class or second
society and Vienna's old aristocrats.

CHAPTER 8

Beethoven's Early Aesthetic Campaigns

A reputation that rests on what an individual says and does to maintain it is perpetually vulnerable, however culturally powerful that individual may be. But there are more secure mechanisms for the renewal and dissemination of reputation, ones that can help to institutionalize social identities and social roles. Over time, pro-Beethoven values were incorporated into the very instruments for musical action and musical discourse within the Viennese musical world during the early 1800s. This chapter discusses how Beethoven's reputation as a musical genius was built into the material and linguistic culture of Viennese musical life.

When viewed with hindsight, Beethoven's innovations appear musically advanced. He is often described, for example, as having anticipated (rather than helped to shape) the modern piano, as if that technology's development occurred autonomously. This evolutionary conception of musical history sidesteps consideration of the socially engaged quality of technological change. By exploring Beethoven's attempts to reform the piano and musical discourse, we can follow his identity as a musical genius as it first became embedded in technological forms. This approach reveals some of the ways that pro-Beethoven values were stabilized outside of specific contexts of action.

THE EXTENT OF BEETHOVEN'S IMPACT
ON PIANO TECHNOLOGY

So far, music historians have not considered the interdependency between Beethoven's reputation and developments in musical discourse and piano technology in Vienna. Yet from 1796 onward, Beethoven campaigned for Viennese piano reform, specifically for "a heavier action, a sturdier instrument and a bigger tone, undoubtedly because he needed an instrument capable of withstanding his animal energies, of projecting his more intense feelings and of compensating for his growing deafness" (Newman 1970, 497).[1] Beethoven was hardly the only musician who had an interest in building a new piano after 1795, however; his impact on piano technology coincided with a growing international trend toward louder and sturdier instruments. Jan Ladislav Dussek also lobbied for piano reform in 1790s London (see Newman 1970, 485; Craw 1964). In fact, from the international perspective of the 1790s and early 1800s, Beethoven's piano preferences appear fairly conservative; he favored the lighter Viennese instruments over their heavier English counterparts (Newman 1970; Winter 1977). Even after the period of Viennese and German piano reform, there were distinctive differences between the continental instruments and their English counterparts. Hummel described these differences in the 1820s in his method book, *A Complete Theoretical and Practical Course of Instruction in the Art of Playing the Pianoforte*: "The German piano may be played upon with ease by the weakest hand . . . it does not impede the rapidity of execution by requiring too great an effort. . . . The English piano . . . does not admit of the same facility of execution as the German. The touch is much heavier" (Schonberg 1963, 19). Friedrich Kalkbrenner, who subsequently made a career as a pianist in London, wrote:

> The instruments of Vienna and London have produced two schools. The Viennese pianists are particularly distinguished for their precision, the clarity and rapidity of the execution. Thus the instruments manufactured in that city are extremely easy to play. . . . The use of the pedals in Germany is almost unknown. English pianos have a fuller sound and a heavier keyboard action. The players of that country have adopted a larger style and that beautiful way of singing that distinguishes them; and it is indispensable to use the large pedal in order to conceal the inherent dryness of the piano. Dussek, Field, and Cramer, the chiefs of that school which was founded by Clementi, use the pedal when harmonies do not change. Dussek above all was responsible for that, for he used the pedal almost constantly when he played in public. (cited in ibid., 20)

It has been suggested that Beethoven preferred Viennese instruments because they were less prone to technical problems.[2] Equally compelling is the argument that the Viennese instrument would have been the type Beethoven was most used to playing. In addition, as Margaret Hood has observed, during the 1790s it "would have been unlikely that any of

Vienna's eminent musicians would have bought pianos from a firm located not only outside the capital but outside the Empire as well" (1986,
3). Whatever the reasons, Beethoven lobbied for a heavier Viennese instrument, though not one that would have been as heavy as its English
counterpart.

During the eighteenth century, the international differences between
instruments were significant. Unlike the Germans, the English were not
a nation of clavichord players. When English manufacturers did begin
to produce pianos, they, like the Italians, conceived of the instrument
as a harpsichord capable of individual tonal nuance. Late eighteenth-
century English pianos were made in the same shops that had been and
were continuing to make harpsichords. The Germans and Austrians, on
the other hand, tended to conceive of the piano as a louder clavichord.
From the first, the English were concerned with maintaining volume but
adding nuance and the Germans with maintaining nuance but adding
volume. Furthermore, the action that English craftsmen developed was
heavier; it was modeled on a technique developed but rejected in Germany. The German harpsichord maker Silberman had developed an
early piano but abandoned it after J. S. Bach refused to endorse it on the
grounds that it was too heavy (Dolge 1911; Harding 1973). Silberman
then directed his efforts to perfecting a lighter-acting keyboard, which
set the agenda for subsequent German manufacturers. One of Silberman's apprentices, however, Johann Schroeter, emigrated to England,
where he began to develop Silberman's initial techniques. Thus the heavy
action, abandoned at home, became a basis for development abroad.

Seen from the viewpoint of the music occupation in London during
the second half of the eighteenth century, the louder, heavier English instrument was well suited to London's more commercial musical climate.
During these years, the public concert was emerging in England as a
commercial venture, and it is not coincidental that England is where the
more modern (from our perspective) piano virtuosi make their earliest
and sometimes controversial appearance. The inflated and specifically
English notion of a "grand" piano (the term was first used by Broadwood in 1790) gave, as Loesser notes, "a sense of elation to the new
people who were likely to be its purchasers" (1954, 227). In comparison
with the Viennese firm with which Beethoven dealt, which produced
about fifty pianos a year, the London firm of Broadwood produced an
annual average of four hundred instruments (ibid., 234), one indication
of London's far greater commercial music world.

Thus Beethoven's international impact on piano construction is distinct from the impact he had on the Viennese context. In retrospect, the important point is that Beethoven became known internationally as an advocate for the *idea* of a louder, more resonant instrument and that he did so at a time when he was emerging as one of Vienna's premier composers. In contrast to its position in Viennese musical culture, the piano in London was perceived as the instrument of the middle and upper middle class during the 1790s (Milligan 1983, chap. 1); it was decidedly not aristocratic. The public taste for piano virtuosi such as Clementi, Cramer, Dussek, and Field (the members of the "London pianoforte school") was often juxtaposed with the aristocratic preference for "classic" or "ancient" music (see W. Weber 1992).

As Milligan has observed, "advocates of the harpsichord sometimes regarded the piano with contempt" (1983, 16). An anonymous writer to the *Universal Magazine* in 1793 (and a partisan of London's aristocratic Concerts of Ancient Music) described pianoforte instructors as "the idle tasteless masters of the day" and went on to suggest that "Mr. Handel's great genius would not allow him to write for that trifling instrument and out of ten of his oratorios which I have by me, I scarcely find anything fit for it. . . . I deal so little in modern composition that I know nothing either of the Battle of Prague or the Siege of Gibraltar [titles of popular piano works of the time]" (quoted in ibid., 16). In London the piano was, for many aristocrats, tainted with the new commercial musical values. It was not, as in Vienna, associated with the new concern with musical seriousness that Beethoven represented.

The London aristocratic Concerts of Ancient Music featured composers such as Arcangelo Corelli (1653–1713), Pergolesi (1710–36), J. Adolf Hasse (1699–1783), Geminiani (1687–1762), William Boyce (1710–79), and most especially Handel (1685–1759) (see W. Weber 1992). Insofar as members often took part in performance,[3] the organization perpetuated a more traditional patron-dominated or patron-as-equal-participant relationship between musician and patron. Aristocratic musical life in London during the early 1790s left little opportunity for the pianoforte, because the instrument was associated with commercial music culture. Later, however (around the time of the founding of the London Philharmonic Society and beyond), aristocrats and the upper middle class began to converge in their acceptance of the piano as a high cultural instrument, an agreement that occurred around the notion of "great" living composers, particularly Haydn, Mozart, and Beethoven. It was in Vienna that the new piano technology first received its aristocratic seal of approval, and this initial aristocratic endorsement

may have helped to make the new technology appealing to English aristocrats, who eventually became interested in the music of the Viennese
masters.

In the 1790s, London concert series were flourishing. Musicians there
were able to command wider publics as well as a greater degree of financial security. In addition, career musicians and other participants in the
music business, including instrument manufacturers, collaborated more
closely than they did in Vienna. Clementi, Dussek, Cramer, and Field,
for example, were all involved at one time or another in music publishing
and piano manufacture. In general, Viennese career musicians had less
scope for entrepreneurial activity and less control over the conditions of
their work than did their English counterparts. By contrast, because the
bulk of Viennese musical life remained private and sponsored by aristocrats, Viennese musicians' assessments of instruments counted for less,
relative to those of their patrons—the primary purchasers of the more
costly, more individually crafted Viennese instruments. One reason that
Viennese piano technology may have tended to remain more "conservative" during the 1790s, in relation to its London counterpart, was that
Viennese musicians had less scope for constituting themselves as commercial performers, as modern-style virtuosi. Czerny observes that
"Mozart's manner, which was so excellently perfected by Hummel, was
more suited to the German Fortepianos [as opposed to the English]
which combined a delicate and shallow touch with a great clarity, and
thus are *best adapted for general use and for use by children*" (Landon
1970a, 62; emphasis added). Echoing Hummel's views on the German
and English instruments quoted earlier, Czerny tells us that the Viennese
pianos were best suited to light-fingered passage work and, by implication, to pianists such as Wölffl and others known for the "somewhat
weak and pleasant touch" that characterized Wölffl's playing.

BEETHOVEN'S CAMPAIGN FOR PIANO REFORM

The piano firm with whom Beethoven most often dealt was "Nannette
Streicher, Geburt Stein." Frau Streicher had learned the craft of piano
manufacture in Augsburg, as an apprentice to her father. As a woman in
charge of the actual construction of the instruments, her position was
unique in Vienna, and probably internationally. Her husband, Andreas
Streicher, was in charge of the shopfront as director of sales and dem-
onstration. Both Streichers were pianists of repute, and Andreas was also
an amateur composer and teacher. Beethoven always went out of his way

to deal with Andreas rather than his wife on matters of piano business, limiting his interaction with Nannette to domestic concerns. When his nephew came to live with him, Beethoven turned to Nannette for domestic advice, and a brief survey of Beethoven's letters around 1818 reveals a lengthy but fascinating series of correspondence concerning plates of stewed fruit, problems with servants, laundry, and bed linen.

Sometime around or before 1801, Andreas Streicher printed the pamphlet "Notes on the Playing, Tuning and Maintenance of the Fortepiano . . ." (Streicher 1984, trans. de Silva). The second chapter of this leaflet is of most interest to Beethoven studies, because there Streicher explicitly advocates the current Viennese ideals of light playing and "pearly" passagework, so-called because the graduated flow of notes in crescendi and decrescendi was compared to "matched pearls" (the piano commentary is full of references to phrases flowing, sometimes to flowing "like oil").

For Streicher, piano aesthetics were part and parcel of a concern with instrument maintenance. In his exhortations against pounding and "torturing" the instrument, which we considered in chapter 6, Streicher's pamphlet advocates a conservative pianistic approach. In Vienna, the dominant pianistic technique and piano-compositional style were reinforced by piano technology and attitudes about how that technology was meant to be handled.

From Beethoven's perspective, this approach presented a problem. The Viennese piano around 1796 could be understood as holding him back from what he did best; to be sure, it did not flatter his talent to the extent that it did Wölffl's. It may have even made him seem less skilled, because its technical strengths and limits would have inhibited the type of playing to which Beethoven was inclined. If we take the following account from Anton Reicha at face value, it presents Streicher's worst-case scenario. Reicha reported an incident that occurred in 1795, when Beethoven performed a Mozart piano concerto: "He asked me to turn pages for him. But I was mostly occupied in wrenching the strings of the pianoforte which snapped, while the hammers struck among the broken strings. Beethoven insisted on finishing the concerto and so, back and forth I leaped, jerking out a string, disentangling a hammer, turning a page and I worked harder than Beethoven" (1936, 351). It is difficult to assess a report such as this: we do not know whether Reicha was exaggerating, nor do we know anything about the condition of the piano in question. We cannot say that it was Beethoven's heavy playing that exacerbated the problem, though firsthand accounts do refer to Beethoven's tendency toward the strenuous and the dramatic, as opposed to the conventionally lighter and cleaner style.

Yet it does seem that we can meaningfully speak of a personal-stylistic context for Beethoven's interest in a more robust and louder piano. One creative solution was to lobby for a different type of instrument, and Beethoven did. He wrote to Streicher for the first time from Pressburg (then one of the most important Hungarian towns and the modern-day Bratislava) in 1796, where he was embarking on an extremely successful foreign concert tour. Streicher had sent Beethoven an instrument to be played on the tour. Beethoven wrote back to thank him:

> I received the day before yesterday your fortepiano, which is really an excellent instrument. Anyone else would try to keep it for himself; but I—now you must have a good laugh—I should be deceiving you if I didn't tell you that in my opinion it is far too good for me, and why?—Well, because it robs me of the freedom to produce my own tone. But of course, this must not deter you from making all your fortepianos in the same way. For no doubt there are few people who cherish such whims as mine. (Anderson 1961, 1:24)

Beethoven wrote again, later in the same year, from Vienna:

> There is no doubt that so far as the manner of playing it is concerned, the *pianoforte* is still the least studied and developed of all instruments; often one thinks that one is merely listening to a harp. And I am delighted, my dear fellow, that you are one of the few who realize and perceive that, provided one can feel the music, one can also make the pianoforte sing. I hope that the time will come when the harp and the pianoforte will be treated as two entirely different instruments. (ibid., 25)

What Beethoven wanted was a piano capable of a more resonating (less harplike) tone, of registering nuances of touch ("to produce my own tone"), and of withstanding a greater force. Eventually, this led to triple-strung pianos with a firmer action—instruments that more closely resembled their English counterparts. During the late eighteenth century, such an idiosyncratic request would not have been perceived as unusual; it was not uncommon for a Viennese piano manufacturer (though not a London one) to tailor the instrument to the client's needs. The salient point is not that Streicher was willing to make Beethoven the kind of piano the latter most desired (since Streicher tended to build his instruments according to the wishes of his clients), but rather that during the next decade Streicher gradually applied Beethoven's specifications to all of the instruments he produced—to respond to Beethoven's lobby for general policy changes.

In part, Streicher was so receptive to Beethoven's concerns because the name "Beethoven" had increasing cachet during the late 1790s. One measure of this claim is that piano manufacturers were beginning to "lend" the composer pianos[4] (a commonly practiced way for a firm to gain repute). In addition, Beethoven's network of aristocratic admirers was expanding.[5] In light of his increasing cultural capital, Beethoven could not so easily be written off as an eccentric. By the late 1790s, Beethoven was on good footing with the Streichers. Although there is no reason to believe that the friendship between them was not genuine, the Streichers would have lost much if they had alienated Beethoven. This was especially true after 1802, when his piano "platform" acquired, in addition to an important and growing contingent of aristocrats, a further constituency that Streicher could not ignore—namely, the Leipzig firm Breitkopf and Härtel.[6]

At that time, Breitkopf and Härtel occupied a peculiar position in the world of music affairs: they were purveyors of musical instruments and music publishers and they also published the important weekly music magazine, *Allgemeine Musikalische Zeitung* (*AMZ; General Music News*), which first appeared in October 1798. It was, in effect, Breitkopf and Härtel's "house organ" in that it contained reviews of published music, much of it their own.[7] By 1803, the journal had become decidedly pro-Beethovenian,[8] a change that coincided with Breitkopf and Härtel's acquisition of some of Beethoven's works for publication.

During the first years of the nineteenth century, both Beethoven (whose support network by this time contained the musically influential high aristocracy) and Breitkopf and Härtel, who acted as Beethoven's representatives, lobbied Streicher for piano reform, specifically for a bigger, more powerful instrument.[9] Breitkopf and Härtel went so far as to suggest that, from their experience, amateurs preferred a bigger tone and a heavier action (subsequently, around 1811 Breitkopf and Härtel started their own piano firm). Streicher, though he complied with this request, may have been more than a little ambivalent about it. In 1805 he wrote back to Härtel:

> I can assure you from twofold experience that a pianist can become accustomed much sooner to a poor tone, dragging, sticking of the keys and all kinds of other evils than to the heavy action and even less to the deep fall of the keys. This summer I too have manufactured some of such instruments (the action of) which, however is far from the action demanded by Mr. Clementi [i.e., the English action] and now I have every reason to regret it. To be sure, the English pianos gain an advantage over ours if we construct the keyboard

according to their way. . . . . Only it is also certain that then the fortepiano certainly will not be the universal instrument any longer, whereby at least nine-tenths of the keyboard amateurs will have to give up their playing. . . . On several instruments I have taken a middle road between light and heavy but also have been forced to leave this as well since not only local but also foreign amateurs have protested it. (quoted in Newman 1970, 498)

By around 1809, however, the Streichers had responded to the Breit-kopf and Härtel lobby. Johann Friedrich Reichardt (1753–1814), on leave from his post as court conductor to Jerome Bonaparte and touring Vienna, reports:

Streicher has abandoned the softness of the other Viennese instruments, with their too delicate touch and bouncing rolling action, and on Beethoven's advice and request has given his instruments a more resisting touch and elastic action, so that the virtuoso who executes with strength and meaning has more control of his instrument in sustaining and carrying, in the striking and releasing (of the keys). He thereby gives his instruments a stronger and more varied character, so that they should satisfy every virtuoso, who does not seek merely a light brilliance in his playing more than any other instrument. (quoted in ibid., 499)

During the years between 1796 and 1810, then, the Viennese piano at the hands of its most eminent manufacturer was restructured to be more closely aligned to Beethoven's rather idiosyncratic needs. Because of the increasing authority that Beethoven and his supporting constituencies could command, an initially private, personal concern (how to look competent in a pianistic climate that did not flatter his talent but tended to flatter that of his adversaries) could be asserted as a professional interest in structuring the climate in which all musicians worked and in the technical conditions of work. It could also be articulated as a disinterested aesthetic concern. Beethoven's increasing position in the musical world allowed him to expand his concern with piano technology from the personal to the impersonal level, from which traces of the former could be gradually erased.[10]

Meanwhile, the owner's manual that the Streicher-Stein firm first printed sometime during the late 1790s (which they had previously included with the purchase of an instrument) was dropped. Hood observes that "this may be partly because some of the mannerisms it ridiculed characterized Beethoven's aggressive and dramatic style of playing, which the seemingly clairvoyant Streichers saw as the wave of the future" (1986, 1:4).

Thus, by around 1805, after the manual was no longer in circulation and when piano reform was well under way, the positions of the "player who is unworthy of imitation but who will serve to illustrate mistakes which should be avoided" and that of the "true musical artist" were, if not reversed, far more equivocal—the light, solid, neat, and quick playing of the latter being increasingly eclipsed by the former. Pro-Beethoven values had been partially worked into the very hardware and into the means of musical production itself.

Part of what strengthened the Beethoven piano lobby was that, after around 1801, Breitkopf and Härtel stood behind the composer and, as they were the northern German brokers for Streicher pianos, they had at least a little leverage over the Streicher-Stein firm. They were not, however, originally Beethoven advocates. Not until about 1801 did the *AMZ* begin to praise Beethoven's music. When the journal did, its writers tended to praise the composer along new and different lines, which were, moreover, apparently reserved for Beethoven alone. The history of Beethoven in the *AMZ* offers yet another example of how a literary "technology" of musical life—in this case the discourse of musical criticism and aesthetic criteria—was restructured in ways that accommodated Beethoven.

The early *AMZ* criticism of Beethoven's work suggests his music was experienced by *AMZ* writers as incongruent with the categories of value they employed. In the most positive *AMZ* reviews, Beethoven's music was never discussed as "pleasing" but rather as "original" and "in a higher style," expansive terms that had the capacity to hide a multitude of what, from the perspective of eighteenth-century listeners, could be construed as stylistic flaws. The ambiguity of the term *originality* and the concept of "higher" style eventually came to serve as resources for those who wished to praise what was initially seen as Beethoven's "hard, rough" approach, while conversely, those who followed the more specifically defined criteria of lightness of texture and, in the piano performances, precision of execution, wrote Beethoven off as "harsh," "overladen with difficulties," "strange," "obstinate," or "unnatural," to choose just a few of the terms that were applied to his work. These latter criteria were dominant in Vienna of the 1790s, and this state of affairs is reflected in the first written reviews of his music.

TRANSFORMING BEETHOVEN CRITICISM IN THE *AMZ*

The *Allgemeine Musikalische Zeitung* was devoted to presenting reviews of recent music, theoretical articles, and reports from correspondents on

musical life in major European cities.[11] Its first editor was Friedrich
Rochlitz (1769–1842), a writer, amateur composer, and one-time student of theology at the Thomas School in Leipzig. The journal's views on
Beethoven were not necessarily representative of the climate of musical
opinion at large (alternative, and more explicitly critical views, appear
in other German-language culture periodicals during the first decade of
the nineteenth century); however, opinions in the *AMZ* may have carried
more weight because of the journal's initial connection to Viennese aristocratic music patrons and, in particular, to Baron van Swieten, a con-
tributor to the journal's early issues.[12]

Beethoven is first discussed in issue 23 (6 March 1799) in a brief review devoted to two sets of piano variations. Thayer has described this
article as "a perfect reflex of the conventional musical thought of the
period" (1967, 1:277). The writer[13] comments on "certain harshnesses
in modulations" and admits that whether Beethoven is as skilled a composer as he is a pianist is "difficult to affirm." Two months later in the
next review, the Piano Trio op. 11 (*AMZ* 2:34) is described as

> not easier but more flowing than many other pieces by the same author . . .
> the composer, with his unusual harmonic knowledge and love for serious
> composition would provide us many things which would leave many hand-
> organ things (simple, popular works) far in the rear, even those things com-
> posed by famous men, *if he would but try to write more naturally.* (Thayer
> and Forbes 1967, 1:277; emphasis added)

Beethoven's music was not found automatically pleasing, in the main
because of its overly "complicated" approach. Three months later, in
June 1799 (*AMZ* 1:36), in a review of the Sonatas for Violin op. 12,
these sentiments are expressed again in more detail. The critic empha-
sizes the ways Beethoven's music could be perceived as chaotic, overlearned, and a burden on the listener. Obviously this writer at least had
not yet found aesthetic categories within which Beethoven's music could
make sense and be positively evaluated:

> The critic, who heretofore has been unfamiliar with the pianoforte pieces of
> the author, must admit, after having looked through these strange sonatas,
> overladen with difficulties, that after diligent and strenuous labor he felt like
> a man who had hoped to make a promenade with a genial friend through a
> tempting forest and found himself barred every minute by inimical barriers,
> returning at last exhausted and without having had any pleasure. It is unde-
> niable that Hr. Beethoven goes his own gait; but what a bizarre and singular
> gait it is! Learned, learned and always learned—and nothing natural, no
> song. Yes, to be accurate, there is only a mass of learning here, without good
> method; obstinacy, but for which we feel but little interest; a striving for

strange modulations, an objection to customary associations, a heaping up of difficulties till one loses all patience and enjoyment. Another critic (*AMZ,* 24) has said almost the same thing, and the present writer must agree with him completely.

Nevertheless, the present work must not be rejected wholly. It has its value and may be of excellent use for already practiced pianoforte players. There are always many who love difficulties in invention and composition, what we might call perversities, and if they play these Sonatas with great precision they may derive delight in the music as well as an agreeable feeling of satisfaction. If Hr. v. B. wished to deny himself a bit more and follow the course of nature he might, with his talent and industry, do a great deal for an instrument which he seems to have so wonderfully under his control. (trans. Thayer and Forbes 1967, 1:277–78)

Closing out the year of Beethoven reviews in *AMZ* and also clarifying the initial ambivalence of the first critic with respect to Beethoven's ability as a composer, a review of the Piano Variations on a Theme by Salieri WoO 73 describes the work as "still and strained; and what awkward passages are in [it], where harsh tirades in continuous semitones create an ugly relationship. . . . No, it is true; Hr. van Beethoven may be able to improvise but he does not know how to write variations" (ibid., 278).

In these early Beethoven reviews, all of which appeared during the journal's first year (between October 1798 and September 1799), Beethoven is assessed according to norms of general taste. His works are evaluated in terms that best served musicians like Wölffl and other members of the "Mozartian school," as Czerny describes it. Filtered through these criteria, Beethoven's music could logically be classified as less than adequate and his talent could be called into question. Indeed, if these criteria had not been subsequently exchanged for other, more flattering ones, it seems fair to say that Beethoven's place in music history might have been quite different—less prominent or, at the very least, more equivocal than it became.

Four months later, however, the initial *AMZ* framework was revised. In the second issue of volume 2 (*AMZ,* 9 October 1799), an entire page is devoted to a review of the Three Piano Sonatas op. 10. The writer says, by way of praise, "It is not to be denied that Hr. v. B. is a man of genius, possessed of originality and who goes his own way. In this he is assured by his extraordinary thoroughness in the higher style of writing and his unusual command of the instrument for which he writes, he being unquestionably one of the best pianoforte composers and players of our time" (Thayer and Forbes 1967, 1:278). The writer has found a new category for Beethoven, distinct from that of composers at large: from this time on in the *AMZ*, Beethoven is described as a connoisseur's musician, and this, it appears, allows the notion of going "his own way" or "his own gait" to be reconceived as acceptable.

The critic then goes on, however, to voice reservations which, for the most part, place his review in line with those that preceded it:

> His abundance of ideas, of which a striving genius never seems to be able to let go so soon as it has got possession of a subject worthy of his fancy, only too frequently leads him to pile up his ideas, etc. Fancy, in the extraordinary degree which Beethoven possesses, supported too by his extraordinary knowledge is a valuable possession and indeed an indispensable one for a composer. The critic who after he has tried to accustom himself more and more to Hr. Beethoven's manner has learned to admire him more than he did at first, can scarcely suppress the wish that . . . it might occur to this fanciful composer to practice a certain economy in his labors. . . . This tenth collection, as the critic has said, seems deserving of high praise.

This October 1799 review (seven months after the Beethoven-Wölffl duel) provided the kinds of linguistic tools that could shift the reception of Beethoven's works from one discursive context to another. The reviewer outlines a new way of conceiving of Beethoven—a discourse in which Beethoven's "harsh" and "overlearned" compositions can be seen as worthy. At the same time, the transition is not total—the writer also wonders (rather wistfully, it seems) whether a little less "fancy" might not be all for the better. This is the first review in which a writer, for whatever reason, informs his readers that he has "tried to accustom himself more and more to Hr. Beethoven's manner" and has "learned to admire him more than he did at first." Was this writer a Beethoven advocate? It seems unlikely. A more plausible approach is to perceive him as wavering in the face of persistent musical authority from Beethoven's growing aristocratic network of sponsors, personally not overly enamored of what he calls the "higher style of writing," yet willing to acknowledge it as such, perhaps grudgingly. In any case, this is the first time in the *AMZ* (apart from the anonymous correspondent on the Beethoven-Wölffl duel) that a critic frames Beethoven's work as in any way desirable. It is also the first time that Beethoven's name is linked in a publication to the concept of "higher" music.

A NEW MODEL GAINS MOMENTUM

The first elaboration of Beethoven as a composer of "higher" music concerns the internal aesthetic unity of a piece, as opposed to an adherence to external compositional conventions. In the 19 February 1800 review of Piano Sonata op. 13, the "Pathétique" (*AMZ* 2:21, col. 373), the critic judges the piece "on its own terms," so to speak, that is, as a discontinuous "object" which, within itself, makes sense. In the context of events in the musical world at large, such a linguistic move could be a practical way of coping with Beethoven's persistence—of resolving the tension between, on the one hand, Beethoven's increasing presence in the Viennese (more particularly, aristocratic Viennese) music world and, on the other, conventional late eighteenth-century evaluative categories. It is not enough to point to the fact that the reviewers may have varied and that some would be likely to prefer Beethoven more than others. Indeed, the shift seems to be independent of the literary personnel, which suggests that something more systematic is at work.

In 1801, Breitkopf and Härtel and Beethoven began to enter into negotiations to publish some of his works. Whether or not the publishers admired Beethoven's work, it made sense for them to add Beethoven to their list of authors since, by this time, a case could be made by his supporters that, next to Haydn, Beethoven was the star of the Viennese musical world. It was probably with this in mind that Breitkopf and Härtel approached Beethoven sometime in 1800. Beethoven, however, appears to have used the publishers' interest in his work as an opportunity for encouraging them to solicit more sympathetic reviews from the *AMZ* reviewers. Thus he writes to Breitkopf and Härtel in April 1801, informing them that he is "very sorry not to be able to accept [their proposal] at the moment" (Anderson 1961, 1:48). He proceeds to outline his credentials and the ways that he is in demand as a composer by referring, in an offhand way, to other publishers who have already sought him out:

> In regard to your proposal about some of my compositions, I am very sorry not to be able to accept it at the moment. But please be so kind just to inform me what types of composition you would like to have from me, namely, symphonies, quartets, sonatas and so forth, so that I may be guided by your wishes and, should I happen to have the works you require or desire, be able to supply them. *Mollo* here is going to publish, with my consent, seven or eights works; and *Hoffmeister* in Leipzig is also publishing four works.—In this connection I merely point out that Hoffmeister is publishing *one of my first concertos,* which of course is not *one of my best compositions.* Mollo is also publishing *a concerto which was written later,* it is true, but which is also *not one of my best compositions of that type.*[14]

This passage immediately followed by a complaint (perfectly reasonable from Beethoven's point of view) about the quality of the reviews he has so far received in the pages of *AMZ:*

Let this serve merely as a hint to your Musikalische Zeitung about reviewing these works, though indeed, if one can hear them and, I should add, well performed—one can then best form an opinion— . . . Advise your reviewers to be more circumspect and intelligent, particularly in regard to the productions of younger composers. For many a one, who perhaps might go far, may take fright. As for myself, far be it from me to think that I have achieved a perfection which suffers no adverse criticism. But your reviewer's outcry against me was at first mortifying. Yet, when I began to compare myself with other composers, I could hardly bring myself to pay any attention to it but remained quite calm and said to myself: "They don't know anything about music." (Anderson 1961, 1:52–53)

Beethoven goes on in the next paragraph to praise Bach's music and the ongoing charity work in aid of J. S. Bach's only surviving child. He then offers, "How would it be if I were to publish some work by subscription for the benefit of this person and, in order to protect myself against all attacks, to inform the public of the sum collected. . . . You could do most for this object." This suggestion was a good way of further extending his reputation and contributing to a charitable cause (the cause itself well suited to dramatizing Beethoven's status as a musician devoted to the spirit of J. S. Bach—one of the few "masters" Beethoven was willing to recognize).

Thus, "at the moment" Beethoven could offer Breitkopf and Härtel none of his (highly sought-after) works, but proposed, via the Bach plan, a way that he could in the future. That Beethoven could be manipulative when it served his career should not surprise us; rather we should recognize that he was a pioneer in the use of entrepreneurial tactics in the musical field.[15] At a time when business relations were more personal and on a smaller scale than they are now, it would not have made sense for the *AMZ* to criticize, systematically, a composer published by its parent company. After 1800, as Beethoven's reputation (and circle of aristocratic admirers) continued to grow, it no doubt began to seem easier to "bend" the existing musical criteria to accommodate Beethoven than to attempt to maintain the more traditional construction that his music was inadequate (see also Wallace 1986, 9).

By May 1802 (*AMZ* 4, col. 569), the transition in aesthetic criteria was more or less complete, even to the point that the "new" aesthetic was constructed as if it were continuous with the old:

The original, fiery and intrepid spirit of this composer, which even in his early works could not escape the attention of astute observers, but which did not always find the most cordial reception, probably because it sometimes sprang forth in a manner that was ungracious, impetuous, dismal and opaque is now

becoming even clearer, ever more disdainful of all obstacles, and without losing its character, ever more pleasing. (trans. in ibid., 10)

Robin Wallace has observed in his discussion of this review that "the
tone has changed completely . . . [Beethoven] is now recognized, not only
as a gifted composer, but as a creative personality whose idiosyncrasies
are valued in their own right, for the pleasure which they can afford to
discriminating listeners" (10).[16] One month later, the new approach is
well established. An *AMZ* reviewer states: "Less educated musicians,
and those who expect nothing more from music than a facile entertainment will take up these works in vain." Only three years earlier, it must
be remembered, Beethoven's supporters had been called a "fringe"
group, "who love excessive difficulty in invention and composition; that
which one might call perverse" (ibid., 11). By 1802 the old aesthetic vocabulary had been exchanged for the new. Within the pages of the *AMZ,*
Beethoven's idiosyncrasies and previously problematic style were discussed as a "higher" form of music, aimed at a select group of listeners.
No longer portrayed as on the periphery of the music world, these listeners could now be constituted as a group at the forefront of musical taste.

CHAPTER 9

Beethoven and the Resources of Cultural Authority

On at least one occasion by 1803, Beethoven's name and reputation were apparently secure enough to take precedence over the works lodged within them. According to Beethoven's pupil Ferdinand Ries:

> I was . . . able to observe the fact that for most people the name [Beethoven] alone is sufficient for them to judge everything in a work as either beautiful and perfect or mediocre and bad. One day, tired of playing from memory I played a March just as it came into my head. . . . An old Countess went into raptures of admiration because she imagined it was a new piece by him. In order to have some amusement . . . I hastened to assure them that this was so.[1]

To Ries's embarrassment, Beethoven soon arrived at the same household, where "he then received extravagant panegyrics on his genius. . . . Later he said to me, 'look here, my dear Ries! Those are the great connoisseurs. . . . Just give them the name of their favorite: that's all they need'" (Landon 1970a, 39–40).[2]

If we are to take Ries at his word, by 1803 the cultural machinery for producing and reproducing Beethoven's genius had been assembled. Among Beethoven's ever-widening base of supporters, the name "Beethoven" had become compelling in its own right. At the same time, not everyone appreciated Beethoven's talents. To the contrary (as discussed in chapter 7), Beethoven reception appears to have grown more sharply polarized over time; his official success was constructed alongside other, competing versions of his identity.

"A relatively small group," Loesser once observed, "of accomplished amateurs, connoisseurs, snobs and romantically minded devotees of 'the grandiose' as they liked to say, were the carriers of [Beethoven's] repute; they were an official lot that could not be readily opposed. To most people, Beethoven's reputation was an article of superstition" (1954, 146). Loesser's point, though unsupported by evidence, is nevertheless suggestive. It highlights how forms of cultural authority may be privately resisted but publicly allowed to pass. This passage may be due to the fact that cultures are sponsored by individuals or groups who are culturally insulated from challenge (for example, because they have been the traditional leaders in some arena). Alternately, the social means for such challenge may be remote (for example, because potential challengers are not fluent in "appropriate" forms of discourse, or they lack the kinds of material resources necessary for a major campaign).

Because Loesser does not delve into questions of social process, he is only able to caricature the means by which Beethoven became an official success during his first decade in Vienna. That success did not derive simply from the fact that Beethoven's supporters "could not be readily opposed"; indeed, as we have seen, they were opposed. Consequently, the study of Beethoven's success and the construction of his claim to legitimacy needs to be viewed in light of the varieties of communicative media available to his supporters and opponents for constructing his artistic reputation. We should not, in other words, talk about constituencies of taste for and against Beethoven without examining the construction of a cultural, organizational, and technological environment for Beethoven's talent and its perception in Vienna.

Beethoven's claim to legitimate success and recognition became powerful because his exceptional abilities were accompanied by and interacted with a network of practices, musical-critical discourse, and music technology produced over time by Beethoven and his "support personnel"—his patrons and other musical assistants. Beethoven succeeded because a complex network was constructed and oriented to the production and perception of his talent. Opposition to Beethoven was less securely embedded in practices, in discourse, and in technology. As the aesthetic and evaluative musical climate was altered through the structuring activities of pro-Beethoven culture creators, the resources for dissent became, at least for a time, fairly remote.[3]

A discrepancy existed between the reception of Beethoven's talent (which was clearly mixed and possibly polarized) and that reception as it was publicly dramatized by those who believed (or wanted to believe) in it and who helped to ensure that it would be represented in flattering ways. The history of Beethoven's success is thus the history of a culture's creation, the formation and implementation of instruments and devices according to which an image of Beethoven as an extraordinary talent could be broadcast to various audiences. The history of Beethoven's reputation and success among his contemporaries during the late eighteenth and early nineteenth century, therefore, is the history of the *representation* of reputation, and not merely of reputation per se.

To focus on the representation of Beethoven's talent is by no means to depict Beethoven and supporters as hyperrational managers of Beethoven's image, as if they set out from the start to market Beethoven's art. I have meant neither to imply such a cynical interpretation nor to imply that Beethoven and his patrons were marketing a "finished product." Such an account oversimplifies the complex social processes I have described; it also tends to evade the ways in which Beethoven's own artistic activities, his self-perception, and the elaboration of a supportive climate for his reception interacted over time.

In retrospect, Beethoven's talent is viewed in ways that highlight its "extraordinary" quality. But in the making, it was accumulated gradually, practically, and unremarkably, in time and space, neither preordained nor planned in its entirety. To suggest that his success, and the particular configuration of music history to which it gave rise, was the result of his music alone and not of the interaction of that music with its context of reception is to employ a retrospective fallacy: it is to see the events of the past through the wrong end of the telescope, accepting the belief that the past inevitably "leads" to present circumstances. Surely this is an impoverished conception of history.

BEETHOVEN IN THE 1790s AND BEYOND

Without doubt, Beethoven survives today not simply because of his initial success among his Viennese contemporaries,[4] but because the model forged during these years of Beethoven as a prototypically serious composer was discovered as a cultural resource and elaborated by subsequent musicians and music entrepreneurs.[5] Certainly one line of future research (which would shed further light on the issue of the canonic ideology and on the emergence of Beethoven's international reputation) would be a comparative study of Beethoven reception in diverse geographical and historical contexts during the years after 1805. There has been some work done on this topic: Leo Schrade's 1910 classic on Beethoven in France, William S. Newman's consideration of the origins of the "Beethoven mystique" (1983), and, more recently, James Johnson's reexamination of Beethoven reception in France (1991).[6] The importance of Beethoven's first decade in Vienna to his subsequent and posthumous reputation must not be exaggerated. At the same time, Beethoven's initial rise provided a cultural resource for the social transformation of high culture musical aesthetics, repertory, and programming practice during the early nineteenth century. In my consideration of these issues I have stayed close to the level of social action; I would hope that subsequent work on the construction of Beethoven's reputation would move further afield to consider the cultural context more broadly and, in particular, to focus on the ways that literary culture, political ideas and philosophy were implicated in this process. At present we know little about the culturally constructed subjectivity of Beethoven's patrons.

BEETHOVEN, THE CONSTRUCTION OF GENIUS, AND THE RELATIVITY OF VALUE

Little has been written about genius as a social construction. The ideology of genius—that some individuals are endowed with extraordinary gifts enabling them to penetrate and radically transform the logic of their particular intellectual creative field—remains powerful and persuasive in spite of attempts to deconstruct it. The belief, for example, that we know greatness when we see it is a pervasive part of our common sense. Genius continues to be shrouded in mystery. One academic writer has suggested that "no amount of analysis has yet been able to explain the capacities of those rare and gifted individuals who can produce creative work of lasting quality and value" (Murray 1989, 1). It is perhaps not surprising, therefore, that ethnographically and historically grounded explorations of genius as socially constructed have not yet been produced.[7]

Throughout this book, I have tried to illustrate how conventional ways of accounting for Beethoven's success through reference to his individual and charismatic "gift" elide the complex and collaborative processes of mobilizing resources, presentation devices, and practical activities that produced Beethoven's cultural authority. Accounts of Beethoven's success that focus on his talent inappropriately employ a language of attribution, which is an impoverished way of talking, one that obscures the social context in which his identity was initially produced.

We cannot point to Beethoven's "originality" as an explanatory factor for Beethoven's success. To say that Beethoven's music is "better" because it is more original makes a tautological argument: it misses a crucial sociological point—namely, that to recognize something as original is to recognize it as located somewhat outside of (and possibly commenting on) conventional criteria of one kind or another. For difference or "originality" to be valued, it has to be recognized as being aligned with "different" criteria. If this alignment is not recognized, difference risks being perceived as "misdirection" or "nonsense" or "off the mark." To be sure, nearly all of Beethoven's contemporaries perceived his work as "different" and many described it as "original." No automatic connection was made, however, from this perception to the valuing of Beethoven's works, to ranking Beethoven above his contemporaries. That connection had to be *made* by Beethoven and his contemporaries. The reviews of op. 12 (remarking on Beethoven's "bizarre and singular" manner) published in 1799—by which time Beethoven's initial reputation as a "genius" was being consolidated—or the mixed reception of op. 10 (where Beethoven is simultaneously described as a "genius" and "original" and criticized for being overly complex—make the initial equivocality of Beethoven's talent clear. In the 1790s, musical "originality" was not automatically equated with musical value.

To say "it could have been otherwise"—that, for example, there could have been a musical-aesthetic world in which Beethoven's works and reputation would not have "blossomed"—or to say that one can imagine a world in which other types of creative products might be valued more highly is not to say that now, in subsequent musical contexts, alternatives *are* equally valid. The point of this study has been to show precisely the opposite: to describe how a particular musical-evaluative context was cultivated and how this process resulted in making particular types of evaluative tools readily available as "legitimate" musical evaluative categories. Within modern musicological circles, it is quite difficult to construct a convincing argument that the music of Wölffl, for instance, is "better" than Beethoven's, even though some of Beethoven's contemporaries suggested just that. To ask, Who is a genius? or What factors "cause" or inculcate genius? is to travel to the topic with too much a priori baggage. Such an attitude fails to recognize how, in invoking the very category "genius," we presume a hierarchy of talent, as if this distribution existed outside of our attempts to frame questions about it. In this sense, asking who the geniuses are presumes a particular type of hierarchical social organization.

It is an existential fact of life that the social institutions, discourses, and disciplines which enable us to live and communicate with each other simultaneously perpetrate symbolic violence: what is facilitating for some may be constraining for others. Recognizing this double nature of conventions enlivens us to the micro- and macropolitical consequences of matters of taste, talent, and value. Writing about Jan Ladislav Dussek's father, the eighteenth-century music historian Charles Burney alluded to these issues when he invoked a line from Thomas Gray's "Elegy Written in a Country Churchyard" ("Chill penury repressed his noble rage"). The poem's message as it unfolds in the following quatrain is also worth recalling:

> Full many a gem of purest ray serene
> The dark unfathomed caves of ocean bear
> Full many a flower born is born to blush unseen,
> and waste its sweetness on the desert air.

There is much more to learn about how value and extraordinary ability emerge as recognizably "real" entities. We can continue to add to our knowledge by following, as they unfold, the processes through which value is assembled. To do so may lead to a richer awareness of the social bases and social uses of identity. We will understand more about how some individuals become lodged within preferred identities, while there remain others to whom entry is denied.

Notes

CHAPTER 1: BEETHOVEN AND SOCIAL IDENTITY

1. Beethoven's early letters from Vienna to members of his Bonn circle also attest to this. See, for example, Anderson 1961, vol. 1, no. 12, in which Beethoven refers, ostensibly, to his eventual return. This was in 1794. There is no reason to doubt, however, that Beethoven was simultaneously attempting to establish himself on a more permanent basis in Vienna, especially because, after the military victories of the neighboring French in 1794 and the dissolution of the electorate, Beethoven's salary was discontinued. It seems plausible that Beethoven began to explore the possibility of a more permanent career in Vienna around this time, if not before.

2. In particular, see work by the historian William Weber (1986) and the sociologist Paul DiMaggio (1982).

3. Even Mozart was celebrated during the early part of the nineteenth century primarily as an opera composer, whereas Beethoven's name alone provided the binding force for disparate genres (Morrow 1989).

4. Some literary and ethnomethodologically inclined critics may suggest that this history was not "made" by the actors who populate my account, but rather that it is made in and through the textual practices of my account. I do not dispute this claim; however, I believe that the counternarrative I provide of Beethoven's success has helped to rescue certain events and documentary sources sidestepped by more conventional musical historical narratives of Beethoven. I therefore do not propose my account as an ontological "advance" on other versions but as a tool with which to promote an alternative way of viewing Beethoven's career, a project which I believe to be a necessary part of the wider deconstruction of what Pierre Bourdieu has referred to as the "charismatic ideology"—the belief that some individuals succeed and are recognized as special because they "possess" an inherent (and thus inalienable and inexplicable) "gift."

5. For a different case study of the ways in which musical reception may be politically mediated, see Pasler 1987b.

6. See Newman 1983 and Comini 1987 for discussions of the Beethoven mystique and Beethoven imagery in the plastic arts.

7. For discussions of this issue as it applies to sociology of the arts, see Griswold 1987 and Radway 1984.

8. For a more detailed discussion of these issues and a critique of the cultural constructivist position, see DeNora and Mehan 1993.

CHAPTER 2: THE EMERGENCE OF
SERIOUS MUSIC CULTURE, 1784–1805

1. For information on Mozart's concertizing see Moore 1991. Press references to Mozart can be found in Deutsch 1965; compilations of "all the available documents relevant to Mozart's life" (Deutsch 1965, vii), with the exception of his letters, are published separately (see Anderson 1938).

2. See, for example, Sadie 1980, King 1955, Olleson 1967, and DeNora 1991, and see Braunbehrens's comment (1989, 497n.): "Every Mozart biography concludes from this remark that the composer had lost his public in Vienna; this seems to me a very arbitrary interpretation."

3. Deutsch's documentation has been supplemented in Eisen 1991.

4. Of course, it is not possible to say definitely that Zinzendorf was bored *by* the opera or that he was simply bored, as he says, *at* the opera, perhaps for some other reason. In the context of his diary overall, and given the social role opera attendance played in Viennese society, Zinzendorf's boredom may have arisen for nonmusical reasons (Dexter Edge, personal communication).

5. Dexter Edge, personal correspondence.

6. See, for example, discussions in *Magyar Hirmondo, Der Himliche Botschafter,* and *Prague Neue Zeitung,* all reprinted in Deutsch 1965, 467.

7. Quoted in *Allgemeine Musikalische Zeitung* (1801) and in Wallace 1986, 11.

8. This list has been compiled from several archival studies of Viennese concert life, including Schönfeld's *Jahrbuch* of 1796. It has also been cross-checked with lists of Beethoven's dedicatees, with a list of the subscribers to Beethoven's Piano Trios op. 1 (Landon 1970a, 64–65), diaries, letters, and musical memoirs of foreign travelers in Vienna during this time (Anderson 1961; Rosenbaum 1968; Burney 1775; Bright 1818; Gardiner 1838), and with Constantin Wurzbach's *Biographisches Lexikon des Kaiserthums Oesterreich 1750–1850,* as well as with other music historical studies less specifically focused on aristocratic patrons (Hanson 1985; Stekl 1973; Thayer and Forbes 1967; A. Schindler 1966; Jahn 1882).

9. Van Swieten was also the librettist for Haydn's *Seasons* and *Creation.*

10. Olleson adds, "It has to be faced that, for all his good qualities, van Swieten was a bore." (225)

11. See, for example, DiMaggio 1982, Levine 1988, Sennett 1978, W. Weber 1986.

12. In this context, the term *public* does not refer exclusively to concerts

open to anyone who could afford or cared to attend, but also refers to quasi-public subscription series and to concerts which were larger than most private ones and which were held in a theater or hall rather than in a private dwelling (there were no purposely built concert halls in Vienna until 1831).

13. Counting repeated concerts and also counting the number of times a composer is featured on a given concert program, more than one hundred performances of Haydn's works are listed in Morrow's (1989) concert calendar, over eighty each of works by Mozart and Beethoven. No other composer was performed with anywhere near this frequency. The fourth most frequently performed composer listed in Morrow's calendar is Ferdinando Par, whose music was performed about half as frequently as any one of these three. The number of Haydn, Mozart, and Beethoven performances listed could be merely an artifact of selective record keeping and data preservation on the part of later, nineteenth-century scholars; this does not, however, appear to have been the case (which does not negate the magnification of these composers to star status by retrospective scholarly practice). First of all, many of these concert program announcements were preserved at the time of issue in theater archives (though there are gaps during which all sources are missing). Second, and this is the case for the middle-class theater in Leopoldstadt as well as for the Theater an der Wien, theater record keeping is buttressed by diaries kept by theater kapellmeisters. Third, other contemporaries noted that Haydn, Mozart, and Beethoven had star status over and above their fellow musicians (see, for example, Schönfeld, if only for the amount of space he accorded to these three in 1796). Morrow may be over-confident in suggesting that "the preservation of source material seems to have been largely random, so that, except for a few cases that have been noted, the resulting data is not obviously weighted toward any one composer or genre" (1989, 148). The star status of Haydn, Mozart, and Beethoven does not appear to be an artifact of preservation biases.

14. Even if the number of performances given during 1808 are discounted, however, Beethoven still ranks as the third most performed composer during this period.

15. See Morrow (1989, 347–52) for concert details for 1808.

16. George Frederick Handel (who, at this time was seen within the serious music ideology as the Shakespeare of music) began to appear on Theater an der Wien concert programs only after 1806, when its affairs were directed by "serious" music aficionados.

17. Zinzendorf, for example, occasionally attended performances at the Leopoldstadt theater (Dexter Edge, personal correspondence), as did members of the Liechtenstein family (see Moore 1987).

18. Because relatively few Leopoldstadt concert programs survive, generalizations about the repertory there must remain speculative.

19. During the eighteenth century, symphonies were typically programmed at the beginning and end of concerts, which has led Zazlaw (1989) and Edge (personal communication) to suggest that the symphony was considered a less important genre. If these critics are correct in their speculation, it is possible that the Universitätssaal and other GAC-controlled concerts helped to redefine the role of the symphony by shifting its status closer to our modern notion of it as a

"major" genre. Also see Morrow's discussion of the consensus within the musical critical press that concerts at the Leopoldstadt were of generally low quality (1989, 215, 156–57, 84). Morrow here views genre through twentieth-century lenses, though elsewhere she is at pains to avoid projecting modern analytical categories on eighteenth-century musical life.

CHAPTER 3: MUSICAL PATRONAGE AND SOCIAL CHANGE

1. Dexter Edge, personal communication.

2. These ensembles were linked to individual patrons rather than family dynasties and therefore were continually formed and disbanded during this period (see Abbott and Hrycak 1990). My concern is with the proliferation of the custom of maintaining such ensembles and the eventual decline of this pattern.

3. Concert organization is an area about which we are still learning, and Thayer's "overview" is perhaps premature.

4. This decline was due to hyperinflation, which began in 1796; see the consumer price index in Moore 1987 (245a, b, c) and the data on average annual discounts against the silver gulden for the *bankozettel* (bank notes) (ibid., 123).

5. He founded a kapelle in 1802 and, according to Countess Lulu von Thurheim, "from morn to night he was occupied by music and squandered a large fortune in order to maintain the most outstanding musicians. . . . He died quite young and left his seven small children nothing but a load of debts" (Landon 1970a, 155).

6. We need to bear in mind that Schönfeld was himself an elevated member of the middle class and therefore may have had reasons for including a sizable proportion of middle-class patrons on his list (friends and acquaintances, for example, whom he felt he should mention in print)—a way of giving such members social prominence, listed, as they were, alongside members of the high aristocracy.

7. The average rate for annual ennoblements was 25 for the years 1701–39, 36 for 1740–80, 40 for 1781–89, 66 for 1790–91, and 47 for 1792–1835 (Moore 1987, 76).

8. This was the case in London, which was large enough to support a number of different musical worlds; in the smaller cathedral cities new and old music was often performed on the same programs (David Wyn Jones, personal communication).

9. See Morrow 1989 for a sampling of some of these practices. Beethoven's performances overlapped with this world at least once when he met the so-called charlatan pianist Daniel Steibelt, who was known for pieces such as his "Storm Rondo," which included accompaniment by his wife on tambourine.

CHAPTER 4: BEETHOVEN'S SOCIAL RESOURCES

1. Haydn particularly admired Dussek's work (the two became close friends while Haydn was in London). Haydn went so far as to write to Dussek's father: "You have one of the most upright, moral, and, in music most eminent of men

for a son. I love him just as you do, for he fully deserves it. Give him, then, daily, a father's blessing, and thus will he be ever fortunate, which I heartily wish him to be, for his remarkable talents" (trans. Craw 1964, 429).

2. Beethoven's father had hoped to capitalize on his son as a child prodigy, a second Mozart, although the effort was not successful. This may have been why he appears to have misrepresented Beethoven's age (he reported Ludwig as being two years younger than he actually was). See Solomon 1977a and Thayer and Forbes 1967 on this.

3. The line Burney quotes is taken from Thomas Gray's "Elegy Written in a Country Churchyard" (see chapter 9).

4. See Solomon (1977a, 69), who suggests that Haydn introduced Beethoven to Countess von Thun, the Erdödy family, Prince Nikolaus Esterhazy, Ignaz Pleyel, Krumpholz, Anton Kraft, one of the Wranitzskys, and Ignaz von Seyfried.

5. Dussek was frequently his own publisher during these years, having become partner with his father-in-law (forming Dussek and Corri), so the question of whether the framing of these pieces was his or his publisher's idea is not relevant. Most pertinent here is the London musical climate; when Dussek subsequently returned to the continent this particular mode of framing his pieces became less common.

6. Many of the descriptive titles given to Beethoven's pieces (for example, "Spring" sonata, "Tempest") were given by others and later on.

7. Beethoven could not so easily do so later on. After 1807, when he began to feel the effects of Viennese hyperinflation, he arranged 132 folk songs for George Thomson (secretary to the board of trustees for the Encouragement of Arts and Manufactures in Scotland), who paid him exceptionally well. Included were "Charlie Is My Darling," "Paddy O'Rafferty," "The Damsels of Cardigan," and "Annie in Our Alley." Beethoven did not read or speak English, and these arrangements were made with no knowledge of the songs' subject matter.

8. Beethoven's earliest piano sonatas, of course, were written for either piano or harpsichord. Although he did write several piano variations—an openly popular genre—during these years, they were often criticized for being overly learned.

9. Sadly, the journalists paid no attention, writing two years later that Wölffl's flute sonata was "just the kind of sonata that second rate dilettantes, *especially the English,* will want" (cited in Loesser 1954, 231; emphasis added). There was a similar pressure on English publishers as well. The firm of Longman and Broderip, whose catalogue leaned toward the serious and more complex forms of music, eventually went bankrupt (ibid.).

CHAPTER 5: "FROM HAYDN'S HANDS"

1. I have confined my consideration of the Beethoven-Haydn account here to the years before 1796, because 1796 marked Beethoven's official "arrival" as a significant Viennese-based musician-composer. In this chapter, I am interested in how accounts of Beethoven's relation to Haydn provided a resource for initial claims of Beethoven's special talent and promise at the time of embarking on his Viennese career.

2. I am grateful to David Wyn Jones for information on Haydn's international reception during the early 1790s.

3. We see a more neutral version of this notion worked out in Neefe's comment of the same year for Spazier's *Berliner Musik-Zeitung*. Neefe describes Beethoven as "one of the foremost pianoforte players [who] went to Vienna at the expense of our Elector to Haydn in order to perfect himself under his direction more fully in the art of composition" (Thayer and Forbes 1967, 1:113).

4. The purpose of this letter was (ostensibly) to describe Beethoven's progress over the past year.

5. As I implied in chapter 4, Bonn was one of the major German-speaking centers, outside Vienna, of aristocratic culture.

6. We know that at least one foreign observer (the Swedish diplomat Frederik Samuel Silverstolpe) described Beethoven in 1796 as the musician who "passes for the greatest performer on the piano" (Landon 1976–80, 4:38).

7. Unlike today, musical activity was by no means a peripheral part of aristocratic and political life. Diplomacy was often conducted in part through musical connections (e.g., van Swieten's Berlin post appears to have been won because of his musical ability; see Olleson 1967).

8. See Frau von Berhnard's recollection in Landon 1970a.

9. Mozart wrote to his father in the 1780s, however, that he thought Ignaz Pleyel—Haydn's student in the 1780s—would become the "next Haydn" (Anderson 1938, 3:875).

10. The quartet became Count Razumovsky's resident ensemble in 1808 (it had previously been patronized by Prince Lichnowsky).

11. The only English-language source on Struck is Lonn 1980.

12. According to Landon (1976–80, 4:336), Hänsel may not have begun lessons with Haydn until 1795.

13. Pleyel had been a Haydn pupil during the 1770s and perhaps, apart from Beethoven, can be counted as the most successful of Haydn's students.

14. The pupil in question may have been Struck or Neukomm, since Silverstolpe may have been more likely to have dropped in on a lesson of a pupil whom he was actively patronizing. Although Landon does not speculate on the identity of the pupil in his discussion of the incident (see 1976–80, 4:335), Silverstolpe had some sort of contact with Struck (both were Swedish and, as has been mentioned earlier, according to Lonn 1980, Struck went to Stockholm on Silverstolpe's recommendation). Silverstolpe was also acquainted with Neukomm: in 1806 Haydn wrote to Silverstolpe (Landon 1959, 242), thanking him for a present of tea and passed on greetings to Neukomm ("Please be good enough, *Monsieur,* to give my kind regards to our good Neukomm; I most sincerely wish him all the success which his talent and his character deserve"). On the other hand, since Silverstolpe says he did not know the student's name or what eventually became of him, the pupil seems more likely to have been Lessel, Spech, or Hänsel. The pupil in question was definitely not Beethoven, who was by this time no longer a pupil of Haydn.

15. The social psychology of the relationship between famous teacher and pupil remains relatively unexplored. One area for future research would focus on how being identified as a pupil of a prestigious teacher (or a pupil under some

other prestigious auspice) may boost a pupil's faith in her or his own talent, which may in turn serve as a resource for that pupil's ability to create, not only for practical reasons (e.g., association with a famous teacher may relieve the student of the need to publicize and dramatize his or her abilities) but also because of the confidence and energy for work that prestigious auspices help to construct. Because of these auspices, a pupil may be more likely to pursue vaguely formulated ideas with conviction.

16. *Österreichische Monatsschrift,* 1794 (trans. Landon 1976–80, 3:226). At this point, Haydn had become a vehicle for national identity and a symbol of Vienna's musical greatness as projected abroad.

17. Consequently, even these larger works could be disseminated to wider audiences, amateurs could reproduce them at home on a domestic scale, and, equally important, the pieces could be sold as sheet music and thus provide a source of income.

18. See also David Wyn Jones's introduction to the collected Haydn folksong settings (Haydn 1984).

19. Griesinger acted as a go-between for Haydn and Breitkopf and Härtel, Haydn's Leipzig publishers.

20. In a testimonial for the more senior composer Emanuel Aloys Förster in 1791, however, the imperial court official Augustinus Erasmus Donath wrote, "As regards his skill in keyboard-playing the late, great master Mozard has often publicly averred to the said Herr Förster, both in my presence and that of others, that the latter was certainly the strongest and most skillful master of the keyboard after himself. Further, all musicians grant that the said Herr Förster can, in the art of composition, justly be placed between Hayden and Mozard" (Deutsch 1965, 419). Förster never became recognized as "great" in the sense that Beethoven was, however; he became one of Beethoven's devotees, and his descriptions of hearing Beethoven play often assume a quasi-religious tone.

21. See Dies [1810] 1968, 264n. 136, by Gotwals; see also Landon 1976–80, 4:503, for a further discussion of Beethoven and Haydn's deteriorating relationship.

22. See Berger 1981 for a more general discussion of the interrelationship between ideals and practical circumstances and how individuals engage in forms of "ideological work" to align the ideal with the practical.

23. For good introductory discussions of conversation analysis and the importance of a turn at talk, see Heritage 1984; for a specific consideration of the story in conversation, see Davis 1989.

24. The notion of "floor" (which, in face-to-face interaction, refers to an actual turn at talk) can also be employed as an analytical device for following textual accounts. In this sense, a floor is any attended location where accounts can be deployed. The floor is invoked and located through specific turns at talk.

25. Harold Garfinkel's classic work (1967) on the uses of the documentary method (such as his famous "therapy experiment") also illustrates this point: sense-making practices occur within the bounds of particular events and thereby "realize" these events as sensible, reasonable, natural, accountable instances of the social world. The subjects in the therapy experiment, for example, did the "work" of producing a coherent and orderly therapy event, one in which it

seemed "as if" the "advice" they were being given was rationally motivated rather than, as was the case, offered at random.

CHAPTER 6: BEETHOVEN IN THE SALONS

1. Carl was the son of the musician Wenzel Czerny, at whose house a group of musicians including Beethoven gathered in the 1790s. Czerny's observations of the Viennese music world (and especially the various debates over musical stylistic issues) are particularly helpful, as his playing straddled two schools of pianistic thought, Hummelian and Beethovenian. Czerny was Beethoven's pupil and later the teacher of Beethoven's nephew Karl, though after around 1810, he was more closely associated with the anti-Beethovenian, Hummelian style.

2. Thurheim's memoirs are punctuated with other, even more negative remarks about the Lichnowskys (Thurheim appears to have been, in comparison to the Lichnowskys, aesthetically, socially, and morally more conservative). In reference to Prince Lichnowsky's extramarital sexual relations, she said, "He, a cynical rake and a shameless coward, would have deserved to be cuckolded. In my opinion, people of this kind are beyond the pale" (Landon 1970a, 67).

3. The Zinzendorf diary is one of the few extant diaries of an aristocrat living in Vienna during this time. It is an invaluable resource to music scholars because Zinzendorf regularly listed the music events he attended. It has not yet been published, although excerpts from it have appeared in Olleson 1963–64 and Morrow 1989.

4. See the list of Beethoven's residences by year in the main index of Thayer and Forbes 1967, s.v. "Beethoven: residences." Beethoven rarely remained in a residence for long and appears to have moved far more often than most of his contemporaries.

5. Wegeler (Wegeler and Ries 1987, 32) says Beethoven was still there in mid-1796.

6. These salon concerts provided Beethoven's primary forum from 1795 to 1798. He was involved in only thirteen public concerts in Vienna during his entire career; eleven of these are listed in Solomon (1977a, 59), and Moore has discovered another two (personal correspondence).

7. There were, of course, many more pianists in Vienna at this time than are listed here, both amateur and professional (there are forty-nine listed in Morrow's concert calendar, while the *Allgemeine Musikalische Zeitung* estimated that there were three hundred piano *teachers* in Vienna). I have listed only those who were considered by Beethoven and his contemporaries to be serious rivals and/or influences. I have not listed those professional-caliber amateurs who were not occupational musicians, though dilettante musicians formed an important mainstay of musical life in late eighteenth-century Vienna, at a time when there was less of a distinction between professional and amateur. The group of dilettante pianists during these years included numerous women pianists who were well known in their day and who should be studied separately; they constitute an important and often neglected segment of Viennese musical life.

8. I describe the piano contest as a type of musical event in chapter 7. Beethoven engaged in later contests with Wölffl and Steibelt.

9. Beethoven also wrote piano variations, especially at the start of his career, often for aristocratic women.

10. See Thayer and Forbes 1967, 1:160: ". . . with all the hardness and heaviness of manipulation caused by his devotion to the organ."

11. "Relatively" finite because the corpus can always and at least potentially be revised in light of new discoveries, redating, and authentication, as has most recently been the case in the controversy over Barry Cooper's "reconstruction" of the first movement of Beethoven's "10th symphony" and, more recently, of Beethoven's "symphony" of 1796.

12. Leo Treitler (1991) develops a similar argument.

13. I am not suggesting that we do not share a culture with Beethoven's contemporaries, but simply that we cannot accept in any a priori way that we do. On this point, see Shapin and Shaeffer 1986, chap. 1. Historians, they suggest, "produc[e] accounts that are colored by the member's self-evident method. In this method the presuppositions of our own culture's routine practices are not regarded as problematic and in need of explanation. . . . [They] start with the assumption that they (and modern scientists) share a culture with Robert Boyle, and treat their subject accordingly: the historian and the seventeenth-century experimentalist are both members" (5).

14. For a more thorough discussion of the theoretical basis of these points, see DeNora 1986.

15. This assumption is by no means clear (Bruce A. Brown, personal correspondence).

16. Music scholars could benefit from discussions within sociology of science. For example, Bruno Latour's (1987) programmatic statement of "science in action" describes how the relationship between scientific artifacts and their social "content" can be explored without "black boxing" either artifacts or social content/context. Instead he suggests the relationship be explored "in the making" and in terms of the various practices and resources mobilized for its construction. See also DeNora n.d.b.

17. This argument is also advanced in somewhat different form within the musicological field by scholars whose sympathies lie with social historical models (see Lenneberg 1988; Treitler 1991).

18. I do not mean to suggest that interpretive readings of music are not of interest for their own sake—they clearly are for music appreciation and hagiography.

19. For a basic introduction to current sociology of science and technology, see Woolgar 1988 or Latour and Woolgar 1987. Within sociology of science and technology, criticism is usually made along the following lines: formalisms are flawed because they are unaware of their own selective processes, of how future ways of conceptualizing an object are implicated in the choice of a particular technical approach and of how the choice of a particular analytical mode is bounded by a variety of unexamined factors.

20. This discourse also allows nonmusic specialists to explore music's social meaning. I exploit this loophole: I do not offer any discussion (informed by twentieth-century music theoretical notions of form) about how Beethoven's early compositions did or did not "deviate" from standard Viennese practice.

For readers who are interested, there are many studies from which to draw. See, for example, the excellent studies by Douglas Johnson, Rosen, Lockwood, Blom, Tovey, Newman, Ratner, Ringer, Tyson, Kerman, and Winter.

21. Née von Kissow; she was in Vienna from 1796 to 1800 and lived at the home of a Russian embassy secretary.

22. Streicher is discussed later; he was the husband of the piano maker Nannette Stein and manager of Streicher Geburt Stein, Vienna's premier piano firm.

23. See Czerny's *Vollständige theoretisch-praktische Pianoforte Schule* (*Complete Theoretical and Practical Piano Course*), translated and quoted in Landon 1970a.

24. See Wegeler and Ries 1987, 75: "During his first stay in Vienna, Beethoven had received some lessons from Mozart but, he complained, Mozart had never played for him." There is, however, no record in Mozart's letters or in any of the materials handed down by his wife after his death that Mozart had contact with Beethoven. As the visit to which Ries refers was brief, it is possible that Beethoven's contact with Mozart was negligible. At the same time, it seems reasonable to assume that Beethoven did hear Mozart play, either at a salon or at a public concert.

25. During the second decade of the nineteenth century, a similar problem was solved in France. Schrade ([1910] 1978) argues that, for the idea of Beethoven to be made appealing, the French conception of Mozart had to be reformed, to be separated from the idea of bel canto (Mozart was seen as the forerunner of Rossini). For Beethoven to be seen as something other than "ugly Germanism," a darker aspect of Mozart's music had to be discovered and used as a bridge.

26. The fortepiano was still a relatively new instrument. It had not yet replaced the harpsichord, and it was owned mostly by old and new aristocrats because, in Vienna, it was expensive. See DeNora 1991, 336, and Edge (n.d.), who develops and refines these points.

27. It is worth noting, incidentally, that this passage hints at the possible linkage of Streicher's interest in the survival of his instruments to a moderate pianistic approach and hence a relatively unobtrusive visual display of skill ("no one is even aware"): the effect is smooth and delicate; the pianist would have looked rather like a good typist.

28. Foreign virtuosi and new musicians were always of interest at this time, even as values for old music were being clarified. Contemporary Viennese commentators on the music scene noted that newcomers and visitors were both welcomed by the music public and shunned by local musicians.

29. Landon has discovered that Beethoven made his public debut in 1795 at the elder Prince Lobkowitz's house from a previously unknown entry in Count Zinzendorf's diary, "De la au Concert du Prince Lobkowitz, ou un nomé Bethofen du Bonn fit tous sentir" (see Landon 1976–80, 3:294). The Burgtheater concert was the first fully public debut, however, as it was the first time Beethoven appeared in a public concert venue rather than a private home.

30. The concert took place on 29 March 1795. Beethoven played his piano concerto, later published as op. 19 (see Morrow 1989, 323).

31. Wegeler (1765–1848) was a friend of Beethoven's during his Bonn years,

becoming acquainted with him around 1782. He moved to Vienna in 1794 after the French invaded Bonn, and he remained in Vienna for two years.

32. Ferdinand Ries (1784–1838), also a member of the Bonn kapelle, came to Vienna in 1801. He studied piano with Beethoven and music theory with Albrechtsberger, and in 1805 he toured France, England, Scandinavia, and Russia. In 1813 Ries moved to London, where he was instrumental in making Beethoven's works known to the London public via his connection to the newly formed London Philharmonic.

33. The Baron Nikolaus Zmeskall von Domanowitz (1759–1833) was an official of the Hungarian court chancellery and a fairly close friend of Beethoven's in Vienna.

34. The contract is translated and reprinted in MacArdle and Misch (1957, 15–17) as document #13.

35. Moore (1987) considers the evidence and provides three possible sums Beethoven may have earned.

36. Beethoven seems to have made a substantial profit from the sales of this work (see Moore 1987)—about two years of his Bonn stipend.

37. The list is reproduced in Landon 1970a, 64–65.

38. This is a good point at which to speculate on the role aristocratic family rivalry may have played in music patronage. Families could cooperate to launch a particular musician whom they could take credit for (a carryover from the days of private kapelles). The Waldstein, Razumovsky, and Lichnowsky families were tied together via the Thuns: Waldstein was Countess von Thun's nephew and Razumovsky and Lichnowsky were sons-in-law. The kinship ties between these patrons should be explored in greater detail; it is possible that status of family (vis-à-vis other aristocratic families), as opposed to old aristocrats versus new, or aristocrats versus non aristocrats, is another relevant social category for explaining music patronage.

39. Beethoven's compositions for this event were subsequently published by Artaria, whose advertisement in the *Wiener Zeitung* said that they were, "as is well known, received with applause" (Landon 1970a, 69).

40. In a recent study, Jürgen May (1994) has suggested that the Lichnowsky-Beethoven tour followed the same route as the earlier Lichnowsky-Mozart one because of a Masonic concern for following in the footsteps of an earlier journey.

41. While on this tour Beethoven also began what was to become his ten-year lobby (via his requests to Streicher) for piano reform.

42. See W. Weber 1975, Sennett 1978, Forsyth 1985, and Raynor 1972, as well as specific contemporary accounts too numerous to mention here. For a discussion of how such changes occurred in America (Boston specifically) and their sociological significance, see DiMaggio 1982.

CHAPTER 7: THE BEETHOVEN-WÖLFFL PIANO DUEL

1. For detailed considerations of concert life and music reception during the 1780s and/or 1790s, see Zazlaw 1989; Edge 1992, n.d.; Morrow 1989; and Moore 1987, n.d.b.

2. This comparison comes up again in 1803 during the debate over Beethoven's ballet *The Creatures of Prometheus*.

3. Dolezalek (1780–1858) was a cellist who met Beethoven in 1800.

4. "Guerre des Buffons" refers to the debate over the respective merits of French and Italian opera that occurred in Paris during the middle of the eighteenth century. Rousseau's position, on the side of Italian *opere buffe* (depicted as the more natural style), became the forefront of advanced opinion on the subject.

5. The ballet was performed fourteen times in 1801 and nine times in 1802.

6. Interest in contrapuntal music during the 1760s and 1770s in Vienna appears to have transcended social background (Dexter Edge, personal correspondence).

7. He also appears to have indicated interest in supporting Beethoven, insofar as he was a subscriber to the Artaria publication of Beethoven's Piano Trios op. 1.

8. Count Moritz von Fries was the only second-society member to be counted as a near equal to Vienna's old aristocrats (see Moore n.d.b.).

9. I am grateful to Else Radant Landon (personal correspondences) for providing this information on the various Schönfeld families living in Vienna during the late eighteenth century.

10. Alice M. Hanson (1983) has documented how musical life in Schubert's Vienna was also characterized by separate social/musical worlds.

11. Two eighteenth-century Viennese diaries, one middle class (Rosenbaum's) and one aristocratic (Zinzendorf's), also support this hypothesis. Rosenbaum and Zinzendorf appear to have conducted entirely distinct musical lives, overlapping only at public performances.

12. Bridgetower's limited access to aristocratic circles may have been related to the fact that he was black. Race and ethnicity, like gender, have so far been underexamined topics in the history of high culture music (Julia Moore, personal correspondence).

CHAPTER 8: BEETHOVEN'S EARLY AESTHETIC CAMPAIGNS

1. The changes that Beethoven tried to effect during these early years had little to do with his subsequent deafness. Later on, as his hearing deteriorated, Beethoven did make requests for unusually loud instruments, but his involvement with piano technology during the years discussed in this book was related to his musical preferences and habits, his problems, and the particular projects he focused on.

2. I am grateful to Margaret Hood for calling this fact to my attention (personal communication).

3. The instrumental parts to much of the music of the late seventeenth and early eighteenth centuries were well within the grasp of the amateur performer; during the nineteenth century, this was less often the case.

4. See Beethoven's November 1802 letter to Nikolaus Zmeskall (at the time, Beethoven was attempting to get a piano from the Walter firm at a good price): "The whole tribe of pianoforte manufacturers have been swarming around me

in their anxiety to serve me—and all for nothing. Each of them wants to make me a pianoforte exactly as I should like it. . . . I can have pianofortes for nothing from [them]" (Anderson 1961, 1:82).

5. It may have been that Streicher's own business interests were served through Beethoven during these years. Although he omits any reference to his sources, Arthur Loesser claims that

> advertising in Vienna was . . . subtle. Competition had developed among piano makers. . . . Most of them tried to entice Vienna's many, many piano teachers into helping them dispose of their wares: they offered a commission to any musician who steered a piano sale onto their books. . . . Beethoven had many opportunities [for this] but he never did so; he disapproved of the practice. . . . Nevertheless, he was sometimes willing to use his influence with piano makers to have the price of an instrument reduced for the benefit of his friends. If the maker were ready to pay a commission, figuring it as "selling expense," he could not object to having the sum turned back to the customer. (1954, 134)

6. The firm was established in 1719 by the printer Bernhard Christoph Breitkopf, who died in 1777; the business was continued under the direction of his son, Johann Gottlob Immanuel, who developed divisible movable type, thus making it easier to publish music in larger editions. In 1795, Gottfried Christoph Härtel joined the firm. It was Härtel who founded the *Allgemeine Musikalische Zeitung* (*AMZ*), which "became the leading voice in music criticism in the first half of the 19th century" (see Plesske 1980).

7. In addition, the *AMZ* contained biographical essays and a special *Intelligence Blatt* (information bulletin) devoted to descriptions of instruments for sale, recent publications, and the like.

8. Before 1801, Beethoven was for the most part criticized in its pages—and it is worth noting that this criticism closely resembled Streicher's discussion of "good" and "bad" music in his fortepiano owner's manual (see chapter 6).

9. At the same time, the *AMZ* began to carry articles that praised music expressly written for the new technology. In 1802, for example, Friedrich Rochlitz, the journal editor, reviewed Beethoven's Sonata op. 27, no. 2 (the "Moonlight" Sonata), which he praised, but then cautioned that a very good piano was needed to attain the correct effect. This is the stage in this history where the music was now showing the technology to be "inadequate," rather than the reverse, as had previously been the case.

10. On how traces of the social process of an artifact's construction are erased, see Latour 1987. The more distant that perception of such traces becomes, the more an artifact will appear to be technologically determined and therefore self-justifying or, as Latour puts it, "black-boxed."

11. See Robin Wallace 1986, a valuable contribution to the history of aesthetic philosophy and also one of the best English-language guides to early *AMZ* Beethoven criticism. My discussion is greatly indebted to Wallace's work. See also Bigenwald [1938] 1965.

12. Van Swieten's autobiographical sketch appeared in the first volume of the *AMZ*.

13. The identities of all of the *AMZ* writers remain unknown. It is possible that, after around 1801, *AMZ* writers may have been working within pro-

Beethoven editorial constraints imposed from above by the parent company, Breitkopf and Härtel (see also Wallace 1986, 9). In this chapter, I am less interested in conflict over Beethoven's identity as evidenced in music criticism than in how these *AMZ* reviews reveal that musical qualities initially criticized could be rediscovered as praiseworthy—that is, in the processes that accomplished an aesthetic shift, as this occurred within the pages of *AMZ*.

14. The emphasis here is Beethoven's. It is significant that he is able to tell them that two of his concerti are being published, especially if they are considered "not his best work," since publishers were far less likely to make a profit on concerti and symphonies and other works for large ensembles. The bulk of the market was in piano and chamber works. Thus the fact that two publishers have purchased his concerti helps him to dramatize his own value in the eyes of publishers and, in particular, the value of his name, independent of sales.

15. In his study of early *AMZ* Beethoven criticism, Wallace (1986) has also noted the correlation between the change of policy at the *AMZ* and Beethoven's letter. While Wallace is quick to recognize the correlation between the new editorial policy and this letter from Beethoven, however, he is less quick to perceive the practical and businesslike reasons for both the letter and the response—in part, I think, because of Wallace's deep admiration for Beethoven's works. Beethoven, like many other musicians, had considerable entrepreneurial skills.

16. However, Wallace (who, in the preface to his book, tells us that since he first encountered the scores of Beethoven string quartets at the age of fifteen: "I have been convinced that the supposedly impenetrable late quartets represent the summit of human creativity" [1986, vii]), sees this transformation as only fitting, showing as it does that Beethoven's contemporaries were eventually able to recognize the intrinsic aesthetic truth of Beethoven's works.

CHAPTER 9: BEETHOVEN AND THE RESOURCES OF CULTURAL AUTHORITY

1. Employed by Count Browne, Ries performed Beethoven's pieces to, as he puts it, "an assembly of rabid Beethovenians."

2. See also the composer Tomaschek's comment to Cipriani Potter (a Beethoven fan): "If Beethoven emptied his inkstand upon a piece of music paper you would admire it!" (Thayer and Forbes, 1967, 1:210).

3. This attitude changed later on in the first half of the nineteenth-century in Vienna, as the taste for "lighter" and more overtly popular musical forms was strengthened.

4. By around 1816 the constituency for more explicitly popular and commercial music, the waltz, and the virtuosic style were overshadowing that for "serious" and learned music in Vienna (see Hanson 1985). The important point is that the musical canon of Haydn, Mozart, and Beethoven was first articulated *as ideology* in Vienna. Subsequently, of course, it was drawn on as a resource, by coalitions of aristocrats and members of the upper middle classes, who elaborated and revised it as a vehicle for constituting a new elite. (These processes have been described by William Weber 1986 and Paul DiMaggio 1982.)

5. The model received its first elaboration in London, at the hands of upper

middle-class founders of the London Philharmonic Society (where Beethoven's music was introduced by his friend, pupil, and devotee, Ferdinand Ries, who had emigrated to London in 1813). It was subsequently adopted and partially reformulated in Paris by Hector Berlioz and Franz Liszt.

6. One area I am currently exploring is the early internationalization of Beethoven's reputation as a "great" composer: I am considering the social circumstances of how Beethoven's music came to be imported by members of the London Philharmonic Society during the 1820s and the relation this had to the formation of international professional networks of musicians. (Of particular consideration is the role of Ferdinand Ries, who became known as "the London Beethoven.")

7. The topic of genius has hardly been ignored by scholars, however; on the contrary, over the past few years the topic has been taken up by literary theorists (Murray 1989; Battersby 1990) and social psychologists (Horowitz and O'Brien 1985; Sternberg and Davidson 1986; Radford 1990). For a survey of these works, see DeNora and Mehan 1993.

References

Abbott, Andrew, and A. Hrycak. 1990. "Measuring Resemblance in Sequence Data: An Optimal Matching Analysis of Musicians' Careers." *American Journal of Sociology* 96:144–85.

Adorno, T. 1976. *Introduction to the Sociology of Music.* New York: Seabury Press.

Albrecht, M. C. 1968. "Art as an Institution." *American Sociological Review* 33:383–96.

Allgemeine Musicalische Zeitung, 1798–1806. Berlin: Breitkopf and Härtel.

Anderson, E., trans. and ed. 1938. *The Letters of Mozart and His Family.* 3 vols. London: Macmillan.

———. 1961. *The Letters of Beethoven.* 3 vols. London: Macmillan.

Angermüller, Rudolph. 1980. "Sigismund Neukomm." Pp. 121–23 in *The New Grove Dictionary of Music and Musicians,* vol. 13, edited by Stanley Sadie. London: Macmillan.

Antonicek, Theophil. 1980. "Vienna." Pp. 713–41 in *The New Grove Dictionary of Music and Musicians,* vol. 19, edited by Stanley Sadie. London: Macmillan.

Bach, C. P. E. 1949. *Essay on the True Art of Playing Keyboard Instruments.* Translated and edited by William J. Mitchell. New York: Norton.

Badura-Skoda, Paul, and Eva Badura-Skoda. 1962. *Interpreting Mozart at the Keyboard.* New York: St. Martin's Press.

Balfe, Judith, and Margaret J. Wyszomirski. 1986. "Public Art and Public Policy." *Journal of Arts Management and Law* 15:5–29.

Ballantine, Christopher. 1980. "Beethoven, Hegel and Marx." Pp. 30–48 in *Music and Its Social Meanings.* New York: Gordon and Breach.

Barea, Ilsa. 1966. *Vienna.* New York: Knopf.

Barker, Thomas M. 1974. "Military Entrepreneurship and Absolutism: Habsburg Models." *Journal of European Studies* 4:19–42.

Barzun, Jacques. 1950. *Berlioz and the Romantic Century*. 2 vols. Boston: Little, Brown.

Battersby, Christine. 1990. *Gender and Genius*. London: The Woman's Press.

Baxandall, Michael. 1972. *Painting and Experience in Fifteenth Century Italy*. Oxford: Oxford University Press.

Becker, Heinz, and Richard D. Green. 1980. "Berlin." Pp. 565–78 in *The New Grove Dictionary of Music and Musicians*, vol. 2, edited by Stanley Sadie. London: Macmillan.

Becker, Howard S. 1963. "Labelling Theory Reconsidered." In *Outsiders*. New York: The Free Press.

————. 1982. *Art Worlds*. Berkeley: University of California Press.

Becker-Weidmann, Gudrun. 1980. "Righini." Pp. 20–22 in *The New Grove Dictionary of Music and Musicians*, vol. 2, edited by Stanley Sadie. London: Macmillan.

Berger, Bennett. 1981. *The Survival of a Counter Culture: Ideological Work and Everyday Life among Rural Communards*. Berkeley: University of California Press.

Berlioz, Hector. 1969. *The Memoirs of Hector Berlioz, Member of the French Institute, Including His Travels in Italy, Germany, Russia and England, 1803–1865*. Translated and edited by David Cairns. London: Gollancz.

Biba, Otto. 1980. "Concert Life in Beethoven's Vienna." Pp. 77–93 in *Beethoven, Performers, and Critics*, edited by Robert Winter and Bruce Carr. Detroit: Wayne State University Press.

Bigenwald, Marthe. [1938] 1965. *Die Anfange der Leipziger Allgemeinen Musikalischen Zeitung*. Reprint, Hilversum: FAM Knuf.

Blom, Eric. 1958. "The Prophesies of Dussek." Pp. 88–117 in *Classics, Major and Minor*. London: Dent.

————. 1968. *Beethoven's Pianoforte Sonatas Discussed*. New York: E. P. Dutton.

Blum, J. 1948. *Noble Landowners and Agriculture in Austria 1815–48*. Baltimore: John Hopkins University Press.

Blume, F. 1970. *Classic and Romantic*. New York: Norton.

Bourdieu, Pierre. 1968. "Outline of a Theory of Art Perception." *International Social Science Journal* 20(4): 599–612.

————. 1970. "Intellectual Field and Creative Project." *Social Science Information* 8(2):89–119.

————. 1984a. *Distinction*. Cambridge, Mass.: Harvard University Press.

————. 1984b. "The Social Space and the Genesis of Groups." *Social Science Information* 24:195–220.

Bourdieu, Pierre, and Jean Claude Passeron. [1964] 1977. *The Inheritors: French Students and Their Relation to Culture*. Translated by R. Nice. Chicago: University of Chicago Press.

Branscombe, Peter. 1980. "Lichtenstein, Karl August." P. 285 in *The New Grove Dictionary of Music and Musicians*, vol. 10, edited by Stanley Sadie. London: Macmillan.

Braunbehrens, Volkmar. 1989. *Mozart in Vienna 1781–1791*. Translated by Timothy Bell. New York: Grove and Wiedenfeld.

Bright, Richard. 1818. *Travels from Vienna through Lower Hungary*. Edinburgh: Archibald Constable and Co.

Brion, Marcel. 1962. *Daily Life in the Vienna of Mozart and Schubert*. Translated by Jean Steward. New York: Macmillan.

Brown, Peter A. 1986. *Joseph Haydn's Keyboard Music: Sources and Style*. Bloomington: Indiana University Press.

Broyles, Michael. 1987. *Beethoven: The Emergence and Evolution of Beethoven's Heroic Style*. New York: Excelsior Music Publishing.

Buck-Morss, Susan. 1977. *The Origin of Negative Dialectics: Theodor W. Adorno, Walter Benjamin, and the Frankfurt Institute*. New York: Free Press.

Burney, Charles. [1770] 1969. *Music, Men and Manners in France and Italy*. Reprint, London: The Folio Society.

———. 1775. *The Present State of Music in Germany and the Netherlands and United Provinces*. 2d corrected ed. London: Becket.

———. [1789] 1935. *A General History of Music from the Earliest Ages to the Present Period*. Reprint, New York: Harcourt Brace.

Buzga, J., and Adrienne Simpson. 1980. "Prague." Pp. 192–201 in *The New Grove Dictionary of Music and Musicians*, vol. 15, edited by Stanley Sadie. London: Macmillan.

Cage, John. 1961. *Silence*. Middletown, Conn.: Wesleyan University Press.

Carse, Adam. 1949. *The Orchestra from Beethoven to Berlioz*. New York: Broude Brothers.

Chartier, Roger. 1988. *Cultural History: Between Practices and Representations*. Oxford: Polity.

Cicourel, Aaron V. 1968. *The Social Organization of Juvenile Justice*. New York: Wiley.

Cicourel, Aaron V., and Hugh Mehan. 1984. "Universal Development, Stratifying Practices and Status Attainment." *Research in Social Stratification and Mobility* 4:3–27.

Cicourel, Aaron V., and Karin Knorr-Cetina, 1981. *Advances in Social Theory and Methodology*. London: Routledge and Kegan Paul.

Comini, A. 1987. *The Changing Image of Beethoven: A Study in Mythmaking*. New York: Rizzoli.

Cooper, Martin. 1970. *Beethoven: The Last Decade, 1817–27*. London: Oxford University Press.

Crabbe, J. 1982. *Beethoven's Empire of the Mind*. Newbury: Lovell Baines Print.

Craw, Howard Allen. 1964. "A Biography and Thematic Catalog of the Works of J. L. Dussek (1760–1812)." Ph.D. dissertation, University of Southern California.

Czerny, Carl. 1956. "Recollections from My Life." *Musical Quarterly* 42:302–17.

Dahlhaus, Carl. 1982. *Aesthetics of Music*. Translated by William Austin. Cambridge: Cambridge University Press.

D'Andrade, Roy. 1984. "Cultural Meaning Systems." Pp. 88–119 in *Cultural Theory: Essays on Mind, Self and Emotion*, edited by Richard W. Shweder and Robert A. Levine. New York: Cambridge University Press.

Davis, Kathy. 1989. *Power under the Microscope*. Utrecht: Foris Publications.

Dawes, Frank. 1980. "Steibelt." Pp. 101–3 in *The New Grove Dictionary of Music and Musicians,* vol. 18, edited by Stanley Sadie. London: Macmillan.

Dean, Winton. 1980. "Criticism." Pp. 36–50 in *The New Grove Dictionary of Music and Musicians,* vol. 5, edited by Stanley Sadie. London: Macmillan.

DeNora, Tia. 1986. "How Is Extra-musical Meaning Possible? Music as a Place and Space for 'Work.'" *Sociological Theory* 4(1):84–94.

———. 1991. "Musical Patronage and Social Change in Beethoven's Vienna." *American Journal of Sociology* 97 (September): 310–46.

———. n.d.a. "Deconstructing Periodization: Sociological Methods and Historical Ethnography in Late 19th Century Vienna." *Beethoven Forum,* forthcoming.

———. n.d.b. "The Musical Composition of Reality? Music, Action and Reflexivity." *Sociological Review,* forthcoming.

DeNora, Tia, and Hugh Mehan. 1993. "Genius: A Social Construction." Pp. 157–73 in *Constructing the Social,* edited by J. Kitsuse and T. Sarbin. Los Angeles and London: Sage.

Deutsch, Otto Erich. 1934. Austrian Currency Values and Their Purchasing Power." *Music and Letters* 15:236–38.

———. 1965. *Mozart: A Documentary Biography.* Stanford: Stanford University Press.

Di Chiera, David. 1980. "Sacchini." Pp. 370–73 in *The New Grove Dictionary of Music and Musicians,* vol. 16, edited by Stanley Sadie. London: Macmillan.

Dies, Albert Christoph. [1810] 1968. "Biographical Accounts of Joseph Haydn." Pp. 67–209 in *Haydn: Two Contemporary Portraits.* Translated and edited by Vernon Gotwals. Reprint, Madison: University of Wisconsin Press.

DiMaggio, Paul. 1982. "Cultural Entrepreneurship in Nineteenth-Century Boston: The Creation of an Organizational Base for High Culture in America." Parts 1 and 2. *Media, Culture and Society* 4:35–50, 303–22.

———. 1987. "Classification in Art." *American Sociological Review* 52:440–55.

DiMaggio, Paul, and Paul Hirsch. 1976. "Production Organizations in the Arts." *American Behavioral Scientist* 19(6): 735–52.

Dittersdorf, Karl. [1896] 1970. *The Autobiography of Karl von Dittersdorf Dictated to His Son.* Translated by A. D. Coleridge. Reprint, New York: Da Capo.

Doernberg, Erwin. 1963. "Adalbert Gyrowetz." *Music and Letters* 44(1): 21–30.

Dolge, A. 1911. *Pianos and Their Makers.* New York: Dover.

Dorian, F. 1971. *The History of Music in Performance.* New York: Norton.

Douglas, Mary. 1985. *Risk Acceptability According to the Social Sciences.* New York: Russell Sage Foundation.

Downs, Philip G. 1970. "Beethoven's 'New Way' and the Eroica." *Musical Quarterly* 56:585–604.

Drake, Kenneth. 1972. *The Sonatas of Beethoven as He Played and Taught Them.* Cincinnati: Music Teachers National Association.

Edge, Dexter. 1991. "Mozart's Fee for Così fan tutte." *Journal of the Royal Musical Association* 116:211–35.

———. 1992. "Review of Mary Sue Morrow: Concert Life in Haydn's Vienna" (with extensive additions and corrections). *Haydn Yearbook* 17:108–66.

———. n.d. *The Concerto in Vienna*. Oxford: Oxford University Press, forthcoming.

Edinburgh Musical Society. 1728–1792. *The Minutes of the Edinburgh Musical Society*. Edinburgh University.

———. 1728–1792. *The Plan Book of the Edinburgh Musical Society*. Edinburgh Public Library.

Ehrlich, Cyril. 1976. *The Piano: A History*. London: J. M. Dent and Sons.

———. 1985. *The Music Profession in Britain since the Eighteenth Century*. Oxford: Clarendon Press.

Einstein, Alfred. 1947. *Music in the Romantic Era*. New York: Norton.

Eisen, Cliff. 1991. *New Mozart Documents: A Supplement to O. E. Deutsch's Documentary Biography*. London: Macmillan.

Elkin, Robert. 1955. *The Old Concert Rooms of London*. London: Arnold.

Etzkorn, K. Peter. 1974. "On Music, Social Structure and Sociology." *International Review of the Aesthetics and Sociology of Music* 5(1):43–51.

Farmer, Henry George. 1947. *A History of Music in Scotland*. London: Hinrichsen Edition.

Feldman, David. 1979. "The Mysterious Case of Extreme Giftedness." *78th Yearboook of the National Society for the Study of Education*. Chicago: University of Chicago Press.

Forbes, Elliot. 1980. "Lichnowsky." P. 824 in *The New Grove Dictionary of Music and Musicians*, vol. 10, edited by Stanley Sadie. London: Macmillan.

Ford, Charles. 1991. *Così? Sexual Politics in Mozart's Operas*. Manchester: Manchester University Press.

Forsyth, D. 1985. *Buildings for Music: The Architect, the Musician and the Listener from the Seventeenth Century to the Present Day*. Cambridge, Mass.: MIT Press.

Freeman, Daniel. 1987. *The Opera Theater of Count Franz Anton von Sporck in Prague, 1724–1735*. Ph.D. dissertation, University of Illinois, Urbana-Champaign.

Freudenberger, H. 1960. "The Woolen Goods Industry of the Habsburg Monarchy in the Eighteenth Century." *Journal of Economic History* 20:383–403.

———. 1967. "State Intervention as an Obstacle to Economic Growth in the Habsburg Monarchy." *Journal of Economic History* 27:493–509.

Frimmel, Theodor. [1926] 1968. *Beethoven Handbuch*. 2 vols. Reprint, Hildescheim: G. Olms.

Funk, Addie. 1927. *Vienna's Musical Sites and Landmarks*. Vienna: Informator.

Gardiner, William. 1838. *Music and Friends or, Pleasant Recollections of a Dilettante*. London: Longman, Orme, Brown, and Longman.

Garfinkel, Harold. 1967. *Studies in Ethnomethodology*. Englewood Cliffs, N.J.: Prentice-Hall.

Garfinkel, Harold, Michael Lynch, and E. Livingston. 1981. "The Work of a

Discovering Science Construed with Materials from the Optically Discovered Pulsar." *Philosophy of the Social Sciences* 11:131–58.

Gartenberg, Egon. 1968. *Vienna: Its Musical Heritage.* University Park: Pennsylvania State University Press.

Geringer, Karl. 1946. *Haydn: A Creative Life in Music.* New York: Norton.

Gilmore, S. 1988. "Coordination and Convention: The Organization of the Concert World." *Symbolic Interaction* 10(2):209–27.

Good, E. 1982. *Giraffes, Black Dragons, and Other Pianos.* Stanford: Stanford University Press.

Goffman, Erving. 1958. *The Presentation of Self in Everyday Life.* Garden City, N.Y.: Doubleday.

Graf, Max. 1945. *Legend of a Musical City.* New York: Philosophical Library.

———. 1946. *Composer and Critic: Two Hundred Years of Music Criticism.* New York: Norton.

Graña, César. 1967. *Modernity and Its Discontents.* New York: Harper Torchbooks.

Griesinger, G. A. 1968. "Biographical Notes on Joseph Haydn." Pp. 5–66 in *Haydn: Two Contemporary Portraits,* translated and edited by Vernon Gotwals. Madison: University of Wisconsin Press.

Grimshaw, Allen, ed. 1990. *Conflict Talk.* Cambridge: Cambridge University Press.

Griswold, Wendy. 1987. "The Fabrication of Meaning." *American Journal of Sociology* 92:1077–117.

———. 1983. "The Devil's Techniques: Cultural Legitimation and Social Change." *American Sociological Review* 48:668–80.

Grout, Donald J. 1973. *A History of Western Music.* New York: Norton.

Grover, David S. 1976. *The Piano: Its Story from Zither to Grand.* London: Robert Hale.

Gusfield, Joseph R. 1973. "The Social Construction of Tradition: an Interactionist View of Social Change." Pp. 83–104 in *Traditional Attitudes and Modern Styles in Political Leadership,* edited by A. R. Davis. Sydney: Angus and Robertson.

———. 1981. *The Culture of Public Problems: Drinking-Driving and the Symbolic Order.* Chicago: University of Chicago Press.

Hamann, Heinz Wolfgang. 1980. "Wölffl." Pp. 508–10 in *The New Grove Dictionary of Music and Musicians,* vol. 20, edited by Stanley Sadie. London: Macmillan.

Hanslick, Eduard. [1869] 1979. *Geschichte des Concertwesens in Wien.* Reprint, New York: G. Olms.

Hanson, Alice Marie. 1983. "Incomes and Outgoings in the Vienna of Beethoven and Schubert." *Music and Letters* 64:173–82.

———. 1985. *Musical Life in Biedermeier Vienna.* Cambridge: Cambridge University Press.

Harding, R. 1973. *The Piano-Forte.* New York: Da Capo.

Hauser, Arnold. 1962. *The Social History of Art.* London: Routledge.

Haydn, Franz Joseph. 1984. *Fifteen Scottish, Welsh and Irish Folksongs, Ar-*

ranged for High Voice (Two Duets), Violin, Cello and Piano. Cardiff: University College of Cardiff Press.

Hebdige, Dick. 1979. *Subculture, the Meaning of Style.* London: Methuen.

Hellyer, R. 1980. "Harmoniemusik." Pp. 167–68 in *The New Grove Dictionary of Music and Musicians,* vol. 8, edited by Stanley Sadie. London: Macmillan.

———. 1984. "The Wind Ensembles of the Esterhazy Princes 1761–1813." *Haydn Yearbook* 15:5–93.

Helm, Ernest Eugene. 1960. *Music at the Court of Frederick the Great.* Norman: University of Oklahoma Press.

Henning, Edward B. 1960. "Patronage and Style in the Arts: A Suggestion Concerning Their Relations." *Journal of Aesthetics and Art Criticism* 18:464–71.

Heritage, John. 1984. *Garfinkel and Ethnomethodology.* Oxford: Blackwell.

Hobsbawm, Eric, and Terrence Ranger. 1983. *The Invention of Tradition.* New York: Cambridge University Press.

Hood, Margaret. 1986. "Nannette Streicher and Her Pianos." *Continuo* (May): 2–5 and (June): 2–7.

Horowitz, F. D., and M. O'Brien, Eds. 1985. *The Gifted and the Talented: Developmental Perspectives.* Washington, D.C.: American Psychological Association.

Hosakowa, S. 1986. "Considerations sur la musique mass-médiatissée." *International Review of Aesthetics and the Sociology of Music* 12:21–50.

Hosler, Bellamy. 1981. *Changing Aesthetic Views of Instrumental Music in 18th Century Germany.* Ann Arbor: UMI Research Press.

Humphries, Charles, and William C. Smith. 1954. *Music Publishing in the British Isles.* London: Cassell and Co.

Jahn, Otto. 1882. *The Life of Mozart.* 3 vols. New York: Kalmus.

Johnson, David. 1972. *Music and Society in Lowland Scotland in the Eighteenth Century.* London: Oxford University Press.

Johnson, Douglas. 1980. "Music for Prague and Berlin: Beethoven's Concert Tour of 1796." Pp. 24–40 in *Beethoven, Performers and Critics,* edited by Robert Winter and Bruce Carr. Detroit: International Beethoven Congress.

———. 1982. "1794–1795: Decisive Years in Beethoven's Early Career." *Beethoven Studies* 3:1–28.

Johnson, James. 1991. "Beethoven and the Birth of Romantic Musical Experience in France." *Nineteenth Century Music* 15(1):23–35.

Jones, Peter Ward, and Peter Williams. 1980. "Longman and Broderip." P. 220 in *The New Grove Dictionary of Music and Musicians,* vol. 11, edited by Stanley Sadie. London: Macmillan.

Kanne, R. 1973. "Aristocracy in the Eighteenth Century Habsburg Empire." *East European Quarterly* 7:1–13.

Kelly, Michael. [1826] 1975. *Reminiscences.* Reprint, London: Oxford University Press.

Kerman, Joseph. 1967. *The Beethoven Quartets.* New York: Knopf.

———. 1970. "Beethoven's Early Sketches." *Musical Quarterly* 65:515–38.

———. 1983. "A Few Canonic Variations." *Critical Inquiry* 10:107–26.

Kerman, Joseph, and Vivian Kerman. 1976. *Listen.* New York: Worth.

Kerman, Joseph, and Alan Tyson. 1980. *The New Grove Beethoven.* London: Macmillan.

King, A. Hyatt. 1955. *Mozart in Retrospect: Studies in Criticism and Bibliography.* London: Oxford University Press.

Knight, Frida. 1973. *Beethoven and the Age of Revolution.* London: Lawrence and Wishart.

Knorr-Cetina, Karin. 1988. "Laboratories: Instruments of World Construction." Paper presented at the symposium Social Studies in the Everyday Work of Scientists, in Rochester, N.Y., 21–22 April.

Komlós, Katalin. 1987. "The Viennese Keyboard Trio in the 1780s: Sociological Background and Contemporary Reception." *Music and Letters* 68 (summer): 222–34.

Kramer, R. 1975. "Notes to Beethoven's Education." *Journal of the American Musicological Society* 28:72–100.

Kuhn, Thomas. 1962. *The Structure of Scientific Revolutions.* Chicago: University of Chicago Press.

Kullak, Franz. [1901] 1973. *Beethoven's Piano Playing.* Translated by Theodore Baker. Reprint, New York: Da Capo.

Lamont, Michele, and Annette Lareau. 1988. "Cultural Capital: Allusions, Gaps and Glissandos in Recent Theoretical Developments." *Sociological Theory* 6:153–68.

Landon, H. C. Robbins. 1970a. *Beethoven: A Documentary Study.* New York: Macmillan.

———. 1970b. *Essays on the Viennese Classical Style.* New York: Macmillan.

———. 1976–80. *Haydn: Chronicle and Works.* 5 vols. Bloomington: Indiana University Press.

———. 1988. *1791: Mozart's Last Year.* London: Thames and Hudson.

———, trans. and ed. 1959. *The Collected Correspondence and London Notebooks of Joseph Haydn.* London: Barrie and Rockcliff.

Lang, Paul Henry. 1960. "Mozart after 200 Years." *Journal of the American Musicological Society* 13:197–205.

Lareau, Annette. 1989. *Home Advantages.* Philadelphia: Temple University Press.

Larsen, Jens Peter. 1967. "Some Observations on the Development and Characteristics of Vienna Classical Instrumental Music." *Studia Musicologica Academiae Scientiarum Hungariae* 9:115–39.

———. 1982. *The New Grove Haydn.* New York: Norton.

———. 1988. *Handel, Haydn, and the Viennese Classical Style.* Translated by Ulrich Kramer. Ann Arbor: UMI Research Press.

Latour, Bruno. 1987. *Science in Action.* Cambridge, Mass.: Harvard University Press.

Latour, Bruno, and Steve Woolgar. 1979. *Laboratory Life: The Social Construction of Scientific Facts.* Beverly Hills, Calif.: Sage.

Le Huray, Peter, and James Day, eds. 1981. *Music and Aesthetics in the Eigh-*

teenth and Early Nineteenth Centuries. New York: Cambridge University Press.

Lenneberg, Hans. 1988. "Speculating about Sociology and Social History." *Journal of Musicology* 4:409–20.

Levien, J. M. 1927. *Beethoven and the Royal Philharmonic Society.* London.

Levine, L. 1984. "William Shakespeare and the American People: A Study in Cultural Transformation." *American Historical Review* 89:34–66.

———. 1988. *"Highbrow/Lowbrow": The Emergence of Cultural Hierarchy in America.* Cambridge, Mass.: Harvard University Press.

Lockwood, Lewis. 1982. "Eroica Perspectives: Strategy and Design in the First Movement." *Beethoven Studies* 3. Edited by Alan Tyson. Cambridge.

Loesser, Arthur. 1954. *Men, Women and Pianos.* New York: Simon and Schuster.

Lonn, S. 1980. "Paul Struck." P. 297 in *The New Grove Dictionary of Music and Musicians,* vol. 18, edited by Stanley Sadie. London: Macmillan.

Lough, John. 1957. *Paris Theater Audiences in the 17th and 18th Centuries.* London: Oxford University Press.

MacArdle, Donald. 1949. "The Family van Beethoven." *Musical Quarterly* 35: 528–50.

———. 1960. "Beethoven and the Philharmonic Society of London." *Music Review* 21:1–7.

———. 1963a. "Anton Felix Schindler, Friend of Beethoven." *Music Review* 24: 50–74.

———. 1963b. "Beethoven and Schuppanzigh." *Music Review* 26:3–14.

———. 1965. "Beethoven and Ferdinand Ries." *Music and Letters* 46:23–34.

MacArdle, Donald, and Ludwig Misch. 1957. *New Beethoven Letters.* Norman: University of Oklahoma Press.

Macartney, C. A. 1968. *The Habsburg Empire 1790–1918.* London: Weidenfeld and Nicolson.

MacKenzie, D. 1981. *Statistics in Britain, 1865–1930: The Social Construction of Scientific Knowledge.* Edinburgh: Edinburgh University Press.

MacKenzie, D., and J. Wajcman. 1985. *The Social Shaping of Technology.* Milton Keynes: Open University Press.

Magani, L. 1970. "Beethoven and the Aesthetic Thought of His Time." *International Review of Music Aesthetics and Sociology* 1:125–36.

Mahling, Christoph Helmut. 1985. "The Origin and Social Status of the Court Orchestral Musician in the 18th and Early 19th Century in Germany." Pp. 221–63 in *The Social Status of the Professional Musician from the Middle Ages to the 19th Century,* edited by Walter Salman. New York: Pendragon Press.

Mann, Alfred. 1970. "Beethoven's Contrapuntal Studies with Haydn." *Musical Quarterly* 56:711–26.

Matis, Herbert. 1967. "Die Grafen von Fries." *Tradition: Zeitschrift für Firmengeschichte und Unternehmenbiographie* 12(1): 484–96.

May, Jürgen. 1994. "Beethoven and the Lichnowskys." *Beethoven Forum* 3: 29–38.

McClary, Susan. 1991. *Feminine Endings: Music, Gender and Sexuality.* Minneapolis: University of Minnesota Press.

———. 1992. *George Bizet's Carmen.* Cambridge: Cambridge University Press.

Mehan, Hugh. 1983. "Social Constructivism in Psychology and Sociology." *Sociologie et Sociétés* 14:77–96.

———. 1986. "Educational Handicaps as a Cultural Meaning System." *Ethos* 16(1):73–91.

Mehan, Hugh, Alma Hertweck, and J. Lee Meihls. 1986. *Handicapping the Handicapped: Decision Making in Student's Educational Careers.* Stanford: Stanford University Press.

Meyer, Leonard. 1973. *Explaining Music.* Berkeley: University of California Press.

———. 1983. "Innovation, Choice and the History of Music." *Critical Inquiry* 9:3.

———. 1984. "Music and Ideology in the Nineteenth Century." The Tanner Lectures on Human Values, delivered at Stanford University, 17 and 21 May.

Milligan, Thomas. 1983. *The Concerto and London's Musical Culture in the Late Eighteenth Century.* Ann Arbor, Mich.: UMI Research Press.

Mills, C. W. 1940. "Situated Vocabularies of Motive." *American Sociological Review* 5:904–13.

Moore, Julia V. 1987. "Beethoven and Musical Economics." Ph.D. dissertation, University of Illinois, Urbana-Champaign.

———. 1992. "Review Essay: Mozart Mythologized or Modernized?" *Journal of Musicological Research* 12:83–109.

———. n.d.a. "800 Gulden Is Not Enough: Mozart and Nine Other Musicians with Similar Salaries." *Journal of the Royal Musical Association,* forthcoming.

———. n.d.b. *Beethoven in the Marketplace.* Oxford: Oxford University Press.

Morrow, Mary Sue. 1989. *Concert Life in Haydn's Vienna: Aspects of a Developing Musical and Social Institution.* New York: Pendragon Press.

Moscheles, Charlotte. 1873. *The Life of Moscheles, with Selections from His Diaries and Correspondence.* 2 vols. Translated by A. D. Coleridge. London: Hurst and Clackett.

Mukerji, Chandra, and Michael Schudson. 1986. "Popular Culture." *Annual Review of Sociology* 12:47–66.

Mulkay, Michael. 1986. *The Word and the World: Explorations in the Form of Sociological Analysis.* New York: Routledge, Chapman and Hall.

Murray, Penelope, ed. 1989. *Genius: The History of an Idea.* London: Blackwell.

Nathanson, C. 1988. "The Social Construction of the Soviet Threat." *Multilingua* 7:241–83.

Neefe, Christian Gottlieb. 1951. "The Life of Christian Gottlieb Neefe." In *Forgotten Musicians,* edited and translated by Paul Nettl. New York: Philosophical Library.

Nersessian, Nancy. 1984. *Faraday to Einstein: Constructing Meaning in Scientific Theories.* Boston: Martinus Nijhoff.

Nettl, Paul. 1956. *Beethoven Handbook.* New York: Frederick Ungar.

————, ed. 1951. *Forgotten Musicians*. New York: Philosophical Library.

Newman, William S. 1963. *The Sonata in the Classical Era*. Chapel Hill: University of North Carolina Press.

————. 1970. "Beethoven's Pianos Versus His Piano Ideals." *Journal of the American Musicological Association* 23:484–504.

————. 1983. "The Beethoven Mystique in Romantic Art, Literature and Music." *Musical Quarterly* 49:354–88.

————. 1988. *Beethoven on Beethoven: Playing His Piano Music His Way*. New York: Norton.

Newmarch, Rosa. 1942. *The Music of Czechoslovakia*. London: Oxford University Press.

Nohl, Ludwig. 1864. *Beethoven's Leben*. 4 vols. Leipzig: Günther.

Nottebohm, Gustav. 1873. *Beethoven Studien, 1*. Leipzig.

Nowak-Romanovicz, Alina. 1980. "Lessel." Pp. 692–93 in *The New Grove Dictionary of Music and Musicians*, vol. 10, edited by Stanley Sadie. London: Macmillan.

O'Boyle, Lenore. 1966. "The Middle Class in Western History, 1815–1848." *American Historical Review* 71:826–40.

————. 1967. "The Middle Class Reconsidered." *French Historical Studies* 5: 53–56.

Oldman, C. B. 1951. "Beethoven's 'Variations on National Themes': Their Composition and First Publication." *Music Review* 12:45–52.

Olleson, Edward. 1963. "Gottfried van Swieten: Patron of Haydn and Mozart." *Proceedings of the Royal Music Association* 89:63–74

————. 1963–1964. "Haydn in the Diaries of Count Karl von Zinzendorf." *Haydn Yearbook* 2:45–62.

————. 1965. "Georg August Griesinger's Correspondence with Breitkopf and Härtel." *Haydn Yearbook* 3:5–53.

————. 1967. "Gottfried, Baron van Swieten and His Influence on Haydn and Mozart." Ph.D. dissertation, Hertford College, Oxford University.

Papendieck, Charlotte. 1837. *Court and Private Life in the Time of Queen Charlotte*. 2 vols. London: Richard Bentley and Son.

Parke, W. T. [1830] 1970. *Musical Memoirs: Comprising an Account of the General State of Music in England from the First Commemoration of Handel in 1784 to the Year 1830*. 2 vols. in one. Reprint, New York: Da Capo

Parker, D. C. 1924. "The Musician, the Patron, and the Audience." *Musical Quarterly* 10:219–35.

Parrish, Carl. 1944. "Criticisms of the Piano When It Was New." *Musical Quarterly* 30:428–40.

————. 1953. *The Early Piano and Its Influence on Keyboard Technique and Composition in the Eighteenth Century*. Superior, Wisc.: Research Microfilm Publishers.

Pasler, Jann. 1987a. "Apaches in Paris: The Making of a Turn-of-the-Century Parisian Art World." Paper presented at the Conference of the American Musical Association, November.

————. 1987b. "Pelléas and Power: Forces behind the Reception of Debussy's Opera." *Nineteenth Century Music* 10:243–64.

Pestelli, Giorgio. 1984. *The Age of Mozart and Beethoven*. Cambridge: Cambridge University Press.

"Pianoforte" and "Piano Playing." 1980. Pp. 71–107 in *The New Grove Dictionary of Musical Instruments*, vol. 3, edited by Stanley Sadie. London: Macmillan.

Plantinga, Leon B. 1977. *Clementi: His Life and His Music*. London: Oxford University Press.

Pleasants, H. 1955. *The Agony of Modern Music*. New York: Simon and Schuster.

Plesske, Hans Martin. 1980. "Breitkopf and Härtel." Pp. 251–53 in *The New Grove Dictionary of Music and Musicians*, vol. 3, edited by Stanley Sadie. London: Macmillan.

Pollner, Melvin. 1987. *Mundane Reason: Reality in Everyday and Sociological Discourse*. Cambridge: Cambridge University Press.

Portnoy, Julius. 1955. *The Philosopher and Music*. New York: Humanities Press.

Postolka, Milan. 1980a. "Gelinek." Pp. 222–23 in *The New Grove Dictionary of Music and Musicians*, vol. 7, edited by Stanley Sadie. London: Macmillan.

———. 1980b. "Lobkowitz." Pp. 101–2 in *The New Grove Dictionary of Music and Musicians*, vol. 11, edited by Stanley Sadie. London: Macmillan.

———. 1980c. "Vanhal." Pp. 522–25 in *The New Grove Dictionary of Music and Musicians*, vol. 19, edited by Stanley Sadie. London: Macmillan.

———. 1980d. "Wranitzky." Pp. 538–40 in *The New Grove Dictionary of Music and Musicians*, vol. 20, edited by Stanley Sadie. London: Macmillan.

Radcliffe, Philip. 1983. "Piano Music." Pp. 325–74 in *The New Oxford History of Music*, vol. 8, *The Age of Beethoven, 1770–1830*. London: Oxford University Press.

Radford, John. 1990. *Child Prodigies and Exceptional Early Achievers*. New York: Free Press.

Radway, Janice. 1984. *Reading the Romance: Women, Patriarchy, and Popular Literature*. Chapel Hill: University of North Carolina Press.

Randel, Don. 1992. "The Canon in the Musicological Toolbox." Pp. 10–22 in *Disciplining Music: Musicology and Its Canons*, edited by Katherine Bergeron and Philip Bohlman. Chicago: University of Chicago Press.

Ratner, Leonard G. 1980. *Classic Music: Expression, Form and Style*. New York: Schirmer.

Raynor, Henry. 1972. *A Social History of Music*. New York: Schocken.

———. 1976. *Music and Society since 1815*. London: Schocken.

Reicha, A. 1936. "From the Unpublished Autobiography of Antoine Reicha." Edited and translated by J.-G. Prod'homme. *Musical Quarterly* 22:339–53.

Reichardt, Johann Friedrich. 1915. *Vertraute Briefe*. Edited by Gustav Gugitz. Munich: Georg Müller.

Rich, A., and D. Foote. 1987. "The Tramp of a Giant." *Newsweek*, 9 March, 69.

Ringer, Alexander L. 1961. "Clementi and the Eroica." *Musical Quarterly* 47: 454–68.

———. 1969. "Mozart and the Josephian Era: Some Socio-Economic Notes on Musical Change." *Current Musicology* 9:158–65.

———. 1970. "Beethoven and the London Pianoforte School." *Musical Quarterly* 56:742–59.

Rosen, Charles. 1972. *The Classical Style*. New York: Norton.

———. 1980. *Sonata Forms*. New York: Norton.

Rosenbaum, Joseph Carl. 1968. *The Diaries of Joseph Carl Rosenbaum, 1770–1829*. Edited and translated by Else Radant. *Haydn Yearbook 5*.

Rosenberg, Hans. 1958. *Bureaucracy, Aristocracy and Autocracy: The Prussian Experience, 1660–1815*. Cambridge, Mass.: Harvard University Press.

Rothenberg, Gunther E. 1982. *Napoleon's Great Adversaries: The Archduke Charles and the Austrian Army, 1792–1814*. London: B. T. Batsford.

Sachs, Joel. 1977. *Kapellmeister Hummel in England and France*. Detroit: Detroit Monographs in Musicology.

Sadie, Stanley. 1980. "Mozart." Pp. 680–752 in *The New Grove Dictionary of Music and Musicians*, vol. 12, edited by Stanley Sadie. London: Macmillan.

Sagarra, Eda. 1977. *A Social History of Germany, 1648–1914*. London: Methuen.

Saint-Foix, Georges. 1931. "Clementi, Forerunner of Beethoven." *Musical Quarterly* 17:84–92.

Salmen, Walter. 1985. "Social Obligations of the Emancipated Musician in the Nineteenth Century." Pp. 265–81 in *The Social Status of the Professional Musician from the Middle Ages to the 19th Century*. New York: Pendragon Press.

Schenk, Erich. 1959. *Mozart and His Times*. New York: Knopf.

Schenk, H. 1953. "Austria." Pp. 102–118 in *The European Nobility in the Eighteenth Century*, edited by A. Goodwin. London: Adam and Charles Black.

Schenk, Johann. 1951. "Johann Baptist Schenk's Autobiography." Pp. 265–79 in *Forgotten Musicians*, edited and translated by Paul Nettl. New York: Philosophical Library.

Schindler, Anton. 1966. *Beethoven as I Knew Him*. Edited by Donald W. MacArdle and translated by Constanze S. Jolly. London and Chapel Hill: University of North Carolina Press.

Schindler, Otto G. 1976. "Das Publikum des Burgtheaters in der Josephinischen Ära: Versuch einer Strukturbestimmung." Pp. 11–96 in *Das Burgtheater und sein Publikum*, vol. 1. Vienna: Verlag der Österreichischen Akademie der Wissenschaften.

Schlauffler, R. H. 1929. *Beethoven: The Man Who Freed Music*. New York: Doubleday.

Scholes, Percy A., ed. 1955. *The Oxford Companion to Music*. London: Oxford University Press.

Schonberg, Harold C. 1963. *The Great Pianists*. New York: Simon and Schuster.

Schönfeld, J. [1796] 1976. *Jahrbuch der Tonkunst von Wien und Prag* (facsimile). Edited by Otto Biba. Reprint, Munich: Emil Katzbichler.

Schrade, L. [1910] 1978. *Beethoven in France*. New York: Da Capo.

Schroeder, D. P. 1985. "Reception and Haydn's Symphonies." *International Review of Aesthetics and Sociology of Music* 16:57–72.

———. 1990. *Haydn and the Enlightenment: The Late Symphonies and Their Audience*. Oxford: Clarendon.

Sennett, R. 1978. *The Fall of Public Man.* New York: Knopf.

Shapin, Steven. 1984. "Pump and Circumstance: Robert Boyle's Literary Technology." *Social Studies of Science* 14:481–520.

Shapin, Steven, and Simon Schaeffer. 1986. *Leviathan and the Air Pump.* Princeton: Princeton University Press.

Slonimsky, N. 1965. *Lexicon of Musical Invective.* New York: Coleman-Ross Co.

Solomon, Maynard. 1968. "Beethoven and Bonaparte." *Music Review* 29(2): 96–105.

———. 1971. "Beethoven, Sonata and Utopia." *Telos* 9:32–47

———. 1972. "Beethoven's Productivity at Bonn." *Music and Letters* 53(2): 165–72.

———. 1974. "Beethoven and the Enlightenment." *Telos* 19:146–54.

———. 1975a. "Beethoven: The Nobility Pretense." *Musical Quarterly* 61: 272–94.

———. 1975b. "The Dreams of Beethoven." *American Imago* 32:113–44.

———. 1977a. *Beethoven.* New York: Schirmer.

———. 1977b. "Beethoven's Class Position and Outlook." Pp. 67–93 in *Bericht über den internationalem Beethoven-Kongress in Berlin,* edited by K. Niemann. Leipzig.

———. 1988a. "Beethoven's Birth Year." Pp. 35–42 in *Beethoven Essays.* Cambridge, Mass.: Harvard University Press.

———. 1988b. "Beethoven's Creative Process: A Two-Part Invention." Pp. 126–38 in *Beethoven Essays.* Cambridge, Mass.: Harvard University Press.

———. 1988c. "The Creative Periods of Beethoven." Pp. 116–25 in *Beethoven Essays.* Cambridge, Mass.: Harvard University Press.

Sonneck, O. G. 1967. *Beethoven: Impressions of Contemporaries.* New York: Dover.

Spohr, Louis. 1969. *The Musical Journeys of Louis Spohr.* Translated by Henry Pleasants. New York: Da Capo Press.

Stadlen, P. 1967. "Beethoven and the Metronome." *Music and Letters* 48:330–49.

Staehelin, Martin. 1984. "A Veiled Judgment of Beethoven by Albrechtsberger?" Pp. 46–52 in *Beethoven Essays: Studies in Honor of Elliot Forbes.* Cambridge, Mass.: Harvard University Press.

Stearns, Peter N. 1975. *European Society in Upheaval: Social History since 1750.* New York: Macmillan.

Stekl, Hannes. 1973. *Osterreichs Aristokratie im Vormarz: Herrschaftsstil und Lebensformen der Furstenhauser Liechtenstein und Schwarzenberg.* Wien: Verlag für Geschichte und Politik.

———. 1978. "Harmoniemusik und 'turkische Banda' des Furstenhauses Liechtenstein." *Haydn Yearbook* 10:164–75

Sternberg, R. J., and J. Davidson. 1986. *Conceptions of Giftedness.* Cambridge: Cambridge University Press.

Streicher, A. 1984. "Notes on the Playing, Tuning and Maintenance of the Fortepiano Manufactured in Vienna by Stein." Pp. 461–70 in *Early Music,* 12: 4, translated by Preethi de Silva.

Strunk, Oliver. 1950. *Source Readings in Music History.* New York: Norton.

Subotnik, Rose Rosengard. 1976. "Adorno's Diagnosis of Beethoven's Late Style: Early Symptoms of a Fatal Condition." *Journal of the American Musicological Society* 29:242–74.

Swidler, Ann. 1986. "Culture in Action: Symbols and Strategies." *American Sociological Review* 51:273–86.

Temperley, Nicolaus. 1985. *The London Pianoforte School: Haydn, Dussek and Contemporaries.* New York: Garland.

Thayer, A. W., and Elliot Forbes. 1967. *Thayer's Life of Beethoven.* 2 vols. Princeton: Princeton University Press.

Tick, J. 1973. "Musician and Mécène: Some Observations on Patronage in Late 18th Century France." *International Review of Aesthetics and the Sociology of Music* 2:245–56.

Tovey, Donald Francis. [1931] 1976. *A Companion to Beethoven's Pianoforte Sonatas.* Reprint, New York: AMS Press.

Treitler, Leo. 1991. "The Politics of Reception: Tailoring the Present as Fulfilment of a Desired Past." *Journal of the Royal Musical Association* 116:280–98.

Tuchman, Gaye, with Nina Fortin. 1989. *Edging Women Out: Victorian Novelists, Publishers, and Social Change.* New Haven: Yale University Press.

Tyson, Alan. 1969. "Beethoven's Heroic Phase." *Musical Times* 110:139.

———. 1973. "Beethoven to the Countess Susanna Guicciardi: A New Letter." *Beethoven Studies* 1: 1–17.

van der Straeten, E., and David Charlton. 1980. "Peter Hänsel." P. 150 in *The New Grove Dictionary of Music and Musicians,* vol. 8, edited by Stanley Sadie. London: Macmillan.

Wagner, Richard. 1872. *Beethoven.* Translated by A. R. Parsons. New York: Schirmer.

Waissenberger, Robert. 1986. *Vienna in the Biedermeier Era, 1815–1848.* New York: Rizzoli.

Wallace, R. 1986. *Beethoven's Critics: Aesthetic Dilemmas and Resolutions in the Composer's Lifetime.* Cambridge: Cambridge University Press.

Weber, Max. 1978. *Economy and Society: An Outline of Interpretive Sociology.* Edited by Guenther Roth and Claus Wittich. Berkeley: University of California Press.

Weber, William. 1975. *Music and the Middle Class.* London: Schocken.

———. 1977. "Mass Culture and the Shaping of European Taste." *International Review of Aesthetics and the Sociology of Music* 8(1):5–21.

———. 1979. "The Muddle of the Middle Classes." *Nineteenth Century Music* 3:175–85.

———. 1980. "Learned and General Musical Taste in Eighteenth Century France." *Past and Present* 89:58–85.

———. 1984a. "The Contemporaneity of Eighteenth Century Musical Taste." *Musical Quarterly* 70:175–94.

———. 1984b. "La Musique Ancien in the Waning of the Ancien Regime." *Journal of Modern History* 59–88.

———. 1984c. "Wagner, Wagnerism and Musical Idealism." In *Wagnerism in European Culture and Politics,* edited by D. Large and W. Weber. Ithaca: Cornell University Press.

———. 1986. "The Rise of the Classical Repertoire in Nineteenth-Century Orchestral Concerts." In *The Orchestra: Origins and Transformations,* edited by Joan Peyser. New York: Charles Scribner's Sons.

———. 1992. *The Rise of the Musical Classics in Eighteenth Century England: A Study in Canon, Ritual and Ideology.* Oxford: Oxford University Press.

Webster, James. 1984. "The Falling-out between Haydn and Beethoven: The Evidence of the Sources." Pp. 3–45 in *Beethoven Essays: Studies in Honor of Elliot Forbes.* Cambridge, Mass.: Harvard University Press.

Wegeler, Franz, and Ferdinand Ries. 1987. "Biographical Notes." Pp. 1–167 in *Beethoven Remembered,* translated by Frederick Noonan. Arlington, Va.: Great Ocean Publishers.

Wellek, René. 1955. *A History of Modern Criticism: 1750–1950,* vol. 1, *The Later Eighteenth Century.* London: Jonathan Cape.

Willets, Pamela J. 1970. *Beethoven and England: An Account of Sources in the British Museum.* London: British Museum.

Williams, Raymond. 1958. "The Romantic Artist." Pp. 30–45 in *Culture and Society, 1780–1950.* London: Chatto and Windus.

———. 1982. *The Sociology of Culture.* New York: Schocken.

Willis, Paul. 1977. *Learning to Labour: How Working Class Kids Get Working Class Jobs.* New York: Columbia University Press.

Winner, L. 1980. "Do Artifacts Have Politics?" *Daedalus* 109:121–36.

Winter, Robert. 1977. "Performing Nineteenth-Century Music on Nineteenth-Century Instruments." *Nineteenth Century Music* 1:163–175.

———. 1984. "The Emperor's New Clothes: Nineteenth-Century Instruments Revisited." *Nineteenth Century Music* 7:251–65.

Woolgar, Steve. 1988. *Science: The Very Idea.* London: Routledge.

Wurzbach, Constantin. 1856–91. *Biographisches Lexikon des Kaiserthums Oesterreich, 1750–1850.* Vienna.

Wythe, Deborah. 1984. "The Pianos of Conrad Graf." *Early Music* 12:447–60.

Young, Percy M. 1965. *The Concert Tradition.* London: Routledge.

———. 1976. *Beethoven: A Victorian Tribute.* London: Dennis Dobson.

Zazlaw, Neil. 1989. *Mozart's Symphonies: Context, Performance Practice, Reception.* Oxford: Clarendon.

Zobel, Konrad, and Frederick E. Warner. 1972–73. "The Old Burgtheater: A Structural History, 1741–1788." *Theatre Studies* 19:19–53.

Zolberg, Vera. 1981. "Conflicting Visions in American Art Museums." *Theory and Society* 10:103–26.

Index

Compositor:	G & S Typesetters, Inc.
Text:	10/13 Sabon
Display:	Sabon
Printer:	Thomson-Shore, Inc.
Binder:	Thomson-Shore, Inc.